Dr. Karyn's Guide to the Teen Years

Dr. Karyn's
Guide to the Teen Years

Understanding and Parenting Your Teenager

Dr. Karyn Gordon
Parent and Teen Coach

Collins

Dr. Karyn's Guide to the Teen Years
© 2008 by DKB Coaching and Wellness Studio, Inc.
All rights reserved.

Published by Collins, an imprint of HarperCollins Publishers Ltd.

First Edition

HarperCollins books may be purchased for educational, business,
or sales promotional use through our Special Markets Department.

HarperCollins Publishers Ltd
2 Bloor Street East, 20th Floor
Toronto, Ontario, Canada
M4W 1A8

www.harpercollins.ca

Library and Archives Canada Cataloguing in Publication
Gordon, Karyn, 1973–
Dr. Karyn's guide to the teen years : understanding
and parenting your teenager / Karyn Gordon.

ISBN 978-0-00-200863-1

1. Parent and teenager. 2. Parenting. 3. Teenagers. I. Title.
HQ799.15.G66 2008   649'.125   C2007-906577-5

WEB 9 8 7 6 5 4 3 2 1

Printed and bound in Canada
Dr. Karyn's Guide to the Teen Years is printed on
Ancient Forest Friendly paper,
made with 100% post-consumer waste.

To Mom and Dad—the two people who first
modelled "inside-out" principles to me.

Thank you for your constant wisdom,
guidance, love and encouragement.

Contents

Introduction: The Six Keys to Parenting Teens

"I never realized how difficult it is to raise teens. Having children was a piece of cake compared to this."

—Howard, father of three

I can't tell you how many times I've heard this! In my public speaking and coaching practice, I talk with thousands of parents and teens every year. And what they tell me confirms that the teen years challenge many families.

But why is this? Why should families who have been moving along so smoothly suddenly hit a bump in the road as soon as their children turn 13 or 14? Why does the emergence of teenagers into a home suddenly turn confident, assured adults into at times doubting, frustrated, even *angry* parents?

Now if we were really being honest, quite often that seemingly smooth road of early childhood has not really been that easy. In some cases, the ride until now has been pretty unsettled. But most parents find that breaking up sibling squabbles or dealing with the crying child who doesn't want to go to bed is a lot less scary than discovering that your 16-year-old son has come home drunk or your 15-year-old daughter is sexually active. Suddenly the problems and challenges of parenting take on a whole new seriousness when kids hit their teen years.

Sometimes, however, early family life *has* been a fairly smooth journey. In families like this, parents are sometimes stunned by the changes brought on by puberty. Their sweet, cheerful daughter now storms out of the kitchen whenever they ask her a question; their enthusiastic, chatty son now hibernates in his room during what little time he spends in the house. What's going on? Why is the parenting approach that seemed to work so well with your grade-school kids now failing you during the teen years?

Well, for starters, teens are not just big children. Nor are they simply young adults. Thanks to recent research, done in large part by Dr. Judith Rapoport and Dr. Jay Giedd at the National Institute of Mental Health in the United States, we now know that the brain goes through a significant period of growth and change during adolescence. (Until fairly recently it was thought that all significant brain growth concluded by about five years of age.) It now appears that the frontal lobe continues to develop throughout puberty, not finalizing its development until young adulthood. This part of the brain controls the "executive functions"—that is, planning, reasoning and impulse control. This suggests that particularly in early adolescence, teens simply are not capable of the same degree of rational thought and judgment that they will be in their adult years. Research has also shown that hormones during puberty appear to cause the amygdala, a structure in the temporal lobes of the brain associated with emotions, fear and gut reactions, to swell temporarily. Teens then may be much more influenced by emotions and emotional swings than adults. Indeed Harvard's Dr. Deborah Yurgelun-Todd has used functional MRIs to show that teens seem to rely on the amygdala rather than on the frontal lobes when performing certain cognitive functions. Not surprisingly, their perceptions are not as accurate as adults'. In adulthood, thinking seems to move exclusively to the frontal lobes where more reasoned perceptions are made.

While the different functioning of teen and adult brains has been observed by a number of international research scientists, it is really not clear if there is a strict cause-and-effect relationship between brain and behaviour. While the brain might still be developing and this might explain some teen responses (such as turbulent emotions, risk taking and a way of looking at the world markedly different from their parents'), other researchers, like Dr. Robert Epstein in his book *The Case Against Adolescence*, point out that the modern·Western teenager may be a product of the way we treat teens—unlike how things were 300 years ago (or unlike in many current non-Western cultures), today's teens are largely kept out of the work world, spend an enormous amount of time with their peers instead of adults, are subject to many, many more restrictions than most adults. We treat teens more like children, yet we expect them to act like adults. And the tension caused by this may cause the differences between how teen brains develop and function in our society as opposed to teen brains subjected to different environmental influences.

In some ways it hardly matters whether environmental factors influence brain development or brain development affects behaviour and therefore the type of world in which teens live. Either way, Western parents are faced with several years during which their teen children are going through intense physical, cognitive and emotional changes.

But just as significant as the teen brain in affecting the way parents and kids interact is the developmental process of growing up. As children hit their teen years, they begin the process of separating from their parents. In order to head out eventually into the adult world, teens begin to stake out their independence, to discover who they are apart from their parents and family. They need to start thinking on their own, to discover their values and to make their own decisions.

And yet in many families, the parenting attitudes, styles and habits simply haven't adapted to these changes on the part of the teens. When children are small, parents need to take responsibility for their health, safety and well-being. Parenting means being a teacher, a nurse, a caregiver and a manager. But as teens move towards independence and adulthood, we need to hand over some of the responsibility and decision-making power to our teens. We need to make the transition from managers to partners. And, as someone once said, if we do our work really well, eventually we will be out of a job altogether!

What's more, as teens struggle with how to separate from their parents, they may have more difficulty talking with their parents or accepting their help or point of view. Communication between parents and teens may not be as easy or straightforward as it once was.

And as most parents realize, even in the teen years, we still need to provide boundaries and consequences. But the time-out chair doesn't work so well for the hulking 16-year-old! As children enter their preteen and teen years, parents clearly need to adjust and fine-tune their skills to meet their teens' changing needs.

Six Keys to Helping Your Teen

In *Dr. Karyn's Guide to the Teen Years*, I have set out six keys that can help parents understand, connect and truly help their teens through these very important transition years. Each key is explained in a chapter. My formal education has been tremendously helpful in preparing this parenting strategy, but to be completely honest, my greatest source of insight has been teens themselves. I've listened to over 7,000 hours of preteens and teens spilling their guts about what they want and need from their parents. These thoughts and feelings have shaped what I see as the principles of effective parenting:

1. Keeping the big picture in mind at all times
2. Acknowledging and adjusting our parenting attitudes
3. Understanding and communicating emotions
4. Building our child's self-esteem
5. Communicating effectively
6. Establishing boundaries and providing structure

All of these keys are applicable to parenting children of any age, but in the following chapters, I have tried to explain how each may be tailored to the needs of teens and their parents. In the "Focus On" sections at the end of each chapter, I discuss specific issues that often challenge parents, basing my advice always on these six keys.

At the heart of all of these keys, however, is my broader parenting philosophy, and that is the importance of being what I call an "Inside-Out Parent." Being an inside-out parent is achieved by doing two things. The first is focusing always on *who* your teen is or is becoming rather than on what your teen is doing or achieving. In this sense, inside-out parenting is recognizing the importance of raising teens with strong, healthy characters and acknowledging that only by valuing what is inside first, will we help our children achieve outward success.

The second, and equally important, aspect of inside-out parenting is taking this same approach with ourselves as parents. Let me explain.

The year I got married, my mom said to me, "Karyn, the irony is that the very person with whom you have chosen to spend the rest of your life, the person who you think is so wonderful, attractive and caring, will be the very person who sees the most egocentric, selfish and unattractive parts of your character. We are all a work in progress. And the difference between surviving marriages and thriving marriages is how those couples handle the work and conflicts. In a merely surviving marriage, people point fingers and blame each other. But in a thriving marriage, they allow the other person to mould their character. So, when conflicts come up, don't get defensive. Instead ask, what is this situation saying about me? What is it saying about my character? What am I learning about myself? How can I use that learning to help me in the future?"

As I've worked with parents over the years, I've thought of those words many, many times. I've come to realize that the idea of turning our focus inward, instead of outward, can be used not just to build a successful marriage, but also to make us all better parents. Howard, the father whose words I quoted at the beginning of this introduction, followed up his words about the difficulty of parenting teens by saying, "It really feels that when you have teens, someone is holding up a mirror to your face, and I just don't want to look at it." But looking at it and responding to it are the only ways we can grow and improve as parents. Responding to our teens and to the challenges they present us with is the best way to be truly effective parents. And looking closely at that mirror, in other words being an inside-out parent, means that instead of just surviving our teens' adolescence, we can build thriving, happy, healthy relationships with our growing children.

But what if your children are well into their teen years? What if you've hit a few bumps in the road already? Can things be changed now? If there's one thing I've learned during my years of working with young people, it is that despite what they may say or do, families are hugely important to teens. I've worked with hundreds of families in which the parent-teen relationships have been transformed. The great news about parenting teens is that it's never too late!

1 The Big Picture

"I wish my parents would get to know the real me. They spend
so much of their time telling me what to do instead of listening
to who I really am and it's really annoying and frustrating."

– Nate, age 16

One of my friends recently told me a great story. When she was a teen
she took a school bus to school. One day, despite leaving her house
with plenty of time to spare, she looked down her street to see the
yellow school bus already approaching the stop. She started running
down the street, waving her arms and shouting. The bus driver saw
her and waited. When she got on, she noticed that he was new. "Hurry
up," he said. "I'm not supposed to wait for students." "But you're early,"
she said. "What's going on?" The bus driver smiled. "There's no traffic
today," he said with satisfaction. She looked around the bus. There
were only a small number of the regular riders on it. As the bus driver
made his way around the route ahead of schedule, there were fewer
and fewer students at the stops, and so he continued to pick up time.
By the end of the trip, there were *no* students at all waiting at the final
stops. As the almost empty bus pulled up to the school doors, the few
kids on the bus were still trying to point out to the driver that there
was a problem. "But I've made such good time!" he protested.

Most of us don't lose sight of the point of what we are supposed to
be doing quite as dramatically as that bus driver, but it is surprisingly
easy to work away at something—whether it is our jobs, our domestic
responsibilities or even parenting—without keeping the big picture

in mind. Certainly many of the parents that I talk with are focused on the particulars of their lives with their teens: "All I want is for my son to focus more on his school work" or "If she'd just pick her clothes off the floor I'd be happy." But of course school work and tidying are not *all* that they want for and from their children. It's just so easy to forget what our primary objectives are when we are trying to get our teens to tell us where they are going, who they are going with and when they'll be back. That's why Key #1, Keeping in Mind the Big Picture, is my favorite key. It is the foundation for all of the other parenting strategies that I will be introducing in the following pages. It is, in my mind, the single most important aspect of parenting any child, but especially of parenting during the often challenging teen years. And yet, the big picture is also the simplest, most straightforward of my six parenting keys.

I use the expression the "Big Picture" to remind us all that we must always keep in mind the objective of parenting. We have to be clear in defining where we want our children to be by the time they reach adulthood. We need to have the big picture in our minds always as we tackle the day to day challenges of parenting. When we have that big picture or mission statement front and centre, we can avoid being reactive or responding impulsively to our teens and to the parenting situations that present themselves.

So, what exactly do I mean by the big picture? How do you know what *your* big picture is?

To figure what your fundamental parenting goals are, you need to ask yourself a couple of questions. If you were to write a mission statement about what you were hoping to achieve by the time your teen finished adolescence, what would it be? How would you define success as it relates to raising your kids?

When I ask these questions of parents, I always hear the same sorts of comments:

- I want my teen to be happy and confident.
- I want my teens to be motivated—to have dreams and to have the courage to go after their dreams.
- I want my teens to be accepting, empathetic, respectful of themselves and other people.
- I want my teen to be responsible, trustworthy, hardworking and to contribute to society.
- I want my teen to be honest, loving and communicative.
- I want my teen to be emotionally balanced and healthy.

All of these descriptions focus on a teen's character—indeed they define a dream character for any child or adult. So, when it comes down to it, what almost all parents want to do is to help their children develop their character. The big picture, then, is all about focusing on the type of people our children are becoming.

Defining Character

What do I mean when I talk about the character of our teens? Dr. Stephen Covey, author of *The 7 Habits of Highly Effective People*, describes character as "a composite of our habits . . . the intersection of knowledge, skill and desire."

Character is more commonly considered the sum of our moral, ethical and mental qualities. In other words, the heart and soul of a person: who they really are when no one is looking. True character comes out in the midst of trials, difficulties and crises. When a person has an authentic character quality, you will see the fruit of that characteristic in his habits and behaviours.

You might be asking yourself, don't most parents want their kids to develop the wonderful characteristics listed above? Of course they do but, troublingly, many parents are not only failing to help their kids move in the direction of developing a happy, healthy character, but are actually, without realizing it, taking their teens in the opposite direction. Let me explain.

Inside-Out vs. Outside-In Parenting Styles

There are two main parenting styles that I see when working with families—one I've dubbed "Inside-Out" and the other, "Outside-In." Parents who are outside in focus on the externals and what their teen is achieving. They often ask questions like:

- Do my kids have good school marks?
- Are they in the right social clubs?
- Do they have the right friends?
- Are they projecting the right image?

These parents put most of their focus on what their teen is doing or achieving as an indication both of their teen's healthy development and of their own success and effectiveness as parents. This is in direct contrast to what I call the inside-out parenting style. An inside-out parent is one who manages to keep the big picture in mind, focusing on *who their teen is becoming* above all else. They ask questions like:

- Is my teen honest, trustworthy, responsible, hardworking, loyal, friendly, etc.?
- What do I need to do as a parent to help my teen develop these characteristics?
- Is my teen trying his or her best?
- Is my teen striving for a life of excellence?

You may be asking yourself what is wrong with paying attention to a child's academic performance or his circle of friends. Wouldn't any responsible parent be concerned if a bright child wasn't achieving at school or if a teenager was hanging out with a group of kids who were doing drugs or in trouble with the law? Of course. But an outside-in parent will focus exclusively on the behaviour and on consequences or punishments to change the behaviour. An inside-out parent will instead ask questions about *why* the behaviour is happening or the lack of achievement occurring. They will be focusing on the teen's self-esteem, his thoughts and feelings, and will try to improve the situation by listening to and working with their teen. What's more, an outside-in parent is likely to be focusing on behaviour and achievement to the exclusion of anything else—even if there are no problems evident.

Let me give you an example. Imagine that your teen has just finished a season of hockey. Outside-in parents might consider goals, assists, amount of ice time, number of winning games and any awards as an indication of their teen's success on the ice. Inside-out parents would be thinking about whether or not their teen enjoyed the year, whether he or she showed up to the games consistently and on time, like a good team player. Did their child try his or her best? Was she a good loser and a gracious winner? Did he display good sportsmanship? Did she encourage the weaker members of the team and congratulate the stronger players? Did she play the game with excellence? If he needed help, did he get more training to improve his skills?

Another good example of the different approaches of inside-out and outside-in parents is how they respond to report cards. Think back to the last time it was report card day in your home. What questions did you ask about the report? The most common questions parents ask are, "How did you do?" or "How many A's did you get?" But both of those questions are focused solely on the external achievement. If the report card has comments as well as grades, an inside-out parent is likely to focus on what the teachers have to say about the teen's effort and attitude rather than on the marks. An inside-out parent might also ask, "Did you try your best?" "How do you feel about what you did?" "Are you proud of your report?" If a teen is disappointed with the results, report card day may be an opportunity for her to brainstorm with her parents about what she needs to do in order to get the results she wants. If the report card suggests that a teen is not doing his best and the teen says he doesn't care about his poor performance, the conversation might focus on what is important to him and why.

My favourite inside-out question for report card day, however, is to ask how the child would grade his effort during the term or year. This kind of question can put those marks clearly in context. For example, one of my clients, Natalie, brought her report in to show me. Rather than looking at the transcript right away, I asked her what grade she would have given her effort in the past term. She said "C+." When I looked at her report card, she had earned straight A's. Natalie was an extremely bright girl, and it was clear that she could achieve excellent grades with minimal effort. But she knew, as I did after she answered my question, that she had been "coasting." And students who coast through school may not be developing the strong character they need to achieve their goals in life. They may not be learning skills such as time management, how to ask for help when it's needed, perseverance, diligence, resilience and a strong work ethic. Without these tools, they are in danger of experiencing extreme stress and anxiety when things do eventually get difficult for them. They may end up crashing, even quitting, when the going gets tough. For some students, this may happen later in high school when the work load gets heavier, in university or even in their first jobs.

Of course, the opposite can also be true. Another client of mine, 12-year-old Riley, answered my report card question by saying he would give himself an A for effort. Riley had a learning disability and his report card was mostly C's. He told me that he had tried his best, had worked on his time management and had moved to the front of the classroom for lessons. And I could see that he was focused, hard-working, diligent, responsible and highly motivated.

Despite Riley's C's, I had every confidence that he was doing well, and developing a strong and resourceful character. With straight-A Natalie, however, there might be cause for concern. Without context, external indications of success can be deceiving.

Coasting and Crashing

When teens are academically and intellectually strong, many parents and teachers assume that their future will be easy sailing. But I see too many kids like these who are "coasting and crashing." I use the term to describe what happens when teens and young adults who have never had rely on hard work to get through school or who have never had to overcome challenges or adversity suddenly run into unfamiliar territory. For example, they've been coasting along in high school, getting their homework done in class or in a few minutes at lunch and are still getting excellent grades. Then they move to a university setting where many of the students are as strong or stronger than they are and the material and expectations are much, much tougher. Suddenly, they have no idea what to do. Without strong work habits, good time management and self-discipline, they end up crashing: doing poorly in school, suffering severe blows to their self-esteem and even quitting. If your teens find school something that they can excel at without much effort, it's important that there are other things in their lives that raise the bar for them. Excellent students might be encouraged to take on more extracurricular activities, add a part-time job to their schedule or do volunteer work. Or they should be encouraged to engage in activities that they are interested in but that they have to work hard to do well at. And even if your teens' grades are good, you may need to work with them on their work discipline and time management. Self-discipline is one of the most important characteristics I want to see teens develop.

The other wonderful thing about asking your child to grade themselves on their effort is that it puts all teens on the same playing field. It doesn't matter whether you've got a teen with a learning disability or a teen who is extremely gifted. Focusing on the marks (external) instead of the effort (internal) is unfair and unrealistic because we can't control the results of our effort. We can't control how hard a test is or how a teacher marks. But we can always control the amount of effort we put into any task. So, focusing on effort is a cornerstone of inside–out parenting.

Your Teen's Character

To be an inside-out parent, you must focus on your teen's developing character rather than on his achievements or on her behaviour alone. Take a little time to think about who your teen is becoming by answering the following:

List at least five to 10 positive attributes of your teen's character. (Read through the list of 103 traits below to help you determine the ones that your feel best describe your child's personality.)

- If you were to ask your teen what two or three attributes of his character need sharpening, what do you think he would say?
- What attributes would you like to help your teen develop?
- What is one habit you can change this week to help your teen develop a part of her character?
- Once you see your teen start trying (effort) to work on his character, what do you need to do to help encourage/ reinforce this change?

Common Character Traits

Accepting	Assertive	Cautious
Accommodating	Attentive	Charismatic
Active	Balanced	Charming
Adventurous	Brave	Cheerful
Affectionate	Brilliant	Clever
Affirming	Calm	Communicative
Ambitious	Capable	Compassionate
Articulate	Carefree	Confident
Artistic	Caring	Considerate

Cooperative	Giving	Passionate
Courageous	Gracious	Patient
Creative	Happy	Persuasive
Curious	Hardworking	Playful
Daring	Healthy	Polite
Decisive	Honest	Reasonable
Dependable	Hopeful	Reflective
Detailed	Humble	Relaxed
Determined	Humorous	Resilient
Disciplined	Imaginative	Resourceful
Easygoing	Inclusive	Respectful
Empathetic	Independent	Responsible
Encouraging	Influential	Self-Assured
Energetic	Intelligent	Self-Controlled
Expressive	Interdependent	Selfless
Fair	Inventive	Sensitive
Faithful	Joyful	Serious
Fearless	Kind	Sociable
Flexible	Loving	Stable
Focused	Loyal	Thoughtful
Forgiving	Motivated	Trustworthy
Friendly	Neat	Understanding
Funny	Objective	Wise
Generous	Optimistic	
Gentle	Organized	

In a world where it is all too easy to get caught up in material success and external benchmarks (how much money we make, what kind of car we drive, how popular we are), inside-out parents will always draw their focus back to what is truly important about their lives and the lives of their teens. They will look at behaviour and achievements not as a ways to judge the success or failure of their teens but rather in the context of what these things might tell them about their teens' healthy development of self and character.

Most of us want to be inside-out parents and help our teens develop great character, but when we look closer at our approach and listen to our conversations, we might find we are actually operating in the outside-in style. And our inadvertent outside-in parenting style may be having more harmful effects on our parent-teen relationship than we realize.

The Potential Risks of Outside-In Parenting

Low Self-Esteem

Megan was intellectually gifted. She worked hard at school and often achieved 80s and 90s in most of her classes. And yet this bright girl struggled terribly with low self-esteem. During one of her sessions with me she told me that she had recently shown her parents her 87 percent math exam. Instead of giving praise, her father's said, "What happened to the other 13 percent?" Megan learned that to her parents, her value was dependent on a number. No matter what she did, it never seemed good enough.

If parents focus too much on what their teens are doing and achieving, teens may believe that their parents only care about them *if* they achieve. These teens often also internalize these beliefs and think that *they* will only be happy *if* they achieve (whether it is a mark, a weight, a relationship). This sort of conditional situation, therefore, means that self-esteem can go up and down like a yo-yo depending on their achievements. If a teen gets an A on a report card, he might feel good for a little bit, but then the feeling of satisfaction passes, and he begins to feel stressed again about achieving. Healthy self-esteem is not based on conditions. People with strong self-esteem will feel great if they do well, but their opinion of themselves won't plummet if they don't. A teen's poor attitude about himself will impact him negatively in all kinds of decisions (e.g., peer pressure, friendships, communication, goal setting, etc.). I'll discuss the dangers of low self-esteem in more detail in Chapter 4.

Overachieving, Perfectionism and Anxiety

If parents focus too much on externals, their teens may push themselves to achieve in order to get their parents' approval. But people who push too hard—expending effort that is excessive or out of proportion to the task at hand—are what are popularly known as overachievers. And one of the problems with overachievers is that they are prone to becoming perfectionists. For a perfectionist, all her work must be "perfect," but because perfect doesn't exist, the perfectionist experiences constant anxiety, panic and low self-esteem. It's like a person trying to run after a train that she cannot ever reach. The more she chases, the higher her anxiety levels grow. Overachieving teens may seem very successful. After all, they are often excelling. But they usually experience an array of problems, from anxiousness to obsessiveness to a poor sense of self.

Remember, achieving is not unhealthy for teens, *unless* it's done for the wrong reasons. If teens are trying to do well at something only to win their parents' approval or because their self-esteem is based on this external success, they are putting themselves in a vulnerable position.

Underachieving

The other extreme is that teens underachieve. Some teens may find the thought of trying and yet failing to achieve just too frightening, so they decide not to try at all. Other teens think their parents will only love them if they achieve, they may decide not to try to earn that love. Often a teen like this will unconsciously or consciously rebel against such outward focus and the more the parent wants him or her to achieve, the more the teen will underachieve. A number of years ago, I coached Laura, an 18-year-old who was underachieving in school. She was bright but rarely applied herself. When I suggested that she place all of her focus on her effort, and not on results, she said, "That's the exact opposite of what my mother has told me all my life. She says that the only thing that matters is the final mark." I was sure that Laura had become an underachiever just to spite her parents.

An even better example of the type of rebellion and underachievement that outside-in parenting can breed is the story of Joanne. At 17, Joanne was significantly overweight. Her mother, Lisa, on the other hand, had been a model years earlier and still had a beautiful figure. Lisa sent Joanne to see me to help her "lose some weight" and "build her self-esteem." Although Joanne was resistant at first, she was happy to have someone whom she could talk openly with. Lisa had, apparently, put Joanne on diet pills at the age of 14, had previously sent her to three other counsellors to get her to lose weight and had repeatedly told her daughter that she would never find a boyfriend or husband if she didn't slim down. Despite all this, Joanne had not succeeded in keeping any of the weight off. One day I asked Joanne, "If you *did* lose the weight, who do you think would win?" She paused and then said, "My mother. My mother would win." For Joanne, gaining weight was a way of rebelling against the perfect image she felt her mother wanted. Being heavy had been a way for Joanne to feel powerful, as if she were in control of her own life. It was, of course, a false sense of control—she was still allowing her mother to determine what the power struggle between mother and daughter was going to be about. And since Joanne was unhappy being overweight and really did want to achieve a healthy body size, her act of rebellion was only damaging herself and her self-esteem.

Lisa may have had the best intentions for her daughter. She did, after all, say she wanted to strengthen her daughter's self-esteem. But notice how she went about it. She asked me first to help with her daughter's weight, and then with her self-esteem. She was focusing on the externals first, thinking that losing weight would improve Joanne's feelings about herself. Instead, she should have been working from the inside out, concentrating on helping Joanne improve her self-esteem so that she might have the courage and motivation to lose weight.

As Joanne's story so clearly shows, underachieving, even if done consciously, can lead to low self-esteem and, of course, a rocky relationship with parents.

Lack of Communication with Parents

The final risk for parents who focus too much on achievement and externals is that their teens may not communicate with them. When teens feel conditional love (which isn't authentic love at all) from their parents, they don't feel safe. And when teens don't feel safe, they don't talk. They will often bottle up their true thoughts and feelings and put all of their focus into their friendships, making these friendships their main family. And when it reaches this point, parents have very little if any influence in their teens' lives.

Outside-in parenting, even if it is unconscious and fairly subtle, can create some real problems within families. But here's the good news: it's never too late to become an inside-out parent (regardless of what age your teens are).

Birth Order and Over/Underachieving

Parents often comment to me that their eldest children are overachievers and the youngest are underachievers. They want to know how that can be. It seems there can only be so many overachievers in a family. It's almost as if the first teen takes the "overachieving trophy" and all the praise, so the next child in line thinks unconsciously, "I can't compete with him, so I'm not even going to try." I've noticed that in outside-in families, I seldom see two consecutive siblings exhibiting overachiever tendencies. Usually whichever extreme the first-born adopts, the second child will do the opposite, if they sense that their parents' approval or love is conditional.

The Rewards of Inside-Out Parenting

Inside-Out Parenting Builds Healthy Self-Esteem

When parents focus more on who their teen is becoming rather than what she is achieving, they are indirectly teaching their teen "I love you for you—no conditions." Teens will often internalize this thinking and believe they are persons worthy of love regardless of the circumstances. When teens adopt this attitude, they have the basis for healthy self-esteem. When teens feel good about themselves, it affects nearly every decision they make, including friendships, dating, peer pressure and goal setting.

Greater Communication and Parental Influence

Monica, age 17, came to see me because her parents were concerned about her underachieving and self-sabotaging habits. They were extremely worried about some of the decisions she was making. After spending some time with Monica, I realized that her parents were operating in the outside-in parenting style. The overwhelming major-ity of their conversations was about what marks she got, why didn't she work harder like her sister and how her life wasn't going to go anywhere if she continued to behave the way she did. As a result, Monica had shut out her parents and had started making her friends her new family. Monica allowed me to share with her parents how she was feeling about the pressure to perform and achieve, and I started working with them to develop an inside-out approach. Part of their problem was that when they saw Monica underachieve or get a bad mark, they blamed themselves, thinking they were doing a terrible job at parenting. And because they were taking responsibility for her performance, they felt enormous anxiety with each low mark. Part of becoming an inside-out parent is learning how to set boundaries for what you can and cannot control. (See Chapter 6 for more on bound-aries.) Her parents could control their encouragement and support of Monica, and they could control the amount of help they offered. They could control how to make the structure of their home *encourage* self-discipline. But they could not control how hard she tried, or how well she did. Within a few weeks of focusing on being her cheerleader and support, their relationship started improving. The parents were feeling much less anxious and angry by not taking responsibility for Monica's school work and saw her improve her efforts slowly but surely.

One of the greatest rewards of her parents' new focus on effort and character, however, was that Monica started to feel comfortable sharing what was happening in her life with them. One night she had a heart-to-heart with her dad about her boyfriend. The topic of physical intimacy came up in the conversation and Monica confessed that she didn't want to engage in sex until she was older. Her dad talked to her about ways she might remind herself of that if she was ever tempted. Three months later, Monica told me that the conversation with her dad had been very important to her and had given her the courage of convictions. She had stuck to her guns, and told her boyfriend that she simply wasn't ready. I asked Monica's permission to share this story with her parents because her dad was questioning how much influence he was having in her life. He was thrilled that he had been of help in his daughter's decision making. Indeed once her parents started changing to an inside-out approach, Monica started listening

The Difference Between Authority and Influence

People who have authority possess it because they are entitled to it. It's a position of power. Police officers have authority. Teachers have authority. Parents have authority. But influence is very different. To have the ability to influence another person, you have to earn that influence. All parents have authority, but not all parents have influence in their teen's life. Parents can use their authority to tell their teen what to do, but whether or not your child listens to you will reflect your degree of influence. And the greatest tool to help parents with the amount of influence they have is the inside-out style of parenting.

to what her parents were saying. Her parents had more positive influence in her life.

One of the greatest rewards of inside-out parenting is that it opens up the communication between parents and teens. If teens know that their parents love them unconditionally, if they know that they will not laugh at them or judge them or tell their secrets to others, if they know that their parents are safe to talk to, they *are* much more likely to talk. And when teens talk more with their parents, parents become a greater source of influence in their lives.

Self-Efficacy: More Motivation, Less Fear

Inside-out parents often come to the key realization that the unwise choices their teens make are not the real issue but rather a symptom of another problem. Poor choice of friends, lack of motivation, doing drugs, promiscuity and so on are a clue that part of their teen's character is not yet developed. Inside-out parents will spend the time to find out what is really going on. They will seek to understand how the teen's character is contributing to the problem and what can be done to help their teen.

A few years ago I worked with a mom, Angela, and her daughter, Stephanie, age 17. Stephanie and her mom had a history of conflict and miscommunication. They rarely talked. Stephanie was bright, hardworking and extremely sensitive. Yet Angela spent most of her conversation with her daughter telling Stephanie what she should be doing. Stephanie had long ago stopped listening, building a wall between herself and her mother. One day, when they came to my office, the tension between them was especially strong. Apparently, despite being a very strong student, Stephanie was procrastinating about applying to university. Angela was angry and frustrated.

An inside-out parent would see the procrastination not as the problem but as a symptom of something else, so I encouraged Stephanie's mom to try to find out what was behind Stephanie's behaviour. After a number of false starts during which Angela kept returning to the idea of the importance of university applications, I asked Stephanie how she felt when she thought about applying. Stephanie was slow to respond, but gradually she revealed that she had been verbally abused every day in grade eight by the most popular girl in her class. The bully called Stephanie stupid and said that she would never get into university and would never do anything with her life. Each time, therefore, Stephanie sat down to complete the university application forms, she began to think of this awful year. She would then abandon the application to avoid dwelling on the painful memory.

Stephanie hadn't realized until she began to talk about her feelings of fear that her grade eight experience had anything to do with

Help Me Understand

"Help me understand" is my favourite line to encourage teens to talk. It's an invitation for a someone to share his thoughts and feelings with the assurance that my intent is to listen and to try to see things from his point of view. And asking "Can you help me understand . . ." can be even more effective, especially if the teen is likely to believe that the "help me" is more of an invitation than a command. When using this phrase in conversation with your children, make sure that your tone is calm and gentle, and avoid using the words to jump to a question about behaviour, performance or other externals. For example, rather than saying, "Help me understand why you didn't study for the math test," you might ask, "Can you help me understand how you feel about math?" or "Can you help me understand how you feel about taking tests?" The emphasis of the question should always be on your teen's thoughts and feelings. Teens are incredibly perceptive and intuitive. If you ask questions or begin conversations in a way that is intended to serve your agenda rather than to listen to them, they will realize this and clam up.

her procrastination. After that "Ah-ha!" moment, followed by a very emotional session, she immediately went home and applied on-line to four universities. Change does not always happen this fast, but for Stephanie this new revelation proved to be motivational.

This is the power of inside-out parenting. When we place our focus first on trying to understand how our teens are feeling and who they are becoming, their actions will follow. That's why it's called "inside-out" not just "inside." When a teen is confident and self-assured she wants to do great things in her life. Once we spent the time to figure out what was happening with Stephanie, she was able to address her thoughts, her fears decreased and her motivation increased.

Stephanie's story is perfect example of the way fear of failure can get in the way of a teen's behaviour or performance, and how an inside-out approach can both identify and address this fear.

No one likes to fail, but managing your fear and addressing the attitudes attached to the fear is part of developing healthy self-esteem. If fear is dealt with effectively, teens are more likely to set goals and pursue them. When teens set realistic goals and achieve them, the experience builds self-efficacy, the sense that they have control in their lives.

Self-efficacy, or an empowered attitude, is the opposite of the victim attitude that leads some people to believe that they have no control over what happens to them in their lives. To help a teen understand the difference between feeling like a victim and feeling empowered, I often suggest that she imagines she is holding a book about her life. The victim will feel powerless, as if the chapters have already been written and she will simply be reading the story. An empowered individual, however, will think of the pages as blank and will understand that she holds the pen and will write the story herself.

One of the greatest rewards of the inside-out parenting style is that it builds a teen's confidence and therefore his motivation. Teens who feel empowered will recognize that they have choices and these choices will govern how their lives will turn out. This confidence increases the motivation to set goals and achieve them, which will reinforce this feeling of self-efficacy.

One final benefit of being an inside-out parent, of focusing on your teens' character instead of their achievements, of keeping the big picture in your mind at all times, is that this approach allows you to bring logic and reason to your parenting. If you know what your goal or mission is as a parent, you can find strategies to reach that goal and you can avoid the type of purely reactive parenting responses that undermine that goal. In the following chapters, I will focus on specific ways you can nurture your teen's developing character and be an inside-out parent in all aspects of your family life.

Focus on Friends and Peer Pressure

Friends are always very important to children, but never more so than in the teen years. As teens make the transition from childhood to adulthood, belonging to a group of friends is often the bridge that carries them from the family home to an independent life in the wider world. And as our children gain their independence and move away from us, aren't we glad they do not have to do it alone?

And yet, so many questions that I get asked by parents have to do with the issue of teen friendships. Parents are often worried about the amount of influence their teens' friends have on them, and they are especially concerned if they don't approve of the friends that their children have chosen.

Connection, Not Control

Many parents feel the need to manage their teens' choices in friends out of a sense that they are losing control (the same reason they may feel the need to read their teens' emails or snoop in their rooms). But this is unrealistic and unfair. All children need to be able to choose whom they befriend, and any unwise choices can often provide important life lessons. If you have concerns about the choices your teens are making in friends, the most effective thing you can do is build a strong relationship with your children—listening to them, connecting with them and understanding them.

It's important for parents to accept that teens choose their groups of friends for a reason—they feel they have much in common or share the same outlook. An inside-out parent would then want to find out why their child is identifying with these other teens. They would not blame these friends for their teens' misbehaviour or poor attitudes, but would attempt to understand why their teens are drawn to social environments where these kinds of activities take place. If parents believe that their child is not being treated well by his peers, or is being coerced into certain behaviours, they have to ask why their teen is allowing him or herself to be treated this way.

Family and Friends

Whether or not you like your teens' friends, what can you do if your children always want to be with friends rather than with family? The best solution is to make it easy for them to do both. Make your home a welcoming place for your children to bring their friends. For teens, a space where they can have a bit of privacy is very important. Inviting your children's friends to stay for dinner will also allow you to spend time together. Some families even find it works to let their teens bring a friend on family holidays or during family activities. You may not get as much time alone with your teens, but in the end you will see more of them! And almost as importantly, you'll get to know your teens' friends.

Knowing your children's friends will give you a stronger sense of what is going on in their lives. Very often, your teens' friends will be more communicative with you than your teens. But talking to your children's friends can sometimes be a bit of minefield. When I began coaching Abigail, she said she didn't like inviting her friends over to the house because her mother always asked them too many questions. She felt as if her friends were being interrogated. When I talked with her mom, however, I thought the questions themselves and their number sounded quite reasonable. But that was missing the point; Abigail thought there were too many questions, and it was making her uncomfortable. If Abigail's mom wanted to get to know her daughter's friends and have Abigail at home more, she was going to have to respect her feelings and reduce the number of inquiries she made when the kids came to her house.

Another mother told me that she has insisted that her son introduce all new friends when he brings them home. While he agreed to do that, he clearly does not want her to talk to the boys as they troop into the rec room. Her teenage daughter, in contrast, is quite happy for her mom to be involved with her friends when they are over, and has even begun to take yoga classes with her mom and one of her friends.

Each child is different, so it's important to pay attention to her reactions and her comfort level when her friends are around. Tailoring your responses to your teens' wishes (within reason) not only respects their feelings, but also makes it easier for them to combine family and friends.

When You Don't Like Your Teens' Friends

There are a number of guidelines you need to consider if you find yourself questioning your teens' friends:

- Don't tell your teens that they can't be friends with someone. They will only rebel and see their friends in secret.
- Don't share with your children negative feelings about their friends. Your teens will feel defensive of their friends, and sense that you are doubting them as well.
- Do, however, talk to your teens about negative behaviour or attitudes that they are developing.
- Be patient—if these friends really are unhealthy, your teens may come to realize this on their own.
- Get to know the friends—you may find your judgments have been unfair.

Groups, Conformity and Peer Pressure

Many parents notice that when their kids hit adolescence, individual friendships seem to give way to groups of kids who travel only in clusters. These cliques or groups may be identified with an activity or a common feature, sometimes with labels like "the jocks," "the skaters" or "the potheads," but their distinctions may be more subtle as well. There is almost always, however, a significant degree of similarity and conformity within the group.

Cliques or groups, although sometimes viewed with suspicion by parents, serve an important function for teenagers. Membership in a group provides young people with a sense of belonging. The group can also be a place of social safety and security where teens, trying to find out who they are, try out new roles and new ideas. A group can give teens approval, support and a measure of independence from parents and families.

But parents often worry that the group dynamic of the teen world can bring more harm than good. They are concerned that membership in a particular group—or the desire of their teens to earn their ways into certain groups—can lead to increased peer pressure.

There a few things that should calm parents' concerns about cliques, conformity and peer pressure. First, the importance of the group and conformity is greatest during early adolescence (grades eight and nine). As teens age and their self-esteem and sense of self strengthen, the importance of the group usually diminishes and teens maintain friendships without the rigid group dynamic.

It's also important to realize that the increasing amount of time teens spend with friends (whether individually or in a group) does not necessarily signal a rejection of family or the values you have tried to raise them with. Most teens listen to their friends about relatively superficial things—fashion, music, activities and their social world. Their parents are still usually the greatest influence on such things as religion, morality and ethics, education and careers.

And finally, we have to remind ourselves that all peer pressure (or peer influence) is not a bad thing. Friends can be powerful positive influences in teens' lives: whether it is encouraging them to do well in school, to keep fit or play sports, or even to become more involved in the community. Teens can model social skills and pro-social behaviour for one another—they can even help each other understand themselves better.

But there's no doubt about it, negative peer pressure is a reality for most teens. And cliques or groups can create problems if belonging to the group requires the teens to skip school, do drugs, bully or otherwise engage in problematic behaviour. There are, however, a number of things that parents can do to help their teens cope. All of the strategies listed below can be employed with older children, but they are most effective if started *before* and continued through those crucial teen years. (Remember, the strongest need to conform happens when kids are in *early* adolescence.)

How to Help Children Resist Peer Pressure

Help Your Teen Recognize Peer Pressure

Talk to your children about what peer pressure is and what it might look like as it is happening. Explain that peer pressure can be very subtle. Sometimes others are openly telling you what to do, but most peer pressure, especially in the youth culture, is what I have termed"silent." Silent peer pressure happens when teens notice that they are the only ones not behaving in a particular way. If they arrive at a party where everyone else is drinking, they may feel they should join in. Or perhaps they suddenly realize that everyone is wearing a certain kind of jeans and feel the need to get a pair themselves. Teens often feel the pressure to conform intensely and so can be influenced by silent peer pressure without even realizing it. You may also want to draw upon your own experiences either as child or an adult. (Remember: peer pressure does not exist only for children. Adults often feel pressure to dress a certain way, drive certain types of automobiles or take part in certain activities.) Encourage your teens to identify the pressures they feel so that they can address them rather than react to them without thinking.

Build Healthy Self-Esteem

The best way to help your child resist negative peer pressure is to make sure they have a strong, healthy self-esteem (see "Self-Esteem and Respect). Teens who feel good about themselves and have confidence in their own judgment and opinions are far less likely to be negatively influenced by others.

Talk about Values

Talk to children about what their values are (listen—don't try to tell them what they should be!). Encourage them to reflect on what is important to them. These may be weighty concepts like honesty, or they may be more specific things that are meaningful to them—like doing well in school, or the type of music they enjoy, or the style of clothes they like to wear. Ask them if they have ever found it tough to stick to one of their values. What did they do? How do they feel about their choice? What would they want to do differently the next time?

Let Teens Make Decisions

Part of being an inside-out parent is allowing teens to have responsibilities and to make decisions for themselves. Not only does this approach raise self-esteem, develop critical thinking skills and help to create boundaries in a family that everyone can agree to and stick with, but it also helps kids deal with peer pressure. Any teen who is used to making decisions for himself will not be as easily led by others.

Brainstorm Responses to Pressure

Encourage your children to brainstorm how they might respond if people ask them to do things they don't want to do. Get them to be specific. How would they respond if someone offered them drugs? Asked them to go shoplifting? Pressured them to have sex? Let them know that it is okay for them to blame you. "I can't. My mom would ground me forever," can be a quick way out of a difficult situation. If they've thought about responses beforehand, they will be better prepared to cope with the situation when it comes.

Teach Kids to Be Assertive

Actively teach your children how to say no. You can model this behaviour yourself (by sticking to boundaries). Encourage kids to say no in an assertive but kind way. Encourage them to find a way of turning down an offer or suggestion that is firm, but feels genuine to them (no way, not my thing, I'll pass, not now, etc.). This may make it easier for them to say no. Also talk about the non-verbal component of their communication—how they hold themselves and position their bodies can undermine or strengthen their assertiveness. Remember that the first place teens are likely to practise their new skill is at home—so don't get too concerned if your teens say no to *you*. If they can be assertive at home, they can be this way with their friends, which is great. The key is to teach assertiveness not aggression.

Encourage Extracurricular Activities

Extracurricular activities are a great way for teens to be involved with others (and join a group) without having to work their way into a clique. But even more important, hobbies and after-school activities can help teens focus on something other than their friends and their friends' opinions. What's more, having to go to a lesson, a practice or a meeting is often a good way of opting out of activities that teens know they shouldn't be involved in. One teen guy I met went to the gym—or said he was going to the gym—whenever his friends were embarking on an activity he didn't want to join.

Lack of Friends

Not all teens belong to big cliques or crowds of friends. Some may have just one or two close friends. If parents are very social, they may worry about this. But there is nothing wrong with being content with a small circle of friends and a relatively quiet social life, and parents should respect the fact that their children have different social needs than they do. If, however, your child has *no* friends, spends all of his or her time alone, or begins to isolate himself from the people around him, then you need to talk with your teen about this. There may be an emotional or social problem that is leading to the isolation. If you suspect there is, take your teen to see a doctor, counsellor or therapist.

Focus on Learning Styles and School

When children and teens have difficulty in school, it is easy to mistake their poor results for a lack of effort, self-discipline or organization. These days, parents and teachers are also likely to suspect learning disabilities. But all too often, the real cause of a student's weak performance in school is simply a disconnect between *how* that student learns and *how* he or she is taught. In order to understand how your teen's learning style might be affecting his or her academic performance, take a look at these three different learning styles and see which seems to describe your teen best.

Visual Learners

Visual learners learn best when they *see* information. They respond not only to material that they read but also to ideas and information that are presented through skits, pictures, graphs, maps and videos.

Concepts often become clearer to visual learners if they can relate them to an image, so metaphors ("our society is a melting pot") and similes ("the stock market moves like a rollercoaster") are particularly strong ways to share information or ideas with these types of learners.

If your child is a visual learner and is having difficulty in school, you may want to encourage her to talk with her teachers about this. I would also recommend that your teen speaks to a guidance counsellor to see if there are any tips, workshops or counselling that they can get. Their instructors may be able to provide course material in visual formats or use more visuals in their lessons. Your teen may also be able to find the visual material (like documentaries for history class) herself.

Visual learners should

- Sit close to the front of the classroom, so they can see the chalkboard and their teachers' body language and facial expressions
- *Always take notes!* Writing out information and ideas will help them visualize the material

- Use an agenda, but choose one that has a good visual of the entire month or week, so that they can see the overall picture of their schedules

Kinesthetic Learners

Kinesthetic learners learn best through *doing*. Usually this involves movement of some sort, including: writing, acting, building models or devices, experimenting, painting, drawing, game playing and other hands-on activities.

Kinesthetic learning is probably the style that is least compatible with the way most teaching is done in our high schools today, and as a result, some kids who are actually kinesthetic learners are labelled ADD or ADHD. If your child is a kinesthetic learner, either you or he might want to talk with his classroom teachers about how lessons and projects might be tailored to fit this learning style. It may also be helpful to explain to teachers that kinesthetic learners find it difficult to sit for too long.

Auditory Learners

Auditory learners learn best through listening. They process information and ideas well when they are conveyed through lectures or discussions, or by listening to CDs or Podcasts.

Generally, auditory learners do well in school, as 80 percent of the lessons in high school are delivered by lectures. Since school often comes easy to this kind of learner, these students may not develop strong work habits, discipline and good time-management skills.

To find out what kind of learning style your teen has (or that you yourself have), try this simple exercise. Suggest that you are going to give your teen directions for how to get from point A to point B. How would he prefer to take the directions?

- Written out (e.g., turn right, turn left)
- Drawn (e.g., an actual picture or a map)
- Walking the route itself with you or someone else

Auditory learners tend to write out directions. Visual learners tend to like maps or pictures. And kinesthetic learners tend to want to travel the route. Many of us have a combination of these different learning styles.

In fact, surprisingly, only 10 percent of the population are auditory learners. Given that so much of the high school curriculum is covered through lectures and discussion, many of the remaining 90 percent of learners may feel stupid, frustrated or unmotivated. If your child is feeling this way, you may want to help him explore ways in which he can study or access information that may work for him. And as inside-out parents, your assessment of his school performance should be on the effort he expends not the grades he brings home.

Different Kinds of Learners

If your teen does well in school without much effort, he might be an auditory learner. If you see your teen trying really hard at school, but her marks don't reflect their effort, it might be because she is primarily a visual or kinesthetic learner.

School Choices

When their children are young, many parents put a great deal of thought into what school their children might go to. Do they want a Catholic school or a public school? A French-immersion program or an English-only program? Would a Montessori, Waldorf or other private school suit their children's needs better than the local school? But by the time high school rolls around, parents may well step back and let their teens make most of their academic decisions. While teens do need to make these decisions, it is important that parents be involved in the process and discuss all of the options with their children.

Even if you live in an area where there is only one high school or no alternative or private schools to choose from, your teen's high school will likely offer some choices in curriculum. In the areas of math and English, for example, there may be different courses designed for students bound for colleges and the trades and those aimed at students headed for university. In some provinces, there are high schools designated commercial, technical or vocational, which generally tailor their offerings to suit college, work or trades-bound students, and academic or "collegiate" schools that provide courses that are prerequisites for university admission. Some high schools offer both types of courses. Middle school and high school counsellors and teachers can provide guidance about which type of high school might suit a student the best, but the decision about courses and schools must be made largely on where the student thinks he or she might want to end up at the end of high school—not an easy thing to foresee for many young people. Encourage your teens to talk with guidance counsellors and career counsellors about courses that might be appropriate both for their interests and abilities and for their post-secondary plans.

In some areas, the choice in high schools goes beyond university-bound and college or trade-bound courses. If you have the financial resources, there may be private schools with specific academic focuses, pedagogical approaches or smaller class sizes that will suit your child better than your local school. In some areas, the public school systems offer schools with specialized focuses including arts, science, technology, International Baccalaureate programs, alternative education and programs that provide smaller teacher-to-student ratios for teens who may have difficulty at the larger schools. The best approach is to find out as much as you can about the choices available to you while your child is in middle school, or if your teen becomes unhappy or unsuccessful in his current school.

Semestered or Non-semestered?

But there are other considerations to take into account when discussing school choices with your teens. For example, high schools operate on either the semester or the non-semester system. In the semestered schools, students usually take three or four courses in each of their half-year terms. In a non-semestered school, the students generally take seven to eight courses that run all year long. As a rule, the semestered schools have fewer subjects each day, in longer periods. The non-semestered schools, more subjects per day in shorter periods. A student who gets bored easily and likes lots of variety may do better in a non-semestered school. A teen who prefers fewer interruptions in a day or a student who may learn better by spending more time on each subject in each session, may have better results in the semestered system. If available in your area, the semestered schools are sometimes also a good choice for students who find organization a bit of a challenge—in each semester they only have to keep track of homework and assignments for three or four subjects. That being said, parents and teens must remember that they may have long stretches of time between courses on the same subject matter when they are in a semestered system. For example, if your teens take math in the first term of grade nine, but then don't get math again until the second term of grade ten, an entire year will have gone by with no math at all. Will your teens remember enough of the grade nine math to succeed in grade ten? If not, will they be willing to put in extra review time to refresh their knowledge?

In Chapter 2, I caution parents about overfunctioning in their teens' lives. And it is certainly possible to overfunction when it comes to your child's high school choice or course options. You need to listen to your teen's thoughts and preferences, and encourage them to make decisions that suit their needs. But it's important to realize that the decisions that need to be made about schools and courses can be confusing and overwhelming—for adults and teens alike. Helping your teens to navigate high school options, curriculum choices and the prerequisites for their post-secondary education or work plans is a good idea. Get your teens to do research, talk with as many people as they can and gather as much information as possible. (If your teen is willing to have you do this as well, the partnership is likely to yield even more information.) Once you've got all the information in front of you, your teen can make wise choices. "Know your options" is what I often tell teens about high school.

How to Help Your Teen Be a Motivated Student

I am often asked by parents how they can help their children become motivated students. Once again, modelling is very important—if you love to learn, they are likely to as well. But there are many other things you can do to help them be hardworking, focused students:

- Make sure you focus on their efforts, not on the end results.
- Praise and affirm their effort when you see it.
- Don't overfunction. If parents are highly anxious about their teen's school work and performance, there is a strong chance your teen will underfunction in reaction. Let them own their school experience.
- Ask what they are learning and studying. Invite them to discuss some of things that have interested them in school.
- Ask if they need any help. Let them know you are available if they need any support.
- If they show an interest in a career choice, do activities with them that might further excite them about that field. For example, if your daughter likes science, take her to a science fair or science centre. If your son is interested in film, take him to a film festival.
- Look for everyday events and family trips to inspire a love of learning. For example, talk about news, music, movies, politics and history.
- Get solution-focused and brainstorm *with them* about what has worked in the past regarding their motivation. For example,

- What environment (e.g., bedroom, computer room, family room, kitchen) helps them be most efficient and focused?
- What time of day do they tend to be most efficient?
- What distracts them? What can they do to reduce those distractions?
- Do they have a good working environment? A suitable desk? A proper light?
- How much time do they need per day to finish their school work and home duties? Look at their schedule with them and help them (if they will allow you) to put together a schedule or routine. (A sampleroutine appears in Chapter 6.)

The key is to partner with your teens and not micromanage them. You want to help your teen discover the unique equation that helps them be focused and efficient.

Attitudes

> "I find it really annoying when my mom reminds me and tells me things I already know. For example, 'You have a test on Friday,' or 'You need to clean your room to do your homework.' I'm well aware of my test on Friday because my teacher told me. I listen in class and I do not need a teacher at home as well."
>
> —Andrea, age 15

In the previous chapter, I explained that being an inside-out parent meant looking at the inner qualities or character of your teen rather outer accomplishments or superficial behaviours. But another essential part of being an inside-out parent is examining your own character. Problems often arise between parents and teens because parents are expecting teens to act in a way that they themselves do not. Or a parent's attitude clashes with a teen's needs. Frequently, parents in these situations are unaware that their parenting style and behaviours are contributing to the problems they are having with their children.

Having coached hundreds of families, I've witnessed over a dozen common parenting attitudes. It's important to realize that these attitudes are not discrete or mutually exclusive—many overlap with one another, and you may have a combination of them, maybe some to a stronger or lesser degree. Most of the attitudes I describe can be problematic, but parents, usually with the very best of intentions, often harbour them without realizing it. However, once they become aware of their attitudes, parents are able to make changes that improve their relationship with their teen.

Parental Attitude Check-Up

As I discuss these different attitudes, I encourage you not only to ask if you see yourself or your spouse in these descriptions, but also to ask what attitude your child or your spouse might say you have.

"It's not only teens who grow. Parents do too. As much as we watch to see what our teens do with their lives, they are watching us to see what we do with ours. I can't tell my teen to reach for the sun. All I can do is reach for it myself."   —Joyce Maynard

---

The Teacher

Parents with the "Teacher" attitude believe that their role is to instruct their teens. Of course, most parents want to use the benefits of their age and experience to share knowledge, wisdom and life lessons with their kids, but teacher parents take this one step further and spend most of their time telling their teens what to do. Moreover, they expect their teens to accept and follow their advice to the letter.

David had brought his 16-year-old son, Brian, to a meeting with me because he was concerned that his son had no motivation, and that they rarely talked with each other. Within three minutes of sitting in my office, David took a deep breath and started: "Brian, you know you just need to buckle down. You just need to really focus and actually start trying. If you could just find some new friends—your friends are just as unmotivated as you are—no wonder you have no direction. You really just need to get to bed earlier. You know if you could get to bed by 10 instead of midnight you might have some energy at school. And what you really need to do is get an agenda book. No wonder you can't keep track of anything. You have no organization. . . ." This went on for another 10 minutes. Even I zoned out.

David was doing all the talking, saying the same thing three differ-ent ways in the hopes that his son would listen and follow his advice.

Brian was sitting silently, but he was not paying attention. Eventually, David said, "Brian have you heard a word I'm saying?" Brian then jumped to his feet, saying, "Dad, if you quit acting like my teacher, always telling me what I should do, maybe I would listen."

Potential Impact

For any of us, constantly being told what to do can be exhausting, irritating and annoying. Not surprisingly, teens in this situation tend to tune out their parents—they learn how *not* to listen. But more harmful even than this breakdown in communication is the impact the teacher attitude can have on a teen's self-esteem. If parents are always telling their kids what to do, they are indirectly telling them, "I don't think you really know how to do this," or "I don't trust you to make good decisions on your own." The teacher attitude, then, disempowers teens instead of empowering them.

The Overfunctioner

This is the most prevalent attitude I see in the parents I work with because it is one of the most common ways in which two people relate to one another. In any relationship, one person may "Overfunction" taking on most of the work involved, while the other person "Underfunctions" as a result. Think of a teeter-totter—as one person goes up, the other goes down.

In the case of a parent-teen relationship, if the parent is the overfunctioner, he or she is doing everything that needs to be done in the teen's life (going one step further than the teacher parent who is simply telling the teens what to do). Overfunctioning parents may be waking their kids up, making their lunches, doing their laundry, nagging them to do their homework, or doing their homework for them.

Parents can overfunction in virtually every area of the parent-teen relationship, including matters of emotion, conflict, friendships and even communication with their teens. They might greet their teen after school by saying, "So what happened in school? Who did you hang out with? What subjects did you have today? What happened in your math test? What happened with your fight with your friends?" They ask millions of questions and are doing all the work. As a result, the underfunctioning teen does very little, perhaps replying with "yep," "nope" and other one-word answers.

Overfunctioning parents are doing all the giving, while their teens are doing all the taking. Overfunctioning parents feel responsible *for* their teen's success and failure instead of responsibility *to* their teen.

Why Do We Overfunction?

Since this is by far the most common attitude I see in today's parents, it worth discussing why so many people behave this way. As you read, ask yourself if any of these apply to you.

Guilt. Many parents do too much for their teens because they feel guilty. Whether it is about their divorce, their long work hours or not providing the type of family life they had hoped for, they're overfunctioning to compensate for their guilt.

Fear. Some parents are afraid to say no to their teens. They fear what might happen if they set limits, stop doing things for their kids or require teens to do more in the family: Will their teens still love them? Will they rebel?

Exhaustion. Let's face it. Most of us are worn out. Sometimes it is just easier to do things ourselves than to ask our children to do them. What's more, teaching children how to do things like laundry and cooking takes time, energy and patience, which may be in short supply at the end of a long working day.

Trying to Be the Dream Parent. Most parents I've worked with have such good intentions. They love their teens deeply and they simply want to give them everything that they themselves did not get. Many parents of teens today who find themselves overfunctioning had parents whom we might call underfunctioners (see below). They are doing too much in their relationship with their children because they are trying to be the parents they wished they'd had. Or they simply want to be a "dream parent." Unfortunately, they don't understand that by doing and giving their teen everything, they are often paralyzing their teen instead of preparing them.

Potential Impact

When parents overfunction there are many potential consequences. For one, parents may be exhausted, stressed out, frustrated or angry. They might tell their kids, "Look at all that I do for you." Teens often see this as nagging and respond negatively. As a result, there can be conflict and distance in their relationship. Overfunctioning highly impacts self-esteem as well. Just as teacher parents are implying a lack of confidence in their child's abilities, so overfunctioning parents are suggesting that their teens aren't capable of doing things on their own. Even if parents say "I know you can do it," if they pick up after their teens all of the time, their teens are more likely to think that their parents don't believe they can do it properly themselves. One of the best ways for teens to build their self-esteem is to have responsibilities. But if a parent steals all the jobs, it doesn't leave anything for the teen.

One of the greatest consequences of overfunctioning is that it creates teens who have an attitude of entitlement. These teens blame their parents for their problems: "It's your fault I was late; you didn't wake me up," or "I failed my math test because you didn't remind me to study."

Their sense of entitlement, however, goes beyond the family. Young adults raised this way are entering the work force with unrealistic expectations and demands. Companies are reporting that Generation Y employees are showing up at their first jobs demanding raises, extra time off and other perks while seeming unaware of what is expected of them.

The important thing to remember is that we should not blame teens or Generation Y for their attitude of entitlement. Our society has greatly contributed to this problem by making things too easy. We've overfunctioned and taught many young people that the world revolves around them.

In Chapter 6, I talk in more detail about how to change from an overfunctioning parent to a healthy-functioning parent to avoid these potential problems with your teens.

When Is It Okay to Overfunction?

Is there ever a situation when it is advisable for parents to overfunction? Yes, absolutely. If you think your teen is in danger of hurting himself or someone else, it is time to step in. Parents always need to make safety their number one concern.

The Mother Bear or Rescuer

The "Mother Bear" or "Rescuer" is really just an aspect of the overfunctioning parent, but I like to discuss it separately as it is such an emotionally driven attitude. All parents hate to think of their children experiencing pain, rejection, disappointment or failure. It's a natural impulse to want to minimize our children's suffering. But rescuers believe that they need to protect their teens from all failure or from any kind of conflict and pain, and in doing so, they usually do just the opposite.

A great example of this situation was my client Jackie. She came from a privileged family and was an only teen. At home, she was the centre of her mother's world. At school, however, this was far from the case. She started having difficulties with other kids by the time she was in grade two. Jackie had never learned how to share, compromise or make friends. But she was really good at making demands, ordering people around and telling people off—all the things she got away with at home. When the school started calling her mother, her mother repeatedly made excuses for Jackie's misbehaviour. She refused to allow the school to impose any sort of consequences, and blamed other children for making up stories because they were jealous. The problems continued and escalated until grade seven or eight. By this time, the kids were fed up with Jackie's "princess attitude." They started avoiding her and excluded her from birthday parties. Her mother, instead of looking at what was causing her daughter's social difficulties, was on the phone with the other mothers, yelling at them for not inviting her daughter to the parties. Jackie, although appearing overly confident, struggled enormously with low self-esteem because of her difficulties with other people, difficulties that were made worse by her mother's rescuer approach.

Rescuers may get involved inappropriately with their children's social lives, school work, assignments and grades, sporting activities and any other area where they feel a disappointing outcome might be avoided. They tend to see all failure as a bad thing that should be minimized at all costs. Like Jackie's mother, the rescuer therefore sidesteps any natural consequences for her children, robbing them of tough but crucial life lessons.

Potential Impact

Children and teens who are constantly rescued from their failures and protected by their parents lose many opportunities to learn about how to get along in the world. They may not develop skills such as problem solving, decision making and resilience. They often struggle with independence and becoming their own person. In the worst cases, teens become almost fused to their parents, thoroughly dependent on them because they've learned that they need their parents to fix all problems. Sometimes, however, teens react with anger, pushing their parents away.

And just like the children of any overfunctioning parent, teens of rescuers suffer from self-esteem issues brought on by their parents' seeming lack of confidence in their abilities.

The Underfunctioner

If you are reading this book, it's unlikely that you are an "Underfunctioning" parent. The opposite of overfunctioning parents, underfunctioning parents do not do enough work in their relationship with their teens. They do not believe they are responsible *to* or *for* their older children. They do very little in the way of helping, connecting or guiding their teens.

Sometimes parents underfunction because they are preoccupied with their own concerns (depression, alcoholism, marriage problems, affairs, career demands, insecurity, etc.). Often, underfunctioning parents simply believe that their teens do not need parenting at all. They may be under the impression that teenagers have all the rational and emotional tools necessary to manage on their own. And they may mistake a teen's desire for independence as proof of that child's ability to be completely independent.

Potential Impact

The greatest consequence of being an underfunctioning parent is that your teens grow up too fast; because their parents underfunction, these teens tend to overfunction. Teenagers in this type of family take on adult responsibilities and lose out on a normal and healthy childhood and adolescence. As a result, many of these teens feel anxious, depressed, overwhelmed and burdened. These kids rarely if ever confide in their parents or go to them for advice and support. Not only do these teens hold age-inappropriate responsibilities, but they may also begin acting like parents, telling their mothers and fathers what they should and should not be doing. In the long run, children of underfunctioning parents may turn to drugs and alcohol to help them cope, or they may become highly stressed and unhappy overachievers.

The Basket Case

Josie was a sensitive, compassionate and perceptive 11-year-old when she first came to see me. Her parents had been having marital difficulties and were fighting and yelling in front of her. To make matters worse, her mother, who kept to herself and didn't have a lot of friends, had started to turn to Josie for support. Josie told me her mom was highly emotional, crying all the time, irritable and suffering from mood swings. She would come into Josie's room at night, tuck her into bed and start complaining to Josie about her husband—Josie's father. Several times, Josie's mom even cried on her daughter's shoulder. Josie loved her mom and wanted to help her, so she continued to listen, gave advice and tried to be supportive of her mother. But it was too big of a job for her. She felt overwhelmed, burdened and depressed. When her mother was upset, Josie felt she had failed her. Eventually, reacting to the stress, Josie developed an eating disorder, which had prompted her parents to bring her to me.

Josie's mother is what I term a "Basket Case" parent. The basket case is a variant of the underfunctioning parent. Many parents may be struggling with problems in their lives, such as divorce, separation or marriage woes, illness, death, work or financial crises and so on. These parents can suffer from stress, depression, anxiety, anger or exhaustion. What makes some parents in these situations basket cases, however, is that they allow their personal difficulties to make them completely self-absorbed and self-obsessed. They no longer take into account the needs of their teens or how the family situation might be affecting their children. They may be highly emotional in front of their children and, in the most extreme cases, basket case parents may also unload their problems on their teens, looking to their children for support. If their teens share something happening in their own lives, often these parents quickly turn the conversation back to themselves.

Potential Impact

If there is one thing teens have really taught me, it's how incredibly bright, intuitive and perceptive they are. We don't give teens nearly the credit they deserve. If teens see that their parents are emotionally unstable or fragile, the teen is unlikely to share their own feelings and concerns. They will assume that if their parents are struggling with their own problems, they won't be able to handle any concerns their teens might bring up. Not only does this cause a real breakdown in communication between parent and child, but it also leaves teens without any parental support. This situation is particularly intense if a teen is emotionally sensitive. Sensitive teens often take their parent's problems on as their own. As a result, they feel burdened, overwhelmed and in extreme cases depressed. What's more, if teens are being asked to help emotionally, but believe that they are not able to solve their parents' problems, or make their parents feel better, they may experience a sense of failure—a severe blow to their developing self-esteem. I cannot stress how important it is for parents *never* to go to your teen for your emotional support. Get a counsellor. Talk to a friend. Join a support group. Find other adults who can be your support team, but that support must *never* be your teen—it's unfair and damaging to your teen.

The Blamer

Sometimes when parents and teens are not getting along or when a family is undergoing difficulty, the parents resort to blaming their teens for the problems. Rather than seeing the crisis as one to which everyone is contributing and everyone needs to help solve, parents will focus on the teens' role exclusively. The "Blamer" parent acts as if the teen is the problem and therefore "needs to be fixed." Some will send their children to counselling hoping that this will do the trick.

These parents rarely agree to join in the counselling, nor do they make concessions or offer apologies for their own behaviour, as they believe that the blame for the family discord lies squarely with their teens.

Potential Impact

Nothing discourages teens more from talking than being attacked. Teens with blamer parents don't feel safe, and when they don't feel safe, they don't talk. When they do talk, these teens often lie to avoid the immediate consequences.

Not only is all the blame and criticism an obvious blow to the teen's self-esteem, but it also may lead teens to rebel, overtly or covertly (including drug use, skipping school and other poor choices). And who could blame them? If a parent already thinks of her teen as a problem, a teen might find himself thinking, *Why not deliver?*

The Sergeant

When Rebecca and her parents first came to my office, I noticed immediately that there was no eye contact, no warmth and no connection between them. Rebecca's father talked loudly, making demands of everyone and allowing no room for negotiating. This attitude apparently helped him in his corporate job as president of a successful company. But this strategy definitely was not working with his daughter. Rebecca was overtly rebelling— ignoring her school work, doing drugs, dating a guy her parents "hated." Rebecca had so many wonderful qualities—she was caring, compassionate, understanding and a great friend. But her communication with her father was now limited to yelling and slamming doors.

Rebecca's father had arranged for family coaching in the hopes that I would get Rebecca to bow to his authority. Rebecca's father had I what I call the "Sergeant" attitude.

For someone with a sergeant attitude, parenting is all about being in charge. Of course every parent is morally and legally responsible to their child, so in many ways, they are in charge. But sergeants exercise their authority through intimidation. They often shout, yell and scream to get their point across. Parents with this attitude set down rigid boundaries and rules and rarely if ever negotiate with their teens. They often think that teens are supposed to be seen and not heard. They seldom apologize. Often they believe that praising children will make their kids "big-headed." They may also believe that kids need to be toughened up by having their weaknesses or things they need to work on pointed out. (I sometimes also talk about a "Closed Door" parent, who is very much like the sergeant, but without the intimidation. Like the sergeant, closed door parents are excessively authoritarian, think they hold all the answers, don't listen to feedback from their children and are extremely defensive when it comes to criticism of their own behaviour.)

Potential Impact

When teens think that they can't negotiate with their parents, or offer a different point of view, they tend to withdraw. They bottle up their feelings and thoughts, and because of this their parents never really get to know them. The resulting gap can mean that teens don't feel safe—they think they have no one to go to for support and under-standing when they need help. What's more, because sergeant parents don't listen to their teens, their teens often don't feel valued, and they may struggle with low self-esteem. If a sergeant parent withholds praise and is generous with criticisms, teens may believe that nothing they do is ever good enough.

The Babbler

Within five minutes of arriving in my office with her son, Michael's mother told me that Michael had, before coming in for coaching, begged her not to babble. Within 10 minutes I understood why. Michael's mom talked non-stop. She started on one topic, which reminded her of another topic, which reminded her of a third topic. As you can imagine, Michael zoned out. His dad stared towards the floor. I stopped the mom after a while and said, "Okay, I've got an idea of how you see the situ-ation—let me hear from the other two people in this room." Michael's dad had only been talking for a couple of minutes when Michael's mom took a deep breath and interrupted her husband. I gently reminded her that it was the dad's turn. I had to do this four times in the next 10 minutes. Michael seemed disconnected from his mother. And I wasn't surprised. How can anyone build a relationship with someone who talks non-stop and cuts off others when they start talking?

Michael's mother was what I call a "Babbler." And while an overly chatty parent may seem to be more annoying than anything else, in reality, he or she can create real problems in the parent-teen relationship. In fact, what babblers hold in common with teachers, sergeants (or closed doors), blamers and basket cases is that they are more focused on themselves and their own opinions and concerns than on their teens. Babblers believe they have a lot of important things to say, and they often think that their opinions are more important that what others think or feel. Babblers are almost always poor listeners.

Potential Impact

Like the children of teachers, sergeants and blamers, teens of babblers may come to believe that their opinions are not as important as their parents'. As well as the resulting self-esteem issues, teens of babblers are unlikely to have a strong relationship with their parents, as the communication is going chiefly one way. Unable to talk with their parents about their ideas, their concerns or even the routine details of their lives, these teens may not be getting all the guidance and support they need.

The Weather Reporter

Seventeen-year-old Sam was struggling with low self-esteem when he started coming to my practice. After a few sessions together, it became clear to me that Sam had a very disconnected relationship with his parents, so much so that he complained about feeling "lonely" at home. He knew his parents loved him and were proud of him, but he didn't know *why*. "They've never told me," he said. He also observed that his parents never asked him any questions. "They never ask me how I'm feeling about certain parts of my life. We talk about the weather and sports. Dinner times are really quiet."

Sam's parents were good people, but they had no idea how to connect with their son in an intimate and meaningful way. Both seemed more comfortable keeping their communication at an impersonal level. I dub parents like these "Weather Reporters."

Weather Reporter parents think that building a good relationship with their teen means talking about weather, sports, movies and other superficial topics. They may fear that asking personal questions of their teen is too invasive, or they may not know how to discuss things that intimate or emotional in nature. In some cases, weather reporters may simply see no value in talking about feelings with other people.

Potential Impact

If a parent doesn't initiate discussions about personal thoughts and feelings, teens may think that they can't raise these topics either. As a result, weather reporter parents never really know how their teens are feeling, what they are stressed about or what their dreams are. I can't count how many times I hear parents say, "I don't feel I really know my kids." That's what happens if all we talk about is the weather. And for the teens, this distance in the relationship may mean that regardless of how loving and supportive the parents want to be, the teens may not think they can seek comfort or guidance from them. The weather reporter attitude can also affect teens' self-esteem. If the parents don't affirm and praise their teens (and I've never met a teen who doesn't want this), the teens never know if they measure up to their parents' love and expectations.

The Friend

The "Friend" is a parent who believes the way to build a relationship with their teens is to be their buddy. Parents with this attitude think that the days when a parent's role was to discipline or dictate are gone. Rather than replace the sergeant approach of old with the inside-out parenting of love, guidance, support and boundaries, these parents follow the lead of their kids, seldom saying no or providing rules. They are often also indulgent—buying their teens whatever they want. Many think that their openness prevents their children from lying to them, although this is often not the case.

A parent I met at one of my workshops told me about how her

husband had responded to the growing difficulties he was having with their 15-year-old daughter. Desperate to have her talk to him and to know what was going on her life, he adopted the kind of permissive attitude a friend might have with another friend. When his daughter asked him to buy her alcohol to take to a party, he was terrified to say no. Instead he bought her and her friends wine with a low percentage of alcohol, rationalizing that by doing so he had prevented her from going to the party and drinking other liquor with higher alcoholic content. Despite being an intelligent man, he was completely unaware at how his lack of boundaries was negatively impacting his daughter.

Potential Impact

The irony of the friend attitude is that it almost always backfires. Most teens have plenty of friends. They are not looking to their mother or father to be one more. They expect their parents to be parents, and when they fail to fill this role, the teens lose respect for them. And teens don't talk with people they don't respect.

But just as important, the children of friend parents often have real difficulties setting boundaries for themselves. They find it difficult to delay gratification and to be self-disciplined. Children learn about how to set boundaries and stick to them by watching their parents do the same thing. But if parents don't set limits and don't provide consequences when boundaries are breached, children have no models for this kind of self-discipline—the kind of self-discipline it takes to say no when it is difficult to do so. If a parent agrees to a request from their teen to buy alcohol, how can the parent expect the teen to say no the hard sell of a drug dealer?

And of course, a lack of self-discipline will have a negative impact on a teen's sense of self. One of the most important ways to build self-esteem is to have responsibilities and to follow through with those tasks. If a teen lacks self-discipline, he won't achieve his goals and as a result, he will struggle with low self-esteem.

The Doormat

"Doormat" parents behave very much as friend parents do, but for different reasons. These parents seldom say no (or feel guilty if they do), not because they want to be buddies with their teens, but because they believe they have lost all power in the parent-teen relationship. They may have given over their power because their self-esteem is so low they don't feel confident to be any kind of authority. Or they may feel unprepared to cope with the conflict that they fear will arise if they say no. Other doormat parents simply don't know *how* to say no. Whatever the reason, in a family with doormat parents, the kids are running the show. Doormat parents also don't know how to set boundaries, or if they do, they don't execute any consequences. Many of the doormat parents I've met don't know how to regain their power.

Potential Impact

Like the children of parents with the friend or underfunctioning attitudes, these teens have been given power that is inappropriate for their age. As a result, they often develop false self-esteem and an attitude of entitlement, and they are often short-tempered with their parents.

The Inside-Out Parent

The "Inside-Out" parent is the one most of us want to be. These parents make it their primary objective to raise teens with solid characters.

Inside-out parents know that teens desperately want and need their parents' love, praise and encouragement. They are affirming and encouraging parents, praising their teens often not for what they are achieving but for the positive character traits they are developing. They acknowledge their children's courage, discipline, perseverance, etc., rather than focusing on outside achievements. (They spend much more time talking about effort than school grades and body piercings!)

Inside-out parents really want to *understand* and know their kids—what they like, what they don't like, what motivates them, what frustrates them, what makes them tick.

Inside-out parents recognize that they must hold more authority than their teens, but they also appreciate that their children are people of great value in their own right. They know that they must provide discipline and structure in order for their teens to develop healthy and positive characters. Their brand of structure and the boundaries they provide are fair: their teens know what is expected of them in advance and the parents follow through with what was agreed upon.

Inside-out parents know they are responsible *to* their teen but not responsible *for* their teen. They understand that they can only try their very best at raising their kids, but also that there are other things that will influence children.

Inside-out parents believe that they hold an enormous responsibility to be role models in all areas of their teenagers' lives. They believe it is unfair and unrealistic to expect their teen to learn any skill or character trait without modelling it and creating a structure to encourage it.

Inside-out parents believe that as parents, they are not perfect. If they realize they have done something wrong (which happens to all parents), they have no problem authentically apologizing to their teen because it's loving and fair, but also because they want to model this behaviour for their children.

And most significantly, inside-out parents believe it's important to enjoy their kids: their presence, their stories and their perspectives. They believe in getting to know their teens. In short, these parents are able to form a healthy attitude towards parenting by avoiding the pitfalls described by the other attitudes listed in this chapter.

Potential Impact

There are so many things that are gained when parents have truly adopted this inside-out attitude. First, teens feel valued, loved, adored and special. When teens learn this, they internalize it and often adopt it as their own thinking. This is the foundation of healthy self-esteem. When teens feel confident, they are more likely to choose healthy friends, set realistic goals and have the courage to go after those goals. When teens believe

Margaret Gordon's Top 12 Tips to Being an Inside-Out Parent

I had a radio talk show in Toronto for two years, and on Mother's Day I decided to have my own mother on as a guest to share her top 12 tips for other parents. It was wonderful for me to hear her talk about her own beliefs and attitudes, because I saw these growing up. Each of her 12 tips I had seen lived out, and I knew what an incredible impact they had had on my own self-esteem and my relationship with my parents. I believe these are a great summary of how inside-out parents think and act. In her own words, here is what my mother said:

1. Accept the uniqueness of each of your teens.
2. Be willing to admit your own mistakes and ask for forgiveness if you have hurt your teen.
3. Spend time with each teen;play with them, get to know their likes and dislikes.
4. Help them when you are asked but don't take over! Give them space to develop their own gifts.
5. Affirm them, focus on their good qualities, praise them for effort and work well done.
6. Teach them to be truthful.
7. Set realistic boundaries and rules, but be flexible.
8. Be consistent with your boundaries and rules (this is not always easy but it is important).
9. Be authentic, be real! Kids can tell right away if we are phonies.
10. Teach them to be responsible for their own things like jobs, money and school work.
11. Love them unconditionally; be patient, kind, accepting of who they are as people; separate who they are from what they do.
12. MODEL, MODEL, MODEL what you preach and teach. For example, don't tell them to tell the truth and then ask them to lie for you on the phone (e.g., saying you're not there when you don't want to talk to the caller).

that their parents are approachable, understanding and supportive (that is to say their parents are affirming, willing to apologize, admit to when they are wrong, try to learn and listen from their teen), they are more likely to talk. The most common question I am asked is, "How can I get my teen to talk to me?" This is the key, and it's not really any secret other than good common sense. When teens feel safe, they talk. When teens feel valued, they have strong self-esteem. When teens have strong self-esteem, they are developing their character. When teens have solid character they become disciplined, responsible, honest, reliable, polite, kind., etc., and this helps them live happy and successful lives.

The best example I know of the inside-out attitude are my own parents. I am the person I am today simply because of the love, encouragement and safety I felt as a teen. A couple of years ago, I asked my mom, "What is the most important piece of advice you would give to other parents?" She replied, "Children and teens need lots of love and lots of discipline." That was it—and this became one of my favourite mottos. Teens need lots of encouragement, praise and affirmation but also lots of structure, boundaries, discipline and guidance. When teens have both of these, they feel safe, valued and cherished and become highly responsible, disciplined, motivated and empathetic.

Teen Attitudes

Since we've been talking about attitudes in this chapter, here are a few thoughts about the attitudes of tweens, preteens and teens. In my years of practice, I've noticed that the teens coming into my office hold one of two distinct attitudes. One group has what I call the "Wise" attitude. These teens have a clear goal, whether it is a desire to build their self-esteem, respond more effectively to their parents or increase their motivation. They see me to learn a specific tool to help them reach their goal. Many of them come in with a notebook or journal (I'm not joking—many parents think I am when I say this) and take notes during our sessions. They are seeking wise counsel and then following it. This is a common technique of many successful people. These people learn from other's successes and mistakes, and they find mentors, teachers and coaches who can help them become the best they can be.

The other group has what I term the "Experiential" attitude. Most of them don't really want to be coached. They are reluctant to have anyone tell them what to do. They have no clear goals, and when I ask them what kind of goals that want to set, they say either "I don't know" or "I can't stand setting goals." If I insist that they set goals, I experience resistance.

The parents of experiential teens describe them as people who march to their own drummer. They live life on their own terms. They want to learn from their own mistakes instead of learning from other people's mistakes. They learn primarily through their own experiences.

In my practice, teaching strategies work well with teens who have the wise attitude. But experiential teens do best when I simply listen to them or act as a sounding board for their thoughts and feelings. So how should parents respond to their experiential teens?

Parents who have teens who are experiential often tell me that their teens don't listen to them. What's more, if these parents hold one of the sergeant, teacher or other "I'll tell you what to do" attitudes, their teens are often highly resistant, defensive and rebellious.

Only the inside-out parent is able to really reach and influence the experiential teen. These teens learn through being listened to, having realistic boundaries set for them (since they learn best through experiencing rewards and consequences, not by being told what to do) and having loving parents who give them room to experience life (within safe limits).

Just recently, I realized that I actually had the experiential attitude for many years. I'm now a "wise-convert" but my husband says that even today he can see evidence of my experiential attitude every so often. As a teen, I tried all sorts of activities: ballet, gymnastics, modelling, drama. When I was 16 I announced to my parents that I wanted to act and had made a call to an agent to see if I could get some background work in movies. My mother responded the way she always did. "Well, that's interesting, Karyn," she said, acknowledging my idea without offering her own opinion. She suggested that I do some research into different agents, and then we could discuss who I should see. She offered to go to meet the agent with me.

After I had researched agents, we met with one of them. Despite her initial reservations about the movie business, my mom liked the agent, and that day I got my first job to be an extra in a major movie. For safety reasons, my mom came with me to all the movies I worked on. I did background work for about a year, and then got bored with it. My mother's approach to my acting was a perfect example of how the inside-out parent can respond to the experiential teen. Rather than discouraging me, my mother allowed me to pursue my interests, while encouraging me to take responsibility for my choices by researching the ideas, applying critical thinking to my choices and following through in a safe and informed way. Trying new things, owning the responsibility, then, became an empowering experience for me.

When I talk with audiences of parents about all of these parenting attitudes, I often ask them to put up their hands as I go through the list if they think their kids would nominate them as one type of parent or another. Some parents put up their hand for almost every attitude. (Weather reporters and underfunctioners are the least common, which makes sense as these types of parents are unlikely to come out to a talk on parenting.) It's clear that most of us are not one attitude or another exclusively, and we may have one attitude or another to a greater or lesser degree. Spending some time thinking about how closely your behaviour and attitudes fit any of the descriptions above is an important step to improving your relationship with your teen. Be honest with yourself. The great thing about all of these attitudes is that you are in complete control of them—no matter what kind of family you were raised in and what kind of experiences you have had. It's never too late to change.

Parents who have older children and teens may think that even if it is not too late to change their parenting attitudes, it may be too late for those changes to make a significant difference in their relationship with their teenagers. Not true. But it is going to take some time.

Some parents have told me that when they do initiate a change in attitude towards their teens, their teens respond with skepticism. "What book did you just read?" one teenager asked his parents. It can be very disappointing for parents to find that after they have invested a lot of thought and energy into improving their parenting behaviour, their kids dismiss or distrust the changes. Remember, as I said before, teens are intuitive and perceptive. They want to see you being authentic and genuine. And let's face it—an attitude change for a week, or even a month, can't tell us for sure whether or not someone has changed. Your teens may not respond positively until they experience your new approach consistently, over several months. Be patient with their doubt and skepticism. It will be worth it.

Some Important Questions to Ask Yourself about Your Parenting Attitudes

- What do I think is my role as a parent?
- What is a "healthy" parent? What does he do? What does she say?
- Where did my idea of healthy parenting come from? Where did I learn it?
- What kind of parenting attitude did my parents have?
- How is my parenting style similar to or different from my parents'?
- What do I want to repeat from my parents' parenting style?
- What do I want to change about my parents' parenting style?
- Which of the attitudes listed above sound the most like me today? What about a year ago?
- How has my attitude impacted my relationship with my teens (i.e., the overall relationship, their self-esteem, how much they share with me)?
- What is one thing I can do differently, starting today, to improve my relationship with my teen?

Focus on Privacy and Independence

"Excessive questions really bother me because, although parents should know what's happening in their children's lives and whereabouts, teens need privacy as well. No teenager wants to tell his parents everything."

—Jim, age 16

The reality is that parents are responsible for their teens' safety and well-being. How do we balance our teens' need for privacy with our need to supervise and protect? I think the most sensible way is to approach privacy much as you would driving—it's a privilege, not an inalienable right. When teenagers are behaving responsibly and honestly, they've earned their privacy. If you suspect that your teens are engaged in behaviour that may be harmful to themselves or others, then some of that privacy may have to be forfeited (although I strongly recommend that your teen knows all of this in advance).

Going Out

One of the questions I'm often asked is whether or not parents have the right to know where their teens are going and what they are doing when they aren't at home. Clearly, many teens feel that when their parents are asking these kinds of questions, they are trying to curtail their independence and freedom.

But parents do need to know where their children are and what they are doing—not only is it a matter of safety and legal responsibility, but it's also one of the ways tension and stress can be avoided in a family (ask any parent who has finished cooking a dinner for three children, only to find out that two of them have gone for pizza). If teens are open and honest with this information, parents can then give them flexibility and freedom (within reason).

When teens go out, they should tell their parents

- Where they are going
- Whom they are going with
- What they are doing

And if plans change (which they often do), the teens need to make a quick phone call to let their parents know of the changes.

The key here is partnership. Be clear with your teens that if they do their part (sharing the information), you'll do your part and give them reasonable amounts of freedom.

Computer Use, Email, Diaries and Bedrooms

Another common question I get asked by parents is whether or not it is okay for them to look through their teens' email or search through their rooms. Many say that checking on their children's on-line activities or looking through their things for evidence of smoking or drug use, for example, is the only way they can be sure their kids aren't getting into any trouble. But in truth, most of the parents who read their teens' emails and diaries, or search through their bedrooms, are doing so because they feel a lack of control. They don't know what is going on in their teens' lives. Instead of talking to their children directly (which would be the right thing to do to model honesty), they start snooping around for clues.

What message does it send to teens about their parents' honesty when they learn that their parents have read their emails and diaries? They learn that they can't trust their parents, and yet trust is the foundation and cornerstone of all healthy relationships (see below).

If parents feel out of touch with their teens' lives, they need to become plugged-in parents and work on their communication with their teens. They should *not* be reading diaries, letters or emails, or snooping through their teens' rooms.

That being said, privacy on their computers and in their bedrooms is a privilege for teens. All privileges require responsibility. And if teens are using the privacy they've been granted to hide irresponsible or inappropriate behaviour, a natural consequence is for them lose some of that privacy. To be fair, however, parents need to make their kids aware of what boundaries they are expected to observe and what the consequences will be for breaking those rules, well in advance. (See Chapter 6 for more on boundaries.) Parents should also establish how and when teens can earn back their privacy.

Several years ago I worked with Amanda, who had been caught bullying another girl through email on the family computer. (The bullied girl's parents called my client's parents and told them about it.) Amanda had been told in advance what responsible use of the computer was, so the consequence (which had been established in advance) was for Amanda to go for two weeks without any computer privileges. She also had to write an apology to the girl explaining that she was sorry and why. After she regained her privileges, she was given limited time to use the computer, and her parents also checked her email periodically for some time to make sure she was not breaking any rules.

If a teen has engaged in inappropriate behaviour (which needs to be clarified and defined in each family), then I often recommend that their parents check on them periodically—whether it is occasionally viewing their email, seeing what websites they are accessing on the computer or checking their rooms for drugs. The difference between this type of checking up and snooping is that parents are open about what they expect and are communicating that if certain responsibilities are broken, a fair consequence will follow (e.g., they will be checking their computer use). This boundary not only allows parents to be fair, it also helps teens make decisions. If they know in advance that if they overstep a boundary their parents will start randomly checking their computer use, it often helps them use better judgment. I find that when parents approach situations with this amount of fairness, most teens respond extremely well. (However, I would *never* recommend that parents read their teens' diaries. Teens need a safe place to write out their thoughts. What's more, diaries and journals are very private and contained, unlike email and the Internet, which teens could use to view or send others inappropriate material.)

Trust, Honesty and Privacy

While most parents would recognize that reading their teens' emails or diaries is an invasion of privacy, many regularly disregard the privacy of others without recognizing that they are doing so. Maria came to talk to me because her 12-year-old son Damon didn't seem to trust her. Damon wasn't able to explain to either of us why he felt the way he did. At one point during the session, the conversation got heated and Maria shared something with Damon that another parent had told her in confidence. Suddenly it became clear why Damon felt she couldn't be trusted—he'd seen firsthand that his mother couldn't keep secrets.

Keeping confidences when asked to do so is not only behaving honestly, it's also respecting someone's privacy. But while we might be able to keep the secrets of our friends and spouses, what do we do if our children tell us things in confidence that we feel we should share with their other parent? "If I don't tell my husband when my daughter confides in me," one mother told me, "he won't have a clue about what is going on." She wasn't sure what to do. It's a good question: is our chief responsibility to keep our partners informed or to respect the privacy of our children?

I usually recommend that parents keep their teens' confidences to themselves. First, if your teens know that you are going to share everything with your spouse, there is a high likelihood that they will share less with you. There are some sensitive topics that, for legitimate reasons, teens want to share with only one parent. Second, it's common for one parent to do more of the relationship building, asking the right questions and connecting with their teen. But if that parent then also plays the messenger and tells the other parent everything, that first parent is actually enabling a weak relationship to develop between his or her spouse and the teen. It takes time, energy, a willing spirit and proper skills to develop a healthy relationship with our children. If one parent does all the work and then tells the other parent, the other parent has not earned the right to know that information. And there will be no need for them to build that relationship with their child.

What I recommended to the mother who wondered if she should share her daughter's confidences with her spouse was that she honour her word to her daughter and keep the information to herself. I suggested, however, that she encourage her husband to talk with their daughter—without telling him what specifically he should be talking about. The point of this was to encourage the father to listen to his daughter, to get to know her and to build his relationship with her. Then she might start confiding in him too.

Every couple needs to figure out how they will handle their children's confidences before they encounter situations like this. Once they have established that boundary, they should let their children know what it is. If you've told your teens that you will not share anything they tell you in private with their other parent, then I strongly encourage you to keep that promise. To do anything else would model dishonesty and lying for your children. If, however, you and your partner have agreed not to withhold anything from each other, make sure that your children know about this policy. Then your kids can decide whether or not they tell you things, knowing that it is likely their other parent will hear them too.

The only time I recommend you break a promise of confidentiality to your teens is if they say that they are hurting themselves or others. In situations like this, parents, teachers and counsellors need to put safety and health above the concern for privacy. But even in these situations, I recommend you tell your children, in advance, that this is your boundary, so that there are no surprises. The key to building a foundation of honesty and trust with your teen is that your words match your actions.

Focus on Eating and Eating Disorders

The teen years can be a time when healthy eating becomes a challenge. When children are small, their parents have a great deal of influence over what and how much they consume. But as kids get older, they usually spend more time out of the house and take more responsibility for feeding themselves. Eating may become part of their social life—going for pizza in the evenings for example, or leaving school to buy lunch. To complicate matters, when children hit adolescence they often find that their appetites go into overdrive, making them feel hungry all the time. For many teens, the increased need for calories during periods of intense growth may convince them that they can eat whatever they want and not become overweight. (Usually a teen's appetite will become more moderate again when his or her growth has slowed.) But poor food choices and high calorie intake can become a habit, and teens need to exercise some discipline in their food choices to remain healthy.

On the other sign of the coin, however, many teens become overly concerned about their weight during the teen years. Girls in particular may feel the pressure to be model thin or to have bodies like those of movie and TV stars. Instead of focusing on eating a healthy, well-balanced diet, their desire to be very slender may lead them to various types of diets. Some may become obsessed with counting calories. In extreme cases, teens can develop serious eating disorders like anorexia and bulimia.

How then do you help guide your teen in the right direction? What do you do if you see them making poor food choices or overeating? And how can you tell if your teen is developing an eating disorder?

Overeating and Unhealthy Eating

Being overweight or obese is a growing problem for many teenagers. Statistics Canada notes that in 2004, the overweight rate for teens age 12 to 17 had doubled since 1979, and the obesity rate for these adolescents had tripled. The U.S. Surgeon General has called obesity the greatest threat to health in America today, killing more people than AIDS, cancer and accidents combined.

Overeating can be a habit developed when children are quite young. If parents don't provide appropriate portion control at meals or if there is an abundance of junk food on offer, even small children can become seriously overweight. Some teens may also start overeating during their teens because of their increased hunger (overeating in quantity and also in the sense that they begin to consume significant amounts of food with little nutritional value). But often people overeat to serve an emotional need. Food can be a comfort and a distraction.

If your teens appear to be overeating, it is important to talk to them about why they are overeating. If the teens are unable to discuss with you what is driving them to overeat, consider taking them to a counsellor who may be able to help them fully understand the relationship between their emotions and their eating.

I also recommend that teens

- see their doctor so that their physical health can be monitored
- talk to a nutritionist to make sure they are eating the right foods—your family doctor or local health centre may also be able to provide you with nutritional guidance or tell you about counselling resources in your community
- get involved in a exercise routine—whether it is jogging every day, taking up a sport, joining a gym or seeing a fitness trainer to work on an exercise program

It may also help to create family boundaries around healthy eating. These eating strategies are good ones for everyone interested in eating a balanced diet—not just for overeaters.

Eating Strategies

Don't eat after dinner. Evenings tend to be a time when many people snack on junk, binge eat or thoughtlessly consume far more calories than they need. Eliminating eating after dinner may help us reduce our intake of empty calories.

Get rid of or limit junk food. The reality is that we can't eat junk food if it's not around. Limiting the amount of junk food that is in the house, putting it out of sight (a number of families I know keep their junk food locked up!) or eliminating it from the household altogether can help teens—and everyone else —reach for healthy snacks and meals when they are hungry.

Eat only in the kitchen or dining room. When we are watching TV, reading a book or playing video games our attention is not on what is going into our mouths, so it's easy to lose track of how much we are eating. Eating in the kitchen or dining room (as long as we don't have TV or video games in there) keeps us focused on what and how much we are consuming.

Eat together as a family as often as possible. Spending family time over a meal is important for so many reasons, including the limits it can impose on how much we are eating. When we eat together, the conversation may help us to eat more slowly. (It takes time for our bodies to register that we've eaten. Eating slowly means that we are more likely to notice when we are full and to stop eating at an appropriate point.) Sharing food with family also means that we may be more conscious of the portions we are helping ourselves to—we notice when others have stopped eating, we have to leave enough on the platter for the next person and so on.

Prepare food yourself. Many people find themselves drawn to food that is easy and fast, and junk food, prepackaged food and processed food is just that. Unfortunately some of these foods are also a source of much hidden fat and many nutrition-free calories. Cooking and preparing healthy foods may seem like a lot of work initially, but once we get used to it, the preparation becomes second nature. I encourage all parents to teach their teens how to cook (and even ask their teens to prepare a meal a week). This way, when the teens are hungry and they have to prepare their own food, they won't be limited to only those things they can eat from the bag or pop into the microwave. Making healthy snacking easy is also an essential way to achieve a balanced diet. Ask your teens to go shopping with you and get them to pick out their favourite fruits and vegetables. When you get home, get your teens to wash and cut the fruits and vegetables so they are ready to eat, and store them in the fridge. (Some parents find that leaving veggies and fruit on the counter works better. When their teens see the snacks immediately, they reach for them. When they are in the fridge, they don't tend to get them out.) Making healthy snacking as fast and easy as possible will help create new habits for your teens.

Find out how you can best support your teen. Ask anyone who has struggled with overeating and they will tell you how difficult it is. Whenever we are trying to make changes in our life, we need positive, encouraging and loving support. As a parent, it is important to find out *how* you can support your teens. The best way to do this is to ask them. They may want to do the grocery shopping with you so they can point out the kinds of healthy foods they like. They may ask *you* to model better eating habits! They may suggest that you not have the foods that tempt them the most in the house. Or they may simply want words of encouragement when the going gets tough.

Remember, like trying to change any habit, developing a pattern of healthy eating takes time. It can require a matter of months and many adjustments, so be patient and encourage your teen to stay with the new healthy-eating boundaries.

Dieting

While many teens struggle with overeating and weight gain, others are worrying far too much about their weight. According to the Canadian

Paediatric Society, 50 percent of teenage girls and 25 percent of teenage boys have dieted to try to change their body shape, and sadly approximately 33 percent of girls who are at a *healthy* weight have still tried to diet. Clearly, many teens feel fat, even when they are not.

Dieting is not something that parents should take lightly. The CPS also reports that teens who diet tend to

- have poor a body image, even if they are not overweight
- have poor self-esteem
- feel a lack of control in their lives
- be more likely to smoke, use drugs or have unprotected sex
- engage in dangerous weight loss attempts by using diet pills or laxatives, or by vomiting after eating

What's more, many diets do not provide the balanced nutrition that growing teens need. Some have calorie intakes too low to maintain health. When teens deprive their bodies of proper nutrition and fuel, they are likely to feel fatigued, dizzy or weak, unmotivated, distracted by hunger, obsessed with thoughts of food (which may lead to binge eating) and unhappy. Further, intense dieting has been shown to increase weight, rather than maintain weight loss. When people reduce their calorie intake drastically, the body slows the metabolism (the rate at which calories are burned) in response. This is a survival mechanism to help us sustain our weight during periods of famine or starvation. If, however, our metabolism has been slowed because of a very low-calorie diet, when we return to a normal or healthy calorie intake, we will actually begin to gain weight. The fact of the matter is diets hardly ever work in the long term.

If your teens are dieting, you need to talk with them about this. If they do need to curb overeating or lose weight (which should be determined by a physician or a health care professional), then following the boundaries and advice discussed in the preceding section on "Overeating and Unhealthy Eating" may help. If they are at a healthy weight (again this can be determined by a physician or health care professional), do the following:

- Ask them why they feel the need to lose weight. Encourage them to talk about how they feel about their bodies.
- Encourage them to question and challenge the standards that the media present about attractiveness and weight.
- Model a healthy attitude towards weight and eating yourself. Many teens who diet have parents who are overly concerned about weight.
- Let them know that not getting enough calories while they are growing and developing can cause serious and long-lasting harm to their health.
- Share with them that diets are seldom successful for long.

If your teens continue to limit their food intake in an unhealthy way, take them to see a doctor. They may be developing a serious eating disorder.

Eating Disorders: Anorexia Nervosa, Bulimia and Binge Eating Disorder

Eating disorders are serious and complex emotional and physical illnesses that can be extremely challenging to treat. They are often accompanied by other problems such as depression, drug abuse and anxiety disorders. Unfortunately, they are also a growing trend for teens, especially girls. Ninety percent of people with eating disorders are women between the ages of 12 and 25 and the disorders rank as the third most common chronic illness in teenage girls.

The frightening thing about eating disorders is that they can start so easily. Behaviours that seem fairly harmless, like dieting or cutting back on food intake, can quickly spiral out of control, becoming compulsive and addictive. Before long, a simple effort to control weight gain can develop into an emotional and physical illness that overtakes a person's life and can even be fatal.

Anorexia

Many experts believe that anorexia is largely about control—anorexics think that they can gain control over their lives by controlling their bodies. People suffering from anorexia also

- severely limit caloric intake, avoid eating many foods, or weigh food before eating
- have a compulsion to keep losing weight even if they are underweight
- have a distorted body image so that they feel significantly heavier than they really are
- are obsessed with their bodies—they believe that their appearance is more important than almost everything else
- feel in control of their eating
- sometimes exercise excessively and compulsively to control weight

Many anorexics also say that they are obsessed with food—although they rarely allow themselves to eat, they think about food and calories all of the time.

Potential health hazards of anorexia. The health costs of prolonged periods of anorexia can be severe. They can include:

- slowed heart rate and lowered blood pressure
- hair loss
- dry, pasty skin, yellowing palms of hands and soles of feet
- brittle hair and nails
- frequent feelings of bloatedness
- physical weakness and light-headedness
- mild anemia
- swollen joints

- growth of fine, soft hair over skin
- electrolyte imbalance
- brittle bones
- kidney failure
- heart failure

Bulimia

The eating disorder bulimia is often known as "binging and purging." People eat large quantities of food (often junk food, but it can be anything) in short periods of time, and then rid their bodies of the food shortly after by making themselves vomit or by taking large doses of laxatives and diuretics (drugs which increase urine elimination). Bulimics may also exercise excessively and obsessively in an effort to burn off calories.

Bulimia usually starts as a way to control weight, but binging and purging can become addictive quite quickly. Those suffering from bulimia generally

- binge and vomit at least twice a week over a period of months
- have an obsessive desire to be thin
- feel overweight, even if they aren't
- have an intense fear of gaining weight
- can be normal weight, underweight or overweight
- feel a loss of control over their behaviour
- may purge after eating healthy quantities of food, with little or no binging

While anorexics may not believe that they have a problem, bulimics often feel intense shame about their behaviour.

Potential health hazards of bulimia. These can include:
- erosion of enamel on teeth from repeated vomiting
- inflammation and damage to the esophagus (the passage in the throat that carries food to the stomach) from repeated vomiting

- constipation
- dehydration
- electrolyte imbalance
- swelling of the salivary glands
- swelling of face and cheeks (caused by swollen glands or high blood pressure in the face from vomiting)
- stomach damage, including peptic ulcers
- inflammation of the pancreas
- irregular heartbeat
- malnutrition
- kidney failure
- heart failure

Binge Eating Disorder (BED)

With binge eating disorder, sufferers eat compulsively as bulimics do, but they do not purge, take laxatives or exercise excessively in an effort to rid their bodies of the food. Binging often happens at night, and is marked by a rapid consumption of a large quantity of food, most commonly when the binger is alone. Binge eating may start because a person has been denying himself food in an effort to lose weight or because he is reaching for food as a comfort. Binge eating is not just having a few too many snacks in the evening however. Those with BED do not feel in control of their eating in any way—bingers feel an overwhelming compulsion to keep eating, even if they are full or feeling uncomfortable. Binging often causes the eater to have intense feelings of shame and self-loathing. Unlike anorexia and bulimia, BED affects just as many men as women.

Potential health hazards of BED. Binge eaters often suffer from obesity and all of its attendant problems:
- high blood pressure
- high cholesterol
- fatigue

- joint pain
- type 2 diabetes
- gallbladder disease
- heart disease

Treatment of Eating Disorders

Treating eating disorders is a challenging process that generally takes time and varies according to the patient's needs. All treatment must be done under the direct supervision of a physician and is most effective if the illness is caught early.

- In severe cases, hospitalization or period of hospitalization may be necessary.
- Medical professionals will try to get those who have eating disorders back to a healthy weight.
- Nutritional deficiencies will need to be addressed.
- Treatment for substance abuse may be necessary.
- Antidepressants may be prescribed.
- Intensive therapy will be required to address the emotional roots of the disease and to change behavioural patterns.
- Ongoing nutritional counselling may also be advised.

It's extremely important for parents to realize that eating disorders are serious illnesses. They are not something teens can "get over" on their own. It's essential for parents to model good eating habits for their teens, avoid any critical remarks about body shape and size, and provide plenty of understanding, love and support to their teen, but if your teen has already developed a full-blown eating disorder it is unlikely that these things alone, or any kind simple eating boundaries, will be able to overcome the disease. *Always* seek immediate professional help if you suspect your child has or is developing an eating disorder. Treatment is much more likely to be successful if started in the early stages of the disease.

Warning Signs for Eating Disorders

If you answer yes to even just a few of the following questions, your teen may have a serious eating disorder that requires *immediate* medical attention.

- Does your teen skip family meals or insist on making his or her own food?
- Does your teen play with food instead of eating it?
- Does your teen seem overly concerned with losing weight or very fearful of gaining weight?
- Have you found laxatives or diuretics in your teen's room or belongings?
- Does your teen hide food?
- Does your teen wear loose, oversized clothing that hides body shape?
- Is your teen excessively thin?
- Has your teen lost a great deal of weight in a very short time?
- Have your daughter's periods stopped?

Other Resources

National Eating Disorder Information Centre (Canada):
www.nedic.ca

National Eating Disorders Association (U.S.):
www.nationaleatingdisorders.org

National Association of Anorexia Nervosa and
Associated Disorders (U.S.)
www.anad.org

Emotions

In the last decade or so, science has discovered a tremendous amount about the role emotions play in our lives. Researchers have found that even more than IQ, your emotional awareness and abilities to handle feelings will determine your success and happiness in all walks of life, including family relationships.

—John Gottman, Ph.D,
Raising an Emotionally Intelligent Teen

In the previous two chapters and the Introducion, I explained the concept of inside-out parenting. Working from the inside out as a parent requires attention to your child's character and self-esteem, to your own parenting attitudes and, of course, to your teen's emotions. Indeed, the "heart" of inside-out parenting is to teach our children emotional intelligence and emotional management, and the best way to do this is to model these skills ourselves.

What is emotional intelligence? It's the ability to know, understand and manage our emotions and those of others, as well as to communicate our emotions. And this ability can be hugely helpful during the teen years, when adolescents are often going through an emotionally turbulent time.

There are many reasons the teen years may be fraught with emotional highs and lows. For years, experts heaped most of the blame on hormonal changes that occur in adolescence. In recent years, brain research has also suggested that there may be a neurological component to the emotional rollercoaster. Research using functional MRIs (conducted by a team at Harvard's McLean Hospital led by Dr. Deborah Yurgelun-Todd) have shown that teens may process emotions in a different way than adults do. When young teenagers were asked to identify emotions on pictures of faces, MRIs showed strong activity in the amygdala, a part of the brain that controls fear and gut reactions, instead of in the frontal lobe, which controls reasoning, as would be the case in adult brains. Not surprisingly perhaps, the teens did not do as well at visually identifying emotions as the adults did. If teens' brains are still developing their ability to recognize correctly the emotional cues they see in other's faces, it could explain much of the confusion and conflict in the lives of some adolescents.

But apart from chemical or physical influences on a teen's emotional landscape, there are so many other things in the lives of teens that can illicit strong emotions—and might in any of us! Their bodies are changing, sometimes causing them discomfort and confusion, almost always demanding them to adjust their body image and hygiene habits. There are the academic pressures as well as the sometimes challenging social climate of high school. Adolescence is also a time when teens are feeling the need for independence. They may be taking on new responsibilities and are faced with some very big decisions—including what they might want to do in their adult lives.

So it's no wonder I get a lot of questions about emotions from the parents I speak to. I often hear things such as:

- How can I get my son to manage his anger? He's got so much rage.
- My daughter is so stressed out all the time. What can I do?
- My son seems depressed. Is that normal?
- My daughter's anxiety seems out of control and it's impacting her in so many ways.
- My son puts down his brother all the time. How can I help him feel more empathy towards him?

Our Emotional Nature

Knowing how to manage our emotions is one of the most important life skills we can teach our teens. But we can't teach something if we don't know it ourselves and model it first. That's why it's imperative we apply once again the inside-out model and look at how much we ourselves understand about emotions.

It's interesting to watch the body language of my audience members or clients when the topic of emotions comes up in conversation. Some people are clearly happy to get to a subject they think is important. Others display body language that tells me they are shutting off—probably annoyed that we have moved on to the "fluffy stuff."

Despite some people's discomfort in talking about emotions, the truth is that every person has an emotional component as well as an intellectual one. What's more, while some theorists talk about a set of basic emotions that number anywhere from five to eight, the fact that we have hundreds and hundreds of words for our emotions, each carrying subtle differences of meaning, suggests that our emotional makeup is rich and varied and complex. And yet, clearly, some people are more in tune with emotions than others.

When it comes to emotions and emotional intelligence, I see three different personality types. Emotionally "Plugged In" people manage their own emotions well and are able to help their children with their feelings. These parents not only model healthy emotion management but also recognize, acknowledge and respect the emotions of their kids. There are two other extremes, however, that can contribute to parenting challenges.

The Unplugged Parent

If you identified yourself as a weather reporter, a sergeant or an underfunctioning parent, you may be a person who is "Unplugged" emotionally.

Unplugged people may

- rarely if ever state how they feel
- rationalize any feeling or situation
- honestly answer "I don't know" when you ask them how they are feeling
- have a difficult time articulating how they are feeling
- seem upset or discouraged but seldom voice these feelings
- show very little expression on their faces
- behave as if nothing bothers them but "lose it" from time to time
- find it difficult to show affection
- find it difficult to say "I love you"
- seldom ask their spouses or teens how they are doing or feeling
- find it difficult to have serious talks about important issues
- laugh or make jokes when conversations start getting too emotional or "deep"
- change or overtly avoid topics if the conversation starts getting too emotional

Even people who are unplugged have emotions, but for many of them it is as if their emotions are kept in a vault that is never opened in the presence of others.

Some parents admit that the unplugged description sounds like them, and that they can't quite see what is wrong with that attitude. But people who are disconnected from their emotions are likely to face a number of personal issues. They may

- feel lonely even though they often have people around them
- be unable to resolve deep emotional issues
- have a dissatisfying marriage or relationship because they haven't learned how to share and talk intimately with their partners
- have spouses or partners who feel alone and frustrated because the unplugged ones are not emotionally connecting to them
- have children who don't feel loved by or connected to them

- have children who may spend time with them out of obligation or guilt, not because they really want to
- have kids who may not learn for themselves how to be emotionally connected and therefore may experience the same problems in their own marriage and family

The Overcircuited Parent

The opposite extreme to unplugged parents are those parents who are emotionally overcharged. Melanie and Peter had come to my office to discuss their daughter, Melissa, who was not there with them. They were very concerned about Melissa's anxiety. Within the first 15 minutes, Melanie started crying, shouting and blaming Peter for many of their parenting problems. Melanie is what I called an "Overcircuited" personality. An overcircuited person is often not in control of his emotions and frequently "catches" or adopts the feelings of those around him. As a result, overcircuited people are more likely to be basket case parents, or have a blamer, mother bear or overfunctioning attitude towards their children.

People who are overcircuited may

- get easily worked up over small things
- shout or yell when they are angry
- blame others for their problems or how they are feeling (e.g., "You made me feel angry.")
- start crying for no apparent reason
- feel anxious and stressed a lot of the time
- find it difficult to relax and take time off
- feel easily sensitive and hurt
- attack others verbally when they can't get what they want
- cut others off in conversation (without realizing it) because they are so worked up (due to anxiety or anger) that they are not fully listening to the other person

- speak on behalf of others (e.g., "We feel" or "We think") instead of allowing others to speak for themselves. They assume that they know how others think and feel because they have overidentified with others.
- experience the emotions *of* their teen (i.e., if the teen is anxious, the parent feels anxious; if the teen is upset, the parent is upset)
- experience emotions *for* their teen (i.e., if their child is not invited to a party, the *parents* may feel rejected even when their teen doesn't seem to mind!)
- feel responsible for their teens and therefore get overinvolved in their lives (the overfunctioning attitude)

So what's at stake if a person remains overcircuited? Like being unplugged, being "overcircuited" can cause a number of difficulties. People who are overcircuited may

- feel absolutely exhausted since they believe they are "feeling" for everyone (e.g., their spouse and their kids)
- have dissatisfying marriages because they feel so much anger and resentment towards their partners
- feel anxious so often that they find it difficult to relax and enjoy their partners and kids
- be so focused on how they are feeling (e.g., anxious) that they've lost objectivity about how to handle situations
- have kids who do not feel comfortable or safe talking with their parent because they fear the strong reactions. Therefore their kids may bottle things up or lash out at them
- have partners or teens who are frustrated because they are often being told how they think and feel

Unplugged Spouse, Connected Parent

I have seen many situations in which parents are unplugged with their spouses but much more emotionally connected to their children. I think this happens for a few reasons.

- Children are naturally loving and accepting so often parents who are unplugged emotionally find it much easier to be loving, playful and passionate with their kids.

- While all children need love and attention, young children are not as likely to want to "talk things out." For parents who have difficulty verbalizing their emotions, this can make the relationship easier for them.

- Unless children have gone through a traumatic event, they don't have emotional baggage that has to be taken into consideration. It is easier to just "be" with them, and the unplugged spouse, feels much less pressure as a parent than as a spouse.

- And finally, as the old saying goes, "opposites attract." Often unplugged personalities end up with overcircuited ones. Having difficulty discussing or acknowledging their own emotions, unplugged people may initially be drawn to others who are very open about their feelings, but in the long run the highly emotional nature of their partners may overwhelm them, causing them to withdraw.

Striking the Balance—The Plugged-In Parent

Unfortunately, not only can the unplugged and overcircuited personalities create a host of relationship problems for themselves, but also neither type of parent is likely to raise healthy balanced teens. The key is to become what I call the "plugged-in parent."

People who are emotionally plugged in

- are able to be fully emotionally present and feel empathy and concern for others, without taking on the feelings of others as their own
- are able to separate their thoughts from their feelings
- own their thoughts and take responsibility for their choices
- are able to state how they are feeling (e.g., "I feel . . ."). They do not blame how they feel on someone else
- are able to stay calm and grounded even if their kids are feeling anxious or hurt
- ask how their teens are feeling about different aspects of their lives (e.g., friendship changes, family trips, school marks, passions and interests, etc.)
- teach by words and actions that emotions, including sadness (and therefore crying), are okay. They teach and model that feelings are healthy and normal.

The great advantage of being emotionally plugged in is that it allows you to connect with people. With parents and teens, this connection can lead to a strong, healthy relationship in which the parents truly *know and understand* their children. Emotionally plugged-in parents are therefore also likely to be plugged in to the practicalities of their teens' lives. In other words, they are likely to know

- the names of their teens' best friends
- their teens' favourite colours, sports, music groups, TV shows, foods and so on
- what it is about them that bugs their teens the most
- what their teens' greatest fears are
- what causes their teens the most stress
- what it is their teens dream of
- what their teens' greatest struggles are
- the last time their teens cried about something

Being plugged in is a huge part of the inside-out parent that I talked about in Chapter 2. Plugged-in parents are able to relate to their teens on both emotional and intellectual levels—they know their kids inside and out.

The Importance of Staying Connected

During one of her appearances on my radio talk show, my mother shared a powerful story about one of her neighbours whose teenage son had committed suicide. The father was devastated not only because his son had ended his own life but also because of the light that tragic event shed on their relationship. When the father was cleaning out his son's bedroom, he had discovered, hidden in a closet, stacks of golf magazines. The father did not know that his son had loved golf—and that made him realize that he hadn't known his son well at all. No wonder he hadn't recognized that his son was depressed and in so much emotional pain that he wanted to end his own life. My mom urged parents to stay "plugged in" to their kids' and teens' lives.

I've worked with several families after they've had a teen commit suicide and one of the most common phrases I hear is "I wish I had stayed more connected."

Five Strategies to Help Teens Manage Their Emotions

But how do we become and stay emotionally plugged in with our children? I've found that five simple strategies can help parents and teens recognize, manage and communicate their emotions in order to connect with one another.

Strategy #1: Know the Unspoken Rules

Every family has rules—overt and covert rules. Overt family rules are the rules that are spoken:

"Do your homework or you can't watch TV."

"Wash your hands before you eat."

"There is no swearing in this family."

Unspoken rules are expectations that we believe to be there but that are never verbalized. Just think about the last time you were stuck in an elevator with a bunch of other people. What's the unspoken rule? Don't talk, avoid eye contact and look up at the numbers. No one posts this rule on the elevator door, but most of us do all these things anyway. All families have unspoken rules or expectations about a variety of topics, but the most common ones are around the topic of feelings. These rules are never spoken directly to teens, but they know them all too well. See if any of these rules sound familiar to you and your family:

When Parents . . .	Teens Learn . . .
Say things like "Stop crying" or "Stop being such a crybaby"	It's not okay to show emotions. I'm weak if I cry.
Yell and scream without explaining that they are sad or frustrated	It's okay to *act* angry but not okay to *say* we're upset
Say "Stop being all emotional like your mother"	Girls are emotional; being emotional is a bad thing
Don't express their emotions	I should not share my emotions
Drink because they are depressed or angry	It's okay for me to drink when I'm feeling depressed or angry
Express when they are hurt, sad or frustrated	It's okay for me to share how I'm feeling

Unspoken rules are incredibly powerful—we often experience much more anxiety breaking an unspoken rule than a spoken one. Sadly, many unspoken rules concerning emotions are not helpful or healthy. So think about what the unspoken rules your family has about emotions. Which rules do you want to keep? Which ones do you want to break (for good)? Then have the courage to model the acceptable new behaviour for your kids. If one of your unspoken rules is that no one ever shares how they are feeling, be the first to start sharing with a family member how you are feeling. (But before you do, finish reading this book, especially Chapter 5, on how to communicate effectively, to make sure you're fully prepared!)

Strategy #2: Know the Risks of Bottling Up Emotions

When I am speaking to parent groups, I'm often asked, "What's the big deal if people don't talk about their emotions? Our parents never did, so why is it so important to break this unspoken rule and start talking?" Great question.

There are four potential consequences for those who bottle up their emotions:

Depression

I've worked with hundreds of preteens and teens who were depressed. In some cases there are clearly chemical imbalances that need to be treated by their medical doctors or psychiatrists. However, many teens are depressed because they have never learned how to express their emotions. Keeping painful emotions or thoughts bottled up does not make them go away. Instead the repression can lead to deep depression that is difficult to break. (See "Focus on Mental Illness, Depression, Suicide and Self-Harm," in this chapter for a more thorough discussion of depression.)

Feeling Numb

Zoe, age 16, had been undergoing a lot of change when she walked into my office several years ago. Her boyfriend had broken up with her, her parents were going through a nasty divorce and she was switching schools. When I asked her how she was feeling about all the change, she looked at me blankly and said, "I don't feel anything. I feel numb." Feeling numb is a common response when unexpressed emotions begin to pile up. It's just like when a computer gets overheated and goes into standby—it's a means of self-protection. While feeling numb helps us avoid feelings like sadness or anger, we don't feel any joy or happiness either.

Explosions

Jamie, age eight, was, in his mother's words, "losing it" on a regular basis. He would seem fine for weeks but then would start yelling, crying and swearing at his parents—usually over small things. The problem turned out to be that Jamie bottled up his emotions most of the time in order to appear compliant, well behaved and as if nothing was bothering him. Eventually, however, some small frustration (such as his mom not letting him watch a TV show) would add to his collection of negative emotions, pushing him over the edge. Jamie was not reacting to one situation; he was reacting to everything he had been feeling for weeks. That is why his response was so over the top.

Self-Harm

When people feel overwhelmed by negative emotions, they sometimes attempt to distract themselves from the emotional pain with physical pain. They may cut or burn their arms or bodies, engage in drug or alcohol abuse or even attempt suicide.

Obviously the potential risks of suppressing our emotions are very serious. But how do we make sure that neither we nor our children bottle up our emotions? Following the strategies outlined in this chapter, developing our emotional intelligence and "plugging in" will help us manage our emotions so we don't keep them bottled up. (Remember to model this healthy attitude for your children.) But if you or your teens do find the difficult emotions piling up, you might want to try the following technique.

The Jar of Feelings

I originally developed this game for children, but I discovered that many teens and adults found it very useful. I ask people to imagine that each of us has a jar where we keep all of our feelings. Whenever we experience a feeling, it goes into the jar. We cannot control the feelings that are collecting in the jar, but we *can* control how many stay in there. For example, if I do poorly on a test, I'll probably feel disappointed or frustrated. Those two feelings would go into my jar. But the jar only has so much room. Over time, it is going to get full. The problem is that if the jar is full of unpleasant or painful emotions, that collection of unpleasant feelings may turn into something worse: depression, numbness, explosions or self-harm, as I have outlined. The good news is that we can control what happens by taking the lid off the jar, and emptying it out by sharing how we are feeling with someone who is close and feels safe to us. Each time we feel upset, angry, frustrated, sad or hurt, we need to acknowledge that this feeling is sitting in the jar. If we continue to experience difficult emotions, we should make an effort to get those feelings out by talking about them or sharing them with someone we trust. Sharing regularly, emptying our jar so things don't build up, is one of the best ways that we can manage our emotions instead of having our emotions manage us.

Of course, knowing when your jar is full isn't as easy as it sounds. For example, if you explode over a certain situation, how can you tell if you are really seriously upset about something or just letting loose because you've got too many unresolved feelings in your jar? Here's the trick. Ask yourself, "Was my reaction in proportion to this event?" If the answer is no, then it's likely that you have been bottling up difficult feelings.

Strategy #3: Know the Difference Between Thoughts and Feelings

One of the things I've learned since I began coaching parents and teens is that most of us really don't understand the difference between our feelings and our thoughts. And this failure to distinguish becomes evident in how we communicate.

I was coaching Betty and her 13-year-old son, Brad, who seemed depressed and unmotivated at school. He wasn't communicating with her, and she was having a difficult time knowing what she should or should not say. I encouraged her to express how she was feeling with Brad and to try to get plugged in. So she said, "Brad, I feel as if you should be working harder at school. I feel that you're depressed and I don't understand why. I feel as though you are upset with me."

She stopped there, looking rather proud that she had expressed her feelings. But she hadn't! Anytime someone says the words, "I feel as if . . .," "I feel as though . . ." or "I feel that . . .," they are not expressing their feelings. Instead, they are expressing their thoughts. More accurate statements might have been," I think that you need to be working harder at school," or "I believe you are upset with me."

We went back and forth for several more minutes—me asking for her feelings, and Betty offering thoughts and opinions. She really didn't know the language of emotions—for years she had been expressing her thoughts while she acted out her feelings. And if *she* didn't know how to talk about emotions, there is no way she would have been able to teach and model this to Brad.

With some more prompting Betty eventually said, "I feel *helpless* [feeling] because *I don't know how to help Brad* [thought]." And then, "I feel *alone* and *unsupported* [feelings] because *my husband works a lot* [thought]." She was finally differentiating between feelings and thoughts.

Here's a trick I often use to help figure the difference: feelings can be declared in one word, e.g., "angry" or "frustrated" or "happy" or "content." The moment we have to start explaining ourselves, we've moved into a thought. (Just because we throw the word "feel" into a sentence does not necessarily mean we are expressing our feelings.)

Feelings Are Never Wrong

Once we can identify what a thought is and what a feeling is, we must also acknowledge one basic difference between these two things: thoughts can be mistaken, incorrect or irrational. Feelings, however, are never wrong. The thought that leads to the feeling might be illogical, but the feeling itself is always logical. That's why we should never say that someone shouldn't feel a certain way. For example, your son may think that the time of his curfew is unreasonable and feel angry and frustrated about it. You may try to convince him that you are asking him to be home at a certain time for reasons that are sound. But you should never tell him that he shouldn't feel angry or frustrated. You may think his notion that it is okay for him to be out all night is illogical, but his feelings aren't "wrong." To be inside-out, emotionally plugged-in parents it's imperative that we understand this distinction.

Moving from Unplugged to Plugged In

Following the strategies outlined for being a plugged-in parent and using the tips for talking with teens about emotions can help any unplugged parent become plugged in. But the transformation may be harder than it sounds. If you are having trouble, start small. Even just asking your teen how his day went is a step in the right direction. Add another technique or strategy as you get comfortable with the previous one. If you are finding the new approach very tough, you may want to seek counselling for yourself so that you can get help in acknowledging, understanding and talking about your own emotions while you are attempting to talk with your teens about theirs.

Strategy #4: Speak from the Heart

I mentioned earlier that we have hundreds and hundreds of words for feelings, and yet so many of us simply don't know the vocabulary of emotions. Would I expect someone to speak French if they've never studied French vocabulary? Of course not. Similarly, we can't speak from the heart unless we are familiar with the words.

Here is a list of emotions I sometimes provide to parents and teens when I am asking them about what is in their "jar of feelings."

I encourage you to read over some of these emotion words to help you recognize and describe some of your own feelings.

Adored	Enraged	Paranoid
Aggressive	Envious	Patient
Angry	Excited	Peaceful
Anxious	Exhausted	Proud
Appreciated	Fearful	Prudish
Arrogant	Frightened	Puzzled
Attacked	Frustrated	Regretful
Belittled	Grieving	Rejected
Blessed	Guilty	Relaxed
Blissful	Happy	Relieved
Bored	Hopeful	Sad
Calm	Horrified	Satisfied
Cautious	Hot	Sexy
Cherished	Hurt	Skeptical
Compassionate	Hysterical	Special
Cold	Indifferent	Stressed
Confident	Innocent	Stubborn
Confused	Insecure	Supported
Creative	Irritated	Surprised
Curious	Joyful	Sympathetic
Defensive	Lonely	Thoughtful
Depressed	Loved	Undecided
Determined	Nervous	Understood
Disappointed	Numb	Upset
Disgusted	Optimistic	Valued
Ecstatic	Overloaded	Violated
Energized	Overwhelmed	

Ask yourself:

- How did I feel today? This week?
- How did I feel today regarding my spouse? My kids?
- How did I feel at work?
- What emotions do I remember feeling as I grew up within my family?
- How did I feel towards my mother? Father? Siblings?

And remember, there are no right and wrong feelings. Feelings are just feelings. Listen to them. Pay attention to them.

Explore Feelings Through Writing

For many of us, just knowing how we are feeling and expressing it to someone with whom we feel safe is a helpful and healing process. For many other teens and adults I've coached, writing about what they feel is another excellent way to release what's in their jar of feelings.

I often suggest to people that they keep a journal. I like to distinguish between a journal and a diary—I consider a diary to be more factual. The journal is intimate—a place to express their feelings and how events have impacted them. The process of writing in the journal may also be a way to work through and discover how they *really feel*. For example, when I was first married my husband and I had a disagreement. I was so mad at him—he was so wrong and I was so right, I thought. Instead of trying to resolve the issue at that time, I headed out to a coffee shop with my journal. I wrote about how I felt and what I was thinking. The more I expressed myself, the more I realized I was in the wrong. I had expectations of him that I had not clearly communicated, and so I shouldn't have been blaming him if he didn't meet them. I made my way home, feeling humbled, and apologized to my husband for my part in the argument.

Unspoken Rules, Emotional Intelligence and Gender

Teen Boys

One of the common unspoken rules (in both families and society in general) is that it is okay for men and boys to be angry but not sad. As a result, when I ask teen guys about their emotions, most of their descriptions are of anger. But when we dig deeper, it becomes clear that other emotions, such as rejection, sadness, loneliness and hurt, are simply being expressed as anger because it's the one emotion they think they are allowed to have.

Teen Girls

Even with teen girls, anger is the most commonly described feeling, but again it is often a secondary emotion, masking hurt, sadness and frustration. Most girls, however, believe that it is acceptable to talk about their feelings. The challenge for them is to remain focused on expressing emotions rather than on describing what happened to make them feel that way. They tend to get caught up in the details of events: what time of day it was, who was there, what they were wearing, who said what to whom, etc. In my experience, there's no question that girls are more expressive and have a bigger vocabulary than boys for their emotions, but they are not necessarily skilled in sharing those feelings.

Talking with the Opposite Sex

Another unspoken rule that many teen guys observe is that it is okay to share their feelings with their girlfriends but not their guy friends. For many, therefore, their first romantic relationships involve discovering a new side of themselves. Unfortunately, it also means that if they break up, they've lost their primary emotional support, which sometimes leads to depression. It's therefore important that teen girls and teen boys learn to share their feelings with their families and close friends as well.

Strategy #5: Know the Difference Between Head, Heart and Hand

When parents first contact my office, it's often because they are concerned about their teen's behaviour: their son or daughter is unmotivated, irritated or short tempered, not sleeping or eating, (or perhaps sleeping or eating too much), using alcohol and drugs, skipping school and so on. Parents often don't know what their teen is feeling—but they can certainly see how their teen is acting.

Yet, as may be evident from so many of the anecdotes I've already shared about teens and their families, the heart of the problem is usually an emotional issue, not the teen's behaviour.

Amanda's story demonstrates how parents and their children can get focused on actions (the "hand") instead of on feelings (the "heart"). Amanda, age 16, and her mom, Veronica, were butting heads over a variety of issues. Veronica was upset because she thought Amanda's behaviour was "irrational." Amanda seemed cheerful whenever she was with her friends but with her family she was argumentative, irritable and unpleasant. Indeed, when Amanda got to my office, she leaned back in her chair, folded her arms and started scowling. Without saying a word, she was making it clear she didn't want to be there.

One thing I've learned through working with teens is that the tougher the exterior, the greater the emotional pain on the interior. I was sure we couldn't take Amanda's difficult demeanour at face value.

In order to help both Amanda and her mother discuss what was going on, I got out my chalk and drew a head, a heart and a hand on the chalkboard in my office. I explained to Veronica and Amanda that the head represents our thoughts, the heart represents our feelings, and the hand represents our actions. How we think impacts how we feel. How we feel impacts what we do. I wrote all of Amanda's behaviours on the chart and then asked her to provide some descriptions of her feelings. After many stops and starts (see "Validating Feelings While Lovingly Challenging Thoughts") and a look at the list of emotions I provided on page 93, Amanda admitted to feeling angry, hurt, frustrated and abandoned. I asked her to help us understand why she felt that way. Eventually she said, "I feel angry and hurt when my mom says she's going to be home by 6 p.m. but she doesn't come home or even call till 8 p.m."

Her mother's tardiness may seem like a small thing, but the more we explored the issue, the clearer it became that Amanda was interpreting this action as evidence of her mother's lack of affection and respect for her. Amanda was expected to take care of her younger brother after school, so when her mother got home late, this had a real impact on Amanda's ability to do her homework or have time for herself. What's more, when Veronica got home, she often asked about whether Amanda's homework was done and not how her day was, which Amanda saw as further proof that her mother did not love her as much as her brother.

In order to work through this issue, Amanda and her mother had to recognize the difference between feelings and actions. While they needed to acknowledge that the actions of each had an effect on the other, Veronica had to accept that Amanda's behaviour may have been

Testing the Small Stuff

When Amanda mentioned that she was upset about her mom's late arrivals at home in the evenings, Veronica looked surprised. Was that the real issue? Was that really what was causing Amanda to be so angry? Amanda was doing something I see very often in teens who are working through conflict with their families. They bring up small things to test the waters and watch to see how their parents respond. Do they get defensive? Do they interrupt? Say it's nonsense? Make fun of the concern?

If parents respond in any of these ways, the teens shut down and won't share anything else. As a result, they never open up about the big stuff—the real issues. If the parents really listen instead (and communicate effectively, they have a much better chance of hearing the truly important things that their teens have to say.

volatile and aggressive but that her feelings were ones of sadness and rejection. And Amanda had to learn that her mother's tardiness and thoughtlessness were not about a lack of love for her daughter.

In Chapter 5, I discuss at length how to talk with your teens effectively and meaningfully. All the tips and strategies in that chapter can be applied to discussing feelings. But when we are trying to resolve an emotional conflict with our children, there is one strategy that is essential: *validate feelings while lovingly challenging thoughts.*

How do you do that? Let me use Veronica and Amanda's story as an example of how to talk to teens about their feelings.

Validating Feelings While Lovingly Challenging Thoughts

Use Behaviours as Clues

When Amanda and Veronica came to see me, Amanda's behaviour was a clue that something was not right. Amanda eventually acknowledged that she was short tempered, snappy and withdrawn. But I encouraged Veronica to recognize these as symptoms of another problem. Telling Amanda to just snap out of it would not have fixed the problem. Instead, we discussed her behaviour in order to dig deeper.

Ask How They Feel

We asked Amanda how she was feeling. When she didn't know, I pulled out the list of emotion words I use to discuss the "jar of feelings." For many children and teens, looking at the list of options helps them articulate how they feel. If you don't want to provide a list, offer suggestions to get your teen's mind going: "So how do you feel? Frustrated? Angry? Sad? Upset?" Providing them with options still allows them to make their own choices but gives them a bit of a jump-start.

Validate Their Feelings (Always)

Once Amanda opened up a bit, she shared that she was feeling angry, hurt, frustrated, irritated and abandoned. She was letting us in. We did not minimize these feelings but rather acknowledged them by saying, "Wow—you've got lots of emotions going on inside of you. I'm really impressed with how articulate you are. Did you realize you felt so much?" It's very important to acknowledge that you've heard your teen.

Unlock Their Thoughts

This step is one of the hardest. You now know what emotions your teen is experiencing. You also know how these feelings are impacting her behaviour. But what is happening in her head that is driving her emotions?

After Amanda told us she was feeling angry, hurt, frustrated and abandoned, I said, "Amanda, I want you to take each feeling that you've shared with us and try to help us understand why you feel that way."

Amanda responded, "I feel angry and hurt when my mom says she's going to be home by 6 p.m. but she doesn't even call until 8 p.m."

Restate What's Been Said

Usually when teens first try to explain themselves, what's going on is not yet clear in their own heads so their explanations aren't clear. That's why it's important to restate what we are being told by our teens. Once teens hear their words restated back to them, they can say, "Oh, no, that's not right" or "Yeah, that's right." This step takes some extra time, but is worth it in the end.

Instead of laughing or minimizing or even responding to what Amanda had said, Veronica took the time to restate it: "So, Amanda, you don't want me to work late."

"No, Mom," said Amanda. "That's not what I'm saying."

Return to Their Thoughts

By continuing to restate what she thought Amanda was saying, Veronica was encouraging her daughter to return to her thoughts.

Amanda tried to explain her thoughts again: "I'm saying that I feel angry when you expect me to be home and take care of Jordon, and you don't even call to tell me you are going to be late."

Veronica again restated what she thought Amanda was saying: "So you're angry because you don't want to take care of your brother."

"No, you're not listening," Amanda responded. "You get mad at me if you don't know where I am. And it's really frustrating that you expect me to be home and take care of Jordon and meantime I have no idea where you are and you're always late. It's not really fair and it's a really big job taking care of an eight-year-old all by myself. And then when you get home, instead of thanking me for taking care of him, you first ask me, 'Is your homework done?' I mean, how can I do my homework when I've got to watch him? It's a lot of work. And you don't even bother asking me how my day was. I swear I think you love Jordon more than me."

Now that Amanda was explaining her thoughts more clearly, Veronica was shocked by them, but she was closer to understanding where her daughter was coming from. She restated what she was hearing:

"You're saying that you feel it's a burden to take care of Jordon. That's a huge responsibility for any teenager and you feel frustrated that you can't rely on me. And I also heard you say that you don't think I value you and appreciate what you're doing. You think I love Jordon more than you. And I'm also hearing that you don't feel loved by me because I'm not asking you how you are doing. Is this right?"

Validate the Feelings, Challenge the Thoughts

The more Veronica and her daughter talked, the closer we got to the real issue: Amanda was not feeling loved and appreciated by her mom. Now we had reached an important point. Veronica needed to validate Amanda's feelings while lovingly and gently challenging her thoughts. She started with the feelings:

"Amanda—honestly I had no idea you were feeling that way. Now that I understand what you're saying I can totally understand why you feel so frustrated and angry at me."

Then Veronica gently challenged the thought: "Sweetheart, I do love you. I love you so much. I'm so sorry you believed that I love Jordon more. It's not true. I love you both the same. I think that sometimes since he's smaller he gets more attention but that's no excuse. I really should be more aware of your needs."

Apologize

Veronica needed to be the adult and model for her daughter what taking responsibility for your words and actions sounds like. Veronica apologized, "To be honest, you're absolutely right. I haven't paid as much attention to you as to Jordon. I just never thought about this before. I never really got it. And, sweetheart, I'm really sorry."

Amanda recognized her mother's sincerity, so I asked her to think about what she could have done differently to improve the situation. She said to her mother, "I know I shouldn't have gotten snappy. I think I should have tried to talk with you about this first, and if you didn't listen I could have tried writing you a letter instead of holding onto my resentment. I realize now that withdrawing from you really didn't work. I'm sorry."

Fix the Problem

It's important to note that fixing is the last step. It takes time to understand a problem. And until we completely understand it, we will not be able to fix it effectively. In Amanda and Veronica's case, since the problem was mostly about how Amanda was perceiving her mom's behaviour towards her, I got Amanda to try to think about what things she needed from her mom. Amanda asked her mother to call whenever she was going to be late. She also thought it would be great if Veronica thanked her for taking care of Jordon. Finally, Amanda suggested that her mother ask her how her day went when she got home: "It would show me that you care," she said.

Veronica later shared with me her surprise at how much emotion her daughter had built up. And she realized that she had never taught her daughter about how to express herself. But we can't teach something if we don't know it ourselves. Veronica learned to talk about her feelings with her daughter and this dramatically improved her relationship with

My Top 12 Tips for Teaching Your Teens Emotional Intelligence

To teach your children emotional intelligence, you have to model it. By following these 12 tips, you are not only managing your own emotions, you are also attempting to understand and communicate with others about their feelings.

1. Get to know the language of emotions. Study the words just as you would when learning the vocabulary of any other language.
2. Start using the language of emotions. Explain how you feel using sentences such as, "I feel _____ [emotion] because _____ [thought]."
3. Try taking "angry" out of your emotional vocabulary. Anger is almost always a secondary emotion standing in for hurt, sadness, frustration or other feelings.
4. Start asking yourself how your emotions are impacting your thoughts and behaviour.
5. Take ownership for your feelings and don't ever blame someone else for how you feel (e.g., "I feel mad" instead of "You make me mad"). No one can make you feel anything. We are also responsible for how we think, which impacts how we feel.
6. Differentiate between thoughts and feelings.
7. If you're feeling an unpleasant emotion, ask yourself what you can do differently or how you can think differently to help you feel a positive emotion.
8. Find two or three close and safe people you can share your feelings with.
9. List your feelings, rating them on a scale of 1 to 10. This will give you a good overall understanding of how you are feeling at any given time.
10. Don't tell people how they feel. Ask them how they feel.
11. Show empathy, respect and understanding for the feelings of others. Don't ever minimize or downplay how they feel—feelings are never wrong.
12. Try to imagine how others feel. Think about how you talk to them. How do you think this will affect them?

Amanda. Amanda was able to share in turn. Teens learn the language of the heart so much faster if we can teach and model it to them.

But it takes time to learn these new skills. And they are skills; the more you use them and practise them, the easier and more effective they become. If we can learn how to ride a bike well, we can ride a bike anywhere. It's the same with communicating emotions. If we can learn how to communicate and express our emotions, we are able to deal with any issue that comes up. Problems come and go but the skills we learn to cope with them stay with us.

Focus on Mental Illness, Depression and Suicide

Adolescence can be an emotionally turbulent time. Hormonal and physical changes, academic and social pressures and growing independence can combine to make life an emotional rollercoaster for some teens—and for their families. One father I talked to said that when his daughter turned 15, it was as if he suddenly had two teen girls: happy Kate and angry Kate. Happy Kate would get up from the dinner table for a glass of juice, but much to the family's surprise, the girl who came back from the fridge would be angry Kate. "I never knew which one I was going to see when she got up in the morning," he joked. Most of the time, as with Kate, these emotional highs and lows are simply reactions to all of the changes in teens' lives. But the teen years are also a time when many of the major mental illnesses that plague adults can appear, including depression, bipolar disorder, eating disorders, anxiety disorders, and schizophrenia. So while even the healthiest teen may experience a certain degree of moodiness, anxiety or sadness, parents should be mindful that some emotional and behavioural changes might be signs of a serious medical condition.

Figuring out the difference between intense sadness caused by specific circumstances, like the break-up with a girlfriend, and serious clinical depression is not a simple thing to do. And how do you know if your teen's anxiety about school is a reaction to upcoming exams or evidence of a developing anxiety disorder?

Simply put, the best way to be aware of your teen's mental health is to be an inside-out parent—one who talks regularly with teens about how they are thinking and feeling; one who asks the right questions and encourages teens to share details; one who listens and truly tries to understand what teens are saying.

As an inside-out parent, what you need to assess is behaviour or feelings that appear out of character or that seem to be interfering with your child's ability to cope with life. The following list of possible warning signs is long, but it reflects the wide variety of ways mental illnesses might reveal themselves. (I have compiled this list from a variety of sources, including the mental health websites listed on pages 113. Keep in mind that when professionals are assessing someone for a mental illness, they are looking to see if clusters of these symptoms have been occurring over many weeks. The fact that your child is challenging authority, for example, does not, on its own, suggest any sort of mental illness.

Possible Warning Signs for Depression and Other Mental Illnesses

- withdrawing from friends and things that they used to love to do
- prolonged sadness, hopelessness
- lack of energy
- indecision, inability to think clearly
- change in sleeping or eating patterns
- substance abuse (drugs or alcohol)
- poor self-esteem or guilt
- restlessness or agitation
- problems with authority
- neglect of appearance or personal hygiene
- extreme risk-taking, including doing things that could be life-threatening
- suicidal thoughts, actions or statements
- crying often or uncontrollably
- significant drop in grades
- uncharacteristic behaviour, such as delinquency, thrill-seeking or promiscuity

Additional warning signs for mental illness:
- frequent physical complaints (headaches and stomach aches for example)
- consistent aggressiveness and violations of the rights of others
- frequent outbursts of anger and rage

FOCUS ON *Mental Illness, Depression and Suicide*

- poor concentration, inability to sit still or focus
- marked changes in personality
- a preoccupation with food, weight and weight loss (particularly if the teen is not overweight)
- extreme fearfulness
- frequent anxiety and worry
- feeling life is too hard to manage
- anxiousness about being harmed or hurting others
- Needing to wash, clean or perform certain actions repeatedly in order to "prevent" some sort of harm or danger
- hearing voices
- frequent nightmares
- setting fires
- killing animals

If you notice a number of these things happening with your teen over a period of weeks, take your teen immediately to see a medical professional.

Depression

I talk with hundreds of teens every year, and I can certainly tell you that it is far from unusual for teens to have periods of unhappiness. Teens may be frustrated by school and homework, disappointed by their athletic performance, or upset by setbacks in their dating or social lives. But sometimes that sadness or melancholy is much more than a passing mood. Depression is a relatively prevalent mental health challenge for teens. In fact, one third of people will struggle with some form of depression (whether mild or severe) at one point in their adolescence.

The Canadian Mental Health Association notes that depression is caused by (1) psychological factors like a negative or pessimistic approach to life or (2) a biochemical imbalance in the brain or (3) distressing life events. Mental illnesses often run in families, so if other family members suffer from depression, your teen may have a higher risk of developing this condition.

There are several types of depression. Mild or situational depression is usually brought on by a difficult event (like intense disappointment), a life transition (like a break-up or a divorce) or a crisis or trauma (like a death in the family). While the symptoms may be the same as with more serious depression, situational depression tends to ebb and flow, and eventually lift. It can, however, worsen into clinical depression, and coaching or counselling—by a psychologist or medical doctor—is often warranted.

Clinical depression, or major depressive disorder, differs from situational depression in that it is does not usually have a clear cause, and it is severe and debilitating. People struggling with clinical depression often have thoughts of suicide and may even experience psychotic episodes. Clinical depression may last for long or short periods of time, and while it is rarely a permanent state, it may occur repeatedly or in cycles.

Depression that is broken by intervals of extremely impulsive behaviour, exaggerated happiness and high energy is called bipolar disorder (sometimes referred to as manic depression). The manic phase of this disorder is sometimes accompanied by a reduced need for sleep, high creativity and productivity and feelings of invincibility.

Anyone suffering from clinical depression or bipolar disorder needs *immediate* professional supervision and help, but you should consider getting help for your teen if they exhibit any sort of depressive behaviour, as depression can lead to other problems. Indeed, teens may try to escape feelings of depression by drinking, doing drugs, being sexually promiscuous or aggressive, taking risks and even inflicting violence on themselves (self-harm). Of course, all of these behaviours are only going to make life more difficult for teens and for those around them, and will likely lead to worse physical and mental health outcomes.

FOCUS ON Mental Illness, Depression and Suicide

Teen Suicide

It would be an exaggeration to say that teen suicide is commonplace, but unfortunately it is not as rare as anyone would like. In fact, in Canada, suicide is the second leading cause of death in youth between the ages of 16 and 24 (outstripped only by accidents). In the U.S. it is the third leading cause of death for those between 15 and 24 (following accidents and acts of violence), and the fourth leading cause of death for children between the ages of 10 and 14.

Teens who are severely depressed may think of taking their own lives. But it is important to note that teens about to attempt suicide are not always obviously depressed. Adolescents can move in and out of depression quite quickly, so those around them may not get a lot of warning signs that something is seriously wrong. But there are behaviours and factors that can either put teens at risk for suicide or be signs that they may be thinking of suicide. These include:

- low self-esteem
- being a victim of sexual abuse
- being the victim of severe bullying
- recent death of a friend or family member, especially if by suicide
- stress and conflicted feelings about sexual orientation
- drug and/or alcohol abuse
- unwanted pregnancy
- running away
- increased risk taking
- self-harm, such as cutting or anorexia
- talking or writing about death or suicide (even seemingly in jest)
- hero worship of those who have died of suicide
- giving away valued belongings
- trying out suicidal behaviour, like taking a small quantity of pills, or actual previous suicide attempts

Talking About Suicide

Some people believe that if someone is actually talking about suicide they are not going to attempt it. This is a myth—and an extremely dangerous one. If your teen makes comments about suicide (even if he seems to be doing it to get a reaction from those around him) or if you see any signs that suggest your teen is thinking of suicide, medical help is needed right away. Take him to a doctor or the emergency room *immediately* so that he can be assessed. (Even if your teen is only using talk of suicide to scare or manipulate, a trip to the emergency room is worthwhile. It teaches teens that suicidal statements are very serious and not something that should ever be used as a weapon or to get a reaction from people.) See pages 110–113 for more that you can do if your teen is depressed and suicidal.

Self-Harm

One of the most disturbing ways that some people deal with emotional pain is by physically hurting themselves. The term *self-harm* is used to refer to any sort of repeated, deliberate self-inflicted injury, like burning or cutting the skin, scratching until blood is drawn, hitting oneself (resulting in bruising or broken bones) or consuming poison. While there are no concrete statistics on how many people self-harm (the Public Health Agency of Canada estimates it is less than 1 percent of the population), it does appear that self-harming behaviour usually starts in early adolescence and peaks between the ages of 16 and 25. Young women appear to be more likely to engage in self-harm than young men.

Cutting and other types of self-harm are not intended to end life—they are not suicide attempts (although people who self-harm might also be at risk for suicide). Rather, self-harm is often a way for teens to distract themselves from the emotional pain they are suffering. If their "jar of feelings" is full and teens have no one to share their difficult emotions with, they may find physical pain helps them dissociate from their thoughts and feelings for a time. Sometimes too many unpleasant emotions leave people feeling numb. Self-harm sometimes gives cutters a feeling of control over their lives, and lends them a sense of relief. The relief, however, does not last—painful feelings or numbness will return and the self-harm will start again.

Teens who cut themselves or inflict other self-harm are often very good at hiding their behaviour. They usually hurt themselves in private, on parts of their bodies that can not be seen or that can be covered up. But parents should be aware of the possible signs that their teens might engage in self-injury or *are* harming themselves:

- unexplained injuries (e.g., cuts, burns)
- wearing long sleeves in warm weather
- difficulty expressing their emotions
- difficulty in relationships
- low self-esteem

If You See Signs of Mental Illness, Depression, Possible Suicide or Self-Harm

If you suspect that your teen is mentally ill, depressed, suicidal or self-harming, don't delay in getting medical treatment. A doctor can rule out physical causes for such feelings and behaviours and can refer your teen to a psychiatrist, psychologist or other counsellor. Be sure to ask to be referred to a mental health professional who specializes in teens. If a teen refuses to go to counselling, I recommend that the parents go in order to find out what they can do to help their child.

While depression is a common mental health issue with teens, it is also the most treatable form of mental illness. There are generally three main forms of treatment:

Psychotherapy teaches people coping skills and provides them a safe place to explore possible events or feelings that are painful to them.

Cognitive-behavioural therapy (CBT) helps people recognize and change negative thoughts and patterns of behaving.
Medication must be prescribed by a medical doctor or psychiatrist.

When teens are dealing with depression, I strongly recommend interpersonal or family counselling, which helps them build healthier and more positive relationships with family and friends, which reduces conflicts and provides support.

While professional help is almost always necessary when dealing with any mental illness, parents should never think that their love and support are not essential in helping their teens get better. A parent's role is much, much larger than simply driving his teens to appointments. People dealing with any kind of mental illness frequently experience strained relationships with those around them. They often isolate themselves from others. Sometimes, friends and acquaintances pull away from them because their behaviour is frightening or unnerving. Many teens have no idea how to respond to friends who are struggling with mental health issues. Parents and family need to be a haven of constant and unwavering love and support.

Listen to your teens. Let them express their thoughts and feelings. Be supportive and resist the temptation to lecture them or tell them they shouldn't feel the way they are feeling. Ask them what you can do to help.

You also need to recognize that you may not always be around when they need you, or they may need to talk to others to see them through tough moments. Help them to find a support group and provide them with the numbers of Kids Help Phone or other emergency hotlines (see below). I've also had many clients who found it helpful to make up a list of supportive people in their lives—friends, aunts, uncles and so on— whom they can call or visit when they need to.

If your teen is cutting or hurting herself, make sure that you focus on the feelings behind the self-harm, rather than on the physical damage itself. Remember, even if she stops cutting or burning herself, she may turn to other self-destructive habits (like substance abuse) if the underlying causes are not addressed and dealt with. Encourage your teen to analyze why and when she is hurting herself by examining feelings or events leading up to the abuse. Ask her if there are other ways she might express her pain or anger the next time a similar situation or feeling arises. She might suggest writing, drawing or talking with someone. Also encourage her to brainstorm things she might do to make self-injury more difficult next time she is tempted. Perhaps she can go to a friend's house if no one is at home, or she can call someone instead. Parents of teens who self-harm should try to remove or lock away all items that they might use to hurt themselves. Teens should be encouraged to do the same.

If you suspect that your teen may be suicidal, immediate intervention is essential. Not only should you seek medical attention, but you should also raise the issue of suicide directly with your teen. Try to talk with him about how he is feeling, and ask him about whether he has been thinking of suicide. Don't be afraid to address the issue head-on—it may make your teen feel that you acknowledge and understand his pain; it won't put ideas in his head. If you suspect that your teen may attempt suicide, you should also make sure that your home is as free from possible hazards as possible—get rid of or lock up medications, alcohol, sharp objects and rope.

But whatever else you do, you need to be a safe person for your teens to go to for help. Review the six keys of this book and dedicate yourself to the principles of inside-out parenting. If you are struggling with the challenges of parenting a mentally ill teen, do not hesitate to get counselling for yourself.

To learn more about mental illness, depression and suicide, visit the following websites:

Canadian Mental Health Association
Offers great information related to all areas of emotional health (depression, anxiety, eating disorders, suicide, mental illness, etc.).
www.cmha.ca

Canadian Network for Mood and Anxiety Treatment
Offers thorough information related to depression, anxiety and mood disorders.
www.canmat.org/resources/depression/children.html

Centre for Addiction and Mental Health
www.camh.net

Centre for Suicide Prevention
This Canadian resource provides a comprehensive list of crisis helplines and centres across the country. Visit the website to find the phone number of the crisis centre closest to you.
www.suicideinfo.ca

Kids Help Phone
Offers counselling on depression and other issues such as bullying.
www.kidshelpphone.ca
1–800–668–6868

Depnet
An everyday resource on depression.
www.depnet.ca ·

The Health Center
A great website that offers a variety of information on emotional issues.
www.thehealthcenter.info

Focus on Drinking and Drugs

One of the challenges for teens as they gain their independence and head out into the adult world is to navigate the risky waters of drug and alcohol use. While each of us would like to think that *our* teens will avoid illegal drug use and underage drinking, it is unrealistic to expect that our children will not be exposed to these activities at some point in their adolescence—no matter where we live or what schools our kids go to. As a matter of fact, according to the Centre for Addiction and Mental Health, in 2005, 62 percent of Canadian students in grades seven to twelve reported consuming some alcohol during the previous year. Ten percent of students said they drank once a week.

It is unclear whether quantity or frequency of drinking or drug abuse has been changing over the years, but research suggests that teens are starting to drink at an earlier age than ever before (as noted by the Substance Abuse and Mental Health Services Administration, SAMHSA, in the U.S.). What's more, the number of girls aged 12 to 17 engaged in alcohol and drug use is now the same as for boys, and girls are surpassing male teens in smoking and abusing prescription drugs.

While most of us are aware of the many and varied dangers that illegal drugs can pose to our physical and mental health (from the brain-damaging effects of crystal meth to the highly addictive nature of crack cocaine), all drug and alcohol use can pose significant risks for teens. Teens who drink or do drugs are more likely to engage in unprotected sex and experience problems in school, have behavioural issues and even suffer from depression. They are more likely to be victims of violence (SAMHSA reports that alcohol is linked to two-thirds of teen sexual assaults and date rapes in the U.S.). And as we all know, alcohol and cars are a deadly mix. According to the American Academy of Pediatrics, the number one cause of death for teens ages 15 to 24 in the U.S. is alcohol-related car crashes. Alcohol or drugs often play a role in other teen accidents as well, including drowning.

Moreover, while alcohol and drugs are often used as a way to deal with depression (a very ineffective way, as alcohol and many drugs are themselves depressants), sadly, they can also contribute to mental states that make suicide more likely.

Why Do Teens Drink or Do Drugs?

It is clear there are many risks associated with teen alcohol and drug use—in addition to their being illegal activities. But it is just as important for parents to understand *why* teens consume drugs and alcohol, as it is to determine *if* they are using.

A study by the Annenberg Public Policy Center of the University of Pennsylvania found that teens tend to associate smoking, drinking and doing drugs with popular peers (and not with less popular teens). Since many teens want to be popular or emulate the popular crowd, there is a great deal of silent peer pressure involved in substance abuse. Teens may also use drugs or alcohol to

- improve their mood
- feel more confident
- help them relax
- help them lose their inhibitions
- lose weight
- alleviate boredom
- forget about or escape from problems
- feel creative

Of all the reasons cited above, perhaps the one that should be of most concern to parents is teens' desire to forget their problems. While girls in particular are susceptible to peer pressure about drugs and alcohol, boys often resort to substance abuse to cope with emotional problems. If teens are using drugs or alcohol to suppress unpleasant feelings or difficult thoughts, the underlying issues need immediate attention before they lead to serious substance abuse and dependency, or other physical and mental risks.

But even social drinking or experimentation can lead to addiction.

Early warning signs of substance abuse can include

- changes in behaviour or relationships with parents or other family members
- acting in a secretive way
- withdrawing from activities they used to enjoy
- hanging out with a new group of friends, or not bringing their friends home
- a drop in grades or frequent absences from school
- needing drugs or alcohol to have fun, forget trouble, unwind
- blackouts
- using alcohol or drugs when alone
- needing more of a substance to get high—developing a higher tolerance
- stealing, lying or selling possessions to get money for drugs or alcohol

Teens who are regularly using drugs may also be irritable and experience changes in eating, sleeping or hygiene patterns. Some of these signs might also be signals of depression or other problems. Whatever their cause, they are indications that your teen may need some help.

What Parents Can Do
Talk to Your Kids
The good news is that parents can make an enormous difference in how their children handle exposure to alcohol and drugs. The Substance Abuse and Mental Health Services Administration in the U.S. reports that youth who have had conversations with their parents about drugs, tobacco and alcohol had lower rates of substance use than those who did not talk with their parents. It's important, therefore, to have conversations with your children, preteens and teens about substance use, the earlier the better (don't wait until your teens are in high school, where they may already have been exposed to alcohol and drugs).

By the time our children have reached their teens, they have been bombarded with countless television commercials and school health lessons about the dangers of smoking. Nevertheless, many of them pick up the habit. Sometimes teens smoke to appear older than they are, to seem cool or part of the popular crowd, to help them eat less and lose weight or simply as an act of rebellion. While you can't control your teens' decision to smoke, you can model healthy behaviour by not smoking yourself and you can establish some boundaries about what happens in your home, including the following rules:

- No smoking inside the house.
- No smoking on the home property.
- If teens are under the legal age to buy tobacco products, cigarettes found in the house will be thrown out. If teens are of age to buy tobacco, you need to let them know what you will do if you find cigarettes.

If your teen does smoke and voices an interest in quitting, ask him how you might best help him. If he doesn't know, you might ask the following questions:

- Would he like you to set up an appointment with a doctor or take him to an addiction centre for counselling or information?
- Would he like you to introduce him to someone dying of lung cancer or emphysema? (I know two parents who did this and it was very effective.)
- Would he like you to ask him weekly how his progress is going?
- Would he prefer you not to bring it up with him?
- Does he need more encouragement?
- Would it be helpful for you to put an incentive plan together for him so that when he reaches a certain number of days without smoking, you can celebrate with him?

The key is that you want to partner with him as he goes through this difficult process.

While you may want to raise the subject of drugs and alcohol specifically on a number of occasions, don't miss opportunities to discuss the issues as they arise naturally—whether you are responding to a television show involving drugs or a family party where an adult had too much to drink. Keep in mind that you should avoid lecturing your kids, and you will probably need to educate yourself about the specific risks of drugs and the effects of alcohol before you talk about them. Overstating the dangers or giving inaccurate information will make it easier for your teens to dismiss your concerns.

You may also have some experiences or information that can make the risks real for your teens. One parent I know sat her preteen children down and told them about how, years ago, her teen brother had died in a car accident because he got behind the wheel after he had been drinking. She then took them to visit his grave. Being able to see the long-lasting, real-life tragedy caused by alcohol use was a powerful learning experience for her kids.

Be an Inside-Out Parent

Being an inside-out parent will help your child make wise choices about drugs and alcohol. Review the six keys in the Introduction and commit to listening to your teens, to helping them build or maintain healthy self-esteem and to empowering them with responsibilities and the opportunity to make decisions for themselves. Teens with strong characters are much less likely to fall victim to substance use and abuse.

Talk About Peer Pressure

Discuss peer pressure with your preteens and teens (see "Focus on Friends and Peer Pressure" in Chapter 1). Make a special point of talking about silent peer pressure. One teen I talked with told me that his friends would never pressure another party-goer to have a beer. "There'd only be fewer for us," he said. That may be true, but simply the fact that he and his friends are all drinking sends a powerful unspoken message (whether they intend it or not) to the rest of the teens at the party.

Keeping Safe in Public Places

While it is a good idea to talk with your children about the dangers of specific drugs, you should also make them aware that sometimes people can slip them drugs without their knowledge. (People may do this because they think it will be entertaining to see someone's reaction to an unexpected drug experience or because they want to take advantage of the incapacitated victim.) Caution your teens never to leave their soft drink cans or glasses unattended at dances, parties or all-age clubs. If they do have to leave their beverages on a table when they are on the dance floor or in the washroom, they should abandon the drink and get a new one when they are thirsty.

Model Wise and Cautious Behaviour

There is no doubt about it—many attitudes to drug and alcohol use are picked up at home. I've met so many parents who enjoy throwing wild, boozy parties for their friends, and then are surprised that their teens are doing the same. Or parents who have smoked marijuana, and then can't convince their children about the dangers of illegal drug use. Teens are very observant and quick to pick up any discrepancies between what adults say and do. (You may think they don't know about your pot smoking, but I bet they do!) If we want our children to avoid drug use and underage drinking, we must model wise, cautious and responsible behaviour ourselves. Look at the following questions, and ask yourself if you would like your teens to emulate your behaviour, or not.

- Do you press drinks on dinner or house guests or do you make sure there are plenty of non–alcoholic alternatives when you entertain?

- Is alcohol a part of every celebration or party at your home?
- Do you use illegal drugs?
- Do you use drugs or alcohol to cope with problems or make statements like, "Boy, do I need a drink!" Do you take prescription drugs for reasons other than those the prescription is intended for?
- Do you operate machinery, drive any kind of vehicle or engage in potentially dangerous activities like swimming and diving after consuming alcohol?
- Do you accept rides with anyone who has been drinking?
- Do you drink to excess?
- Do you joke about getting drunk or tell funny stories about drinking or drug use?

Teens are often in a hurry to grow up and enter the adult world. While you may not think you have much influence, you must remember that you are their primary source of information about that world. If you demonstrate a cavalier or irresponsible attitude to drinking and doing drugs, your teens are likely to follow suit.

Encourage Teens to Get Involved

According to the Substance Abuse and Mental Health Services Administration in the U.S., during June and July, there is a 40 percent increase in the rate of young people who try marijuana for the first time. The agency suggests that too much unsupervised time and boredom contribute to an increase in drug use in the summer months. Certainly large amounts of unstructured time can create ample opportunity for your children to engage in risk-taking behaviour of all sorts. Encourage teens to build variety into their schedules—while they need downtime and opportunities to relax, they will also benefit from some structured events, hobbies or group activities. During the summer, encourage part-time jobs, summer camps, volunteer work, sports teams or activities like tennis or sailing lessons or art classes.

Set Boundaries Around Things You Can Control

While you can make it clear that you don't want your teens drinking underage or taking drugs, you can't establish boundaries on their actions because you can't control them. You can, however, establish boundaries about things that happen in your home. For example, you can make it clear that underage drinking and drug use are not allowed on your property, and you can establish a consequence if you find evidence of such activities. You should also have consequences in place in the event that your teen is found drinking or doing drugs outside of your home. (See Chapter 6 for how to work out appropriate consequences with your teens.) You can also establish that alcohol or prescription drugs are not to be taken from your home.

If you have seen evidence of habitual drug use, your teen's privilege of privacy may need to be revoked—at least in part. (This should be made clear to teens beforehand.) I strongly recommend at this point that you take your teen to a counsellor who specializes in drug and alcohol addictions.

Establish Rules About Parties

While you can't stop your teens from experimenting with drugs or alcohol, you can certainly make it more difficult for them. For example, you should establish some guidelines with your teens about both throwing and attending parties. If your teen wants to entertain at your home, make it clear that they can only have groups over when you are there. Give your teens some privacy during the party, but make sure that you are in a location where you can keep a discreet eye on things. Agree ahead of time on the number of guests to be invited. Make sure that your teens know that no uninvited teens should be let into your house and that anyone arriving with drugs or alcohol will be asked to leave.

If your teen wants to go to someone else's party, get the name of the host and his or her parents, their phone number and the street address. You may want to call ahead to make sure there will be a parent at the party. And always make sure your child has a safe way home from the event. If your teen will be relying on a friend for a ride, make sure that your teen knows that they should not get into a car if the driver has been drinking. Let them know that if the driver has been drinking or doing drugs, you will come to pick your teen up—no questions asked. If you don't drive, make sure they have money and a phone number for a taxi. (These rules for a safe way home should be followed whenever your teens go anywhere.)

Letting Your Teens Drink at Home

Over the years, a number of parents have asked me if it was okay to let their teens have a glass of wine with the adults at a family dinner, or a beer while they watch TV with their parents. I understand their uncertainty. In some countries, even children may have a small glass of wine with a meal. But despite these cultural differences, I usually advise against allowing teens to drink at home. For one thing, underage drinking is against the law, and allowing your child to break the law in your home sends mixed messages (What other laws are okay to break? When do you observe the law and when do you ignore it?). Another consideration is that once you allow underage drinking, the boundary lines get very blurry. I have worked with parents who have allowed their teens to drink in the home. Conflict arose when the kids brought their friends home and their parents would not let the teens and their friends have a drink. The teens wanted to know why they could have a beer when they were alone with their parents, but not when they had company. And if they can drink in your presence, does that mean that they can have a drink when they are at someone else's house with you?

Get Your Teen Professional Help

If you suspect that your teen has an alcohol or drug habit, take him or her to a substance abuse counsellor immediately. You can ask your family doctor for a referral or contact an addiction or mental health agency, such as Recovery Counselling Services in the Toronto area (**www.recoverycounselling.on.ca**), the Centre for Addiction and Mental Health (**www.camh.net**) or their 24-hour Drug and Alcohol Information Line at 1-800-463-6273, or the Canadian Health Network (**www.canadian-health-network.ca**), for guidance and referrals. Recovery Counselling Services also has an excellent addiction self-assessment on its website.

A counsellor specializing in drug abuse may recommend regular drug testing for your teen and will work with parents and teens to put together a boundary plan to address the teen's substance abuse.

FOCUS ON *Drinking and Drugs*

4 Self-Esteem and Respect

"I want my parents to understand that I have greater ambitions than they think and expect. The support for those dreams just isn't there. I wish they understood."

—Liam, age 18

In my very first year of private practice, I experienced something that highlighted a key issue of most problems during the teen years. On this particular day I had five different teens scheduled throughout the afternoon. My first client, a 17-year-old girl, came in and started complaining about her life. She was unhappy with her body, claimed nobody liked her at school and said that none of the guys she liked were interested in her. After that, I talked with a 14-year-old girl with a very similar story. The third client, age 18, was an athletic guy who seemed together on the outside but soon revealed that no matter how hard he tried, he was never satisfied. He got a 93 percent average on his last report card and although he felt "amazing" for two minutes, he soon started feeling anxious and scared about keeping up his average. Nothing was ever good enough for him. He was harsh and negative towards himself. Next I saw a 12-year-old boy who told me about all the things he didn't like about himself. He was followed by a 16-year-old girl whose tale was similar to all of the others combined.

As I was sitting in my office, listening to all of their heartaches, I had a revelation. All five of these stories pointed to a similar problem. Each of these teens struggled with low self-esteem—that was the root problem. Their low confidence was having a negative impact how they responded to events in their lives.

When people have healthy self-esteem, they feel confident about themselves, they respect themselves and others, they are more likely to set realistic goals and have the courage to go after those goals. People who have healthy self-esteem tend to choose friends and partners who treat them well. And the key to helping your teens build their confidence and self-esteem is to treat them with respect.

Respect is an important component of inside-out parenting. It's something that teenagers are tremendously aware of and value very highly. I asked a number of teens across Canada to define respect. Here are just a few of the answers I received:

- Respect is showing consideration and equality towards others.
- I guess respect is when you treat a person as an equal you don't judge really and when you can value someone's opinion even if you disagree.
- Respect is the appreciation that one person has for another. It's treating people how you would want to be treated, noticing their high and low points, and not looking down on them.
- In order for a person to be respectful they must be empathetic. I think that's the first step towards respect
- Respect is simple—it's kindness towards others.
- Respect to me is when people listen to what I have to say and treat me nicely and appreciate me.

I was so impressed by their responses. Respect is indeed both the condition of being honoured, esteemed or well regarded and the objective, unbiased consideration and regard for the rights, values, beliefs and property of all people.

We all want to be respected, to be listened to, to be valued, to be seen as an equal and to be appreciated. Respect is so important, in fact, that youth culture has its own word for the lack of it. To "dis" someone is to disrespect them, and while teens may use this word primarily when talking about other teens, there is no doubt that if parents don't respect their teens there can be huge consequences not only for the relationship but also for the teens' self-esteem.

But before I begin to discuss strategies based on respect that can help bolster your teen's self-esteem, perhaps we should look at the ways various types of self-esteem might show themselves in our teens.

Types of Self-Esteem

Low Self-Esteem

People who have low self-esteem feel *inferior* to others. As a result, they often belittle themselves by thinking or saying comments like:

- I'm ugly
- I'm stupid
- I'm fat
- No one wants to be my friend
- Nothing ever goes right for me
- I can't do anything right

I sometimes call this the "Blind" attitude because people with low self-esteem are blind to their own strengths. If you ask them what they are good at they are likely to say, "Nothing." But if you ask them what they are bad at, they will answer, "Lots of things." They cannot see their own talents, their uniqueness and what makes them special. They are incredibly tough on themselves and have very little self-respect. As a result, they often allow other people to walk all over them.

False Self-Esteem

People with this attitude feel *superior* to and lack respect for others. They are cocky, arrogant and often rude. They put people down with no regard for others' feelings. They might make such comments, whether joking or serious, as:

- You're stupid
- You're such a loser
- Why would anyone want to date you?
- You won't do anything in your life
- You're so fat and ugly

Their chief concern is themselves. They don't let others walk over them. If you ask them what they are good at, they will be able to tell you. If you ask them what they are bad at, they are likely to say, "Nothing." They view asking for help as a weakness. I sometimes say that people with false self-esteem have a "Disguised" attitude because they are not as confident as they appear to be, and they use their outward bravado to cover up feelings of insecurity. People with this attitude are the toughest to reach in coaching and counselling because they use all their energy to disguise their emotional weaknesses. They protect themselves by insisting that all problems are caused by someone else. They can act very proud, and rarely, if ever, apologize.

Healthy Self-Esteem

People with healthy self-esteem believe they are *equal* to others—not better, not worse. They don't put themselves down, and they don't put other people down. Those with healthy self-esteem treat themselves and others with respect—even when their opinions differ. They choose to respect all people regardless of age, race, sexual orientation, religion or any other difference. If you ask these people what they are good at, they may answer:

- Well, I've got a lot of strengths including . . .
- I'm proud of the fact that I am . . .
- I'm trying my absolute best at . . .

If you ask people with healthy self-esteem what they are bad at, they may respond by saying something like, "I've got my weaknesses, but I'm trying to work on them."

People with healthy self-esteem show compassion towards themselves and towards others. They know that they are not perfect, so they ask for help and apologize for their part in conflicts. They realize there is much to learn from others and themselves.

Connecting the Dots

You may have recognized yourself or your teen in the descriptions of the three types of self-esteem. But often, it's difficult to see ourselves or each other this clearly. After one of my presentations to high school students, a 16-year-old girl wrote to me, "Most of my friends think I have healthy self-esteem—but really I don't at all."

So how can parents discover how their children feel about themselves? Obviously, our goal in becoming inside-out parents is to be able to talk with our children about their thoughts and feelings (see Chapter 5 for more on this idea). But even before we've achieved this type of relationship with our teens, we can come to some conclusions by properly interpreting their behaviour. How we feel about ourselves impacts nearly every decision that we make (e.g., dating, friendships, goals, motivation, communication, etc.). The following chart summarizes how the three types of self-esteem may affect many key areas of teens' lives. Keep in mind that there are *always* exceptions to the correlations I outline below. Everyone is different. Be your own judge about how many of these apply to you and your teen, and to what extent.

The Three Types of Self-Esteem

FRIENDSHIPS

Low Self-Esteem	Healthy Self-Esteem	False Self-Esteem
• may seek out friends with low or false self-esteem • may be self-absorbed; allows others to walk over him or her • may seek and accept negative feedback • may fight with friends in passive-aggressive ways, like excluding others (more common in girls)	• seeks out a mix of friends, mostly with healthy self-esteem • prefers equal partnerships • often seeks and accepts positive feedback from others	• may seek out friends with low or false self-esteem • may be self-absorbed; takes others for granted • may be physically aggressive

DATING

Low Self-Esteem	Healthy Self-Esteem	False Self-Esteem
• may date people with false or low self-esteem • may tend to be jealous and possessive • may feel incomplete without a partner	• dates people with healthy self-esteem • won't tolerate dating someone with false self-esteem • may want a partner but doesn't think he or she "needs" one	• may date people with false or low self-esteem • may be extremely controlling, jealous and possessive • may feel incomplete without a partner

GOALS and MOTIVATION

Low Self-Esteem	Healthy Self-Esteem	False Self-Esteem
• may set no goals for fear of failure OR may become a perfectionist, setting very high goals but seldom reaching them • may be unmotivated, reticent	• sets high career goals • is motivated and strives for excellence • sets, actively pursues and often achieves realistic goals	• may set few goals for fear of failure OR may become a perfectionist, setting very high goals but never reaching them • may be unmotivated, reticent

COMMUNICATION

Low Self-Esteem	Healthy Self-Esteem	False Self-Esteem
• may exhibit passive or passive-aggressive tendencies (such as "backstabbing") in communication • may play the victim; may think that life is happening to him or her without offering choices • over-apologizes	• exhibits assertiveness in communication • takes responsibility for his or her actions • apologizes when in the wrong (but doesn't over-apologize)	• may exhibit aggression and disrespectfulness in communication • may blame others for his or her problems • rarely, if ever, apologizes or takes ownership of problems

PEER PRESSURE

Low Self-Esteem	Healthy Self-Esteem	False Self-Esteem
• may have a hard time saying no to others • may be desperate for acceptance; may do whatever is necessary to gain it	• says yes to what he or she wants and no to what he or she doesn't want • understands and defends his or her values	• often won't take no for an answer • may be controlling and demanding; may pressure others to do things

BODY IMAGE

Low Self-Esteem	Healthy Self-Esteem	False Self-Esteem
• may base his or her value on looks and weight; may think, "If only I weighed _____pounds, I'd be happy." • may believe teasing remarks or negative comments about body image, even though the comments are not true (e.g., a teenage girl tells herself she is fat although she weighs only 100 pounds)	• is accepting of his or her body shape and size • is respectful and caring towards his or her body	• may base his or her value on looks and weight; may think, "If only I weighed _____ pounds, I'd be happy." • may not be satisfied with or respectful towards his or her body

ANGER		
Low Self-Esteem	**Healthy Self-Esteem**	**False Self-Esteem**
• may get angry and blame self when unfortunate events happen • may direct anger towards self	• voices his or her anger in an assertive way • strives for conflict resolution	• may get angry and blame others when unfortunate events happen • may take anger out on others

DEPRESSION and SUICIDAL THOUGHTS		
Low Self-Esteem	**Healthy Self-Esteem**	**False Self-Esteem**
• may feel depressed, hopeless or even suicidal at times. May lose motivation, sleep too much or not enough, have difficulty making decisions, have less energy, lose appetite and think about suicide • may look for friends, music or environments that reinforce negative emotions • may use drugs or alcohol to numb feelings and provide escape	• does not generally experience depression or suicidal thoughts	• may feel depressed, hopeless or even suicidal at times. May lose motivation, sleep too much or not enough, have difficulty making decisions, have less energy, lose appetite and think about suicide • may look for friends, music or environments that reinforce negative emotions • may use drugs or alcohol to numb feelings and provide escape

DIVORCE		
Low Self-Esteem	**Healthy Self-Esteem**	**False Self-Esteem**
• may blame self for parents' divorce	• doesn't blame self for parents' divorce; understands that it was a decision between the parents alone	• may direct anger over parents' divorce towards others

SELF-DESTRUCTIVE BEHAVIOURS (*applies more often to girls)

Low Self-Esteem	Healthy Self-Esteem	False Self-Esteem
• may smoke* • may engage in self-mutilation to help escape emotional pain • may abuse drugs or alcohol • may show signs of having an eating disorder; may undereat or overeat to feel in control*	• is accepting and respectful of his or her body; cares for physical self • does not abuse drugs or alcohol • doesn't over- or under-eat* • doesn't smoke*	• may smoke* • may engage in self-mutilation to help escape emotional pain • may abuse drugs or alcohol • may show signs of having an eating disorder; may undereat or overeat to feel in control*

ABUSE

Low Self-Esteem	Healthy Self-Esteem	False Self-Esteem
• may blame self for being abused • may learn not to trust own intuition or judgment • may abuse drugs or alcohol • may become sexually promiscuous (may believe he or she is good only for sex) • may develop an attraction to people who are abusive	• has learned (either through personal experience, counselling or reading) that the abuse was not his or her fault • has learned to trust self and others again • is attracted to friends and partners who are loving and kind	• may blame self for being abused but acts out this anger aggressively towards others • may learn not to trust own intuition or judgment • may become sexually promiscuous (may believe he or she is good only for sex) • may become abusive, in turn, to friends and/or partners

Five Strategies to Build Your Teen's Self-Esteem and Self-Respect

When I speak at conferences or to groups of parents, I often ask my audience, "So what's the secret? If we all realize the importance of teaching our teen about confidence, self-esteem and respect, how do we do it? What's the answer?" The parents frequently come up with some good answers, such as:

- Encourage our kids
- Affirm them
- Listen to them
- Let them make their own mistakes

What's fascinating to me, however, is that the best ways to truly build self-esteem are often not mentioned. The four strategies I'm about to share with you are by no means an exhaustive list, but they will certainly get you thinking.

Strategy #1: Preach Less and Model More

In my many years of private practice, I've found that the greatest variable in determining what kind of self-esteem kids have is what kind of self-esteem *their parents* have. When I was describing the different types of self-esteem earlier, I asked you to think about which one sounded the most like you. It's important that we all figure this out for ourselves.

About a year ago when I was speaking at a parent workshop, a mother came up to me afterwards and said that as she watched the skit on stage, she not only saw her teen in the character named Susan (who had low self-esteem) but also herself. That was an important revelation because she realized for the first time how she had been feeling. And although she thought she kept these thoughts and feelings to herself, without realizing it, for years she had been modelling low self-esteem for her daughter.

Ask yourself the following questions:

- Do I put myself down?
- Do I put other people down?
- Do I refuse to apologize even when it is appropriate?
- Do I apologize too seldom?
- Do I respect all people, even people who hold opinions different from mine?
- Do I have difficulty saying no to others?
- Do I have difficulty listening to others or always think that my way is the right way?
- Do I consider myself a perfectionist?
- Do I set goals that are often unattainable?

It's very important to realize that our teens pick up on these messages and often learn unconsciously that this is how they should believe and act.

Fathers and Sons, Mothers and Daughters

What influences teens' self-esteem the most? Many things affect their sense of self, including TV, magazines, friends, friends' parents and so on. But the greatest influence on what type of self-esteem teens develop is their same-sex parent. Girls are most likely to adopt the same attitudes as their mothers, while guys tend to get their self-esteem messages from their fathers. I have seen exceptions to this (as there are always exceptions), but the pattern is surprisingly consistent. This is why we often date people with personalities similar to our opposite-sex parent; we are mirroring the type of self-esteem our parents have modelled for us (unless we have consciously changed it in ourselves).

At workshops I'll often ask the parents in the audience, "Would you want your teen to date somebody like you?" Usually there is silence, and I see an "Oh, no" look on many faces. The truth is if we cannot answer confidently yes to that question, we have some work on ourselves to do first!

I saw the power of modelling at work in Rachel, age 15, several years ago. She came in to see me because she was cutting her arms, unfortunately a popular trend among troubled teens (and one that requires immediate professional attention). As I outlined in Chapter 3, most cutters self-mutilate because they are experiencing such deep emotional pain that the only coping strategy they have found is to inflict physical pain on themselves as a distraction from the emotional pain.

Rachel was very depressed, suffered from low self-esteem and talked very little. She was dating a guy who was verbally abusive to her. Rachel's boyfriend had also been cheating on her. Rachel's parents were just as concerned about this harmful relationship as they were about their daughter's cutting, but as I got to know Rachel and her family, I started to see a pattern. The daughter's relationship with her boyfriend was almost a carbon copy of her parents' relationship. Rachel was simply acting out the role that been modelled by her mom and dad.

Rachel had frequently seen her father belittle her mother and knew that her dad had had at least two affairs. Rachel's mother had never addressed these problems; instead she pretended that nothing bothered her. It was interesting to watch the dynamics between Rachel and her mom in my office. After Rachel's mother tried to convince her daughter to believe in herself and have the courage to end her relationship, Rachel looked her mom straight in the eye and said, "Maybe you should listen to your own advice."

Despite the harshness of Rachel's response, she had a good point. When a parent says one thing but acts a different way, teens will tend not to believe the verbal message if it is outweighed by the actions they are observing. (In Chapter 5 I talk about the importance of congruent communication.) When our actions and words match, our teens are most likely to trust and believe in what we have to say. Rachel's mom's words were not congruent with her actions, so they had no impact on Rachel.

Parents are often overwhelmed when I tell them what an enormous influence their own lives and behaviour have on a teen's self-esteem.

Responsibility vs. Blame

When I see parents who model poor self-esteem for their children, I am careful not to "blame" them for their actions. There's a difference between blaming someone and asking them to take responsibility. Blaming suggests the person caused something to happen. Asking someone to accept responsibility for a situation is asking them to take ownership for how they are contributing to a problem. Rachel's parents did not cause her to cut herself or engage in a bad relationship. Their own behaviour in their marriage, however, did contribute to Rachel's problems.

Many don't want their children mirroring their self-esteem problems. But the fact that a parent's self-esteem is the primary influence on their teen's sense of self can be great news! It means that if parents treat themselves and others with respect (a skill that we can all learn regardless of our education, race or age), there is a high likelihood that their kids will naturally start feeling the same way about themselves. An essential part of being an inside-out parent then is developing, maintaining and modelling our own healthy self-esteem.

Strategy #2: Teach Responsibility

I want you to start listening to your words. Notice whether you often say things like

- I can't
- I have to
- I have no choice
- I must
- I should

What do all of these expressions have in common? They sound like the words of someone who has absolutely no power in his or her life. They sound like the words of a victim. But is that true?

Playing the victim is a habit for some people, and it's a habit that often interferes with healthy self-esteem. People who adopt the role of victim often blame problems on other people and avoid taking responsibility. These behaviours often determine whether a person is acting as an adult or is acting as a child (emotionally speaking) in relationships. Here is how I define the difference.

Those with low or false self-esteem are often emotionally immature. So age does not determine a person's emotional maturity: our habits and thinking do. A person might be 50 years old but still be emotionally immature, while a 17-year-old could be emotionally mature. As parents, we need once again to ask ourselves, "Which one sounds more like me?" As I said earlier, the most powerful way to help

Emotionally Immature	Emotionally Mature
• plays the victim • seldom apologizes (since it's everyone else's fault) *or* apologizes too much (e.g., "Fine, it's all my fault.") • blames events on other people • talks aggressively by using "You" statements (e.g., "You made me feel . . .") *or* talks passive-aggressively and behind people's backs (e.g., "She made me feel . . .") • makes comments like "I can't," "I have to," "I must," "I should," "I have no choice" • sees life as happening to him or her, not something he or she chooses or affects • sees self as being responsible *for* others	• takes responsibility for his or her own actions • can look at a conflict; genuinely apologizes for his or her part but doesn't apologize for something that he or she does not feel responsible for • speaks assertively, dealing with conflict in a direct but respectful way; often uses "I" statements (e.g., "I feel . . ." and "I think that . . .") • takes responsibility for his or her choices (e.g., "I choose to . . ." or "I choose not to . . .") • seldom if ever uses statements like "I can't" or "I have to" • sees life as full of choices • sees self as being responsible *to* others

our teens build healthy self-esteem is to model it ourselves, and part of that means taking responsibility for ourselves—our attitudes, habits and choices—and being emotionally mature. The next best way to help our teens become more emotionally mature is to pay attention when they are displaying emotional immaturity.

I had been working with Brian, age 16, for several months when he mentioned a conflict he was having with his parents. Although Brian was one of those wise teens I mentioned earlier, when he first told what happened, he blamed the entire conflict on his parents. When I asked him what percentage of the conflict he thought was his mom and dad's responsibility, he answered, "About 90 percent." Then I asked him what percentage he would claim. (I always ask this question, even though it sounds like an obvious one, because some people will assign blame to things like the weather, noise and so on.) He accepted the remaining 10 percent. "Okay, Brian," I said, "tell me more about your 10 percent. What could you have done differently? What do you think was your responsibility?"

Over the course of an hour, as we discussed the conflict in detail, Brian gradually began to take more responsibility for his part in it. "Well, hmm, I could have not yelled—that didn't go over very well," he offered. Then he added, "I guess I should not have sworn at them, but they got me mad."

"Hang on," I said. "We'll get back to what they could have done differently. But for now, let's look at what you could have done differently."

Brian suggested that perhaps he shouldn't have barged into the room while they were watching a movie, interrupting them. He was making some good progress. Then I asked, "Brian, what would happen if you approached your parents and apologized first for your part in this conflict? I'm not telling you to apologize for anything that you do not believe is your responsibility—but own up to what you think you could have done differently. How do you think your parents would respond?"

Brian thought that his parents would be shocked because he had never done that before, and he didn't know what to say. I suggested that he tell them what he had told me—that he took ownership for how he voiced his frustration, for his rudeness and his inappropriate interruption. I advised him to tell his parents that he still wanted to talk to them if they were willing to sit and listen.

Brian thought about this and decided to write his parents a letter instead of talking it out. His plan proved to be a very good starting point—his parents responded well and were willing to own up to their part in the conflict. Brian's story illustrates how we can teach responsibility by helping our teens to take ownership for their part when conflicts arise by both describing how this is done and by taking responsibility ourselves.

Let Them Vent!

Here's a little trick I've learned. Allow teens to vent their frustration and anger about a conflict before you ask them to look at what their part is in a conflict and before offering a solution. The trick is to listen, listen, listen. If they don't believe that we have heard their pain and frustration, they are not nearly as willing to accept any responsibility for a problem. And if we have not apologized first for what we could have done differently, they are even less likely to acknowledge what they could have done differently.

Strategy #3: Challenge Negative Thinking

As I said earlier, self-esteem all comes down to how we think about ourselves. The comments we tell ourselves go around and around in our heads—like a soundtrack on a CD. And how we think affects how we feel, and how we feel affects our decisions. So paying attention to how we think is critically important.

A lot of the time, when teens come in to see me they want to talk about an emotional issue. They may be feeling confused, stressed, anxious, depressed or upset. Their parents, however, are more often concerned about their teens' behaviours, such as withdrawing from friends and family or having angry outbursts. My work involves helping these teens and parents understand the link between emotions and resulting behaviour and our cognitive system, or how we think.

Best Friend Technique

When 17-year-old Colleen came in to see me she was feeling depressed, alone, unconfident, disappointed and confused. So I asked her how her feelings were affecting her behaviour. She told me she had been avoiding her family and friends, had stopped showering and hardly left the house. She also said she was no longer motivated in school, was not exercising and didn't really care about her physical appearance anymore.

All of Colleen's behaviours are potential symptoms of depression. My first recommendation was for her to see her family doctor to make sure her physical health was not in jeopardy. Colleen had been very clear about how she was feeling, but I wanted to find out about the thoughts behind those feelings. I asked her to describe how she thought about herself. She was quiet and didn't answer at first. I let her reflect for a few minutes. I asked her again. "Colleen, try to finish this sentence," I prompted. "I feel anxious because . . ." After five or 10 minutes of silence she said, "I feel anxious because I think my work is never good enough. I think I'm fat and ugly. I think I'm never good enough. I have no goals and no passion—and if I was skinnier I'd be happy."

When I wrote down all of these thoughts and feelings on a "head, heart and hand" diagram (see Chapter 3), Colleen stared at them in disbelief. She said she found it a little depressing to see all that had been inside her head spelled out on the chalkboard.

Colleen's response to this exercise is common. Many teens find it difficult—even depressing—to read what is recorded on a head, heart and hand diagram because, for the first time, they are facing *their current reality*. But we cannot change what we don't know or understand.

I explained to Colleen that we cannot control our hearts or how we feel. But we can control how we think and what we do. That means if we want to feel better, we need to learn how to think and act differently.

So how do we think differently? To show Colleen, I used what I call the "Best Friend Technique." Something special happens to most of us when we start thinking about our best friends: we become loving and objective. I asked Colleen to imagine that she had a best friend named Casie. Casie looks like Colleen, talks like Colleen and acts like Colleen. One day, Casie tells Colleen that she thinks of herself as fat and ugly. "What would you say to Casie?" I asked Colleen. "Would you say, 'It's true—you are kind of fat and ugly'?"

Colleen, of course, laughed and acknowledged that she would never treat a friend this way. So I asked Colleen to look at five negative statements she had made about herself and imagine Casie saying them and asking Colleen for advice. I advised Colleen that when she responded to Casie, she needed to be both truthful *and* loving.

Here is what Colleen came up with, with a little help from me.

Old thought: "I think I'm fat and ugly."
New thought: "You are beautiful just as you are."

Old thought: "I think I'm never good enough."
New thought: "You are good enough just as you are."

Old thought: "My work is never good enough."
New thought: "Focus on what you can control—which is how hard you try. Stop putting so much emphasis on some mark. Really try working towards accepting whatever your best is."

Old thought: "I have no goals and no passion."
New thought: "You're young— it takes time to discover your passion. Just be willing to try new things to discover what you're passionate about."

Old thought: "I think if I was skinnier I'd be happy."

New thought: "I love you just as you are—I'm not going to love you any more or less if you lose or gain weight. Focus on being healthy instead of trying to get to some stupid number."

I asked Colleen how she would feel if these new thoughts became her own thoughts. She said, "Confident, encouraged, optimistic, curious and beautiful." Then I asked Colleen how her behaviour would change if she felt these new feelings. She admitted that she would probably exercise more, try harder in school, take care of her appearance, try new things, and spend more time with her family and friends.

I put all of these new thoughts, feelings and actions on the chalk-board beside the old ones. Colleen's look brightened when she read the new words, but she was unsure of how she could make the new thoughts truly her own. I used the CD metaphor, explaining that whatever thoughts are playing in her head will determine how she feels. Her heart, I pointed out, does not know the difference between the truth and a lie. So if a person tells themselves they are fat even though they are only 130 pounds, they will feel fat.

Colleen estimated that she had had those five negative thoughts five to six times each a day for eight to 10 years; in other words, she'd told herself those mean, hurtful and cruel messages over 14,000 times. Meanwhile, she'd told herself the wonderful loving messages just once, in my office.

In order to change her thinking, I asked Colleen to write a letter to Casie, including all the loving new words of truth, and to read that letter at least three times a day. After she had finished the letter, she was to cross out Casie's name and write her own.

I've done this exercise with hundreds of people. On average, I find people have to read these letters around 500 times before their thoughts begin to change. (Many people tell me that at first when they start reading their letter, it is frustrating and feels like a waste of time. I tell clients to stick to the program and keep reading their letter.) Once they start believing their own words, their feelings change and then their behaviour starts changing as well. For those who follow through with the exercise, this is the most rewarding type of work they can do. Often people will start to believe some of the letter after 40 or 50 times; others take longer, depending on how many times they've told themselves the negative thoughts.

I encourage all parents to do this exercise themselves first before encouraging their teens to try it. Teens will probably find it easier to complete in private, without their parents' help. If they are not willing to try it at all, don't force them. Simply take notice when they say any negative comment about themselves or someone else and lovingly but gently challenge their thought. Here are some of the questions I use in these kinds of conversations:

- Is that statement truthful?
- Is that statement loving?
- Would you say that to your best friend?
- If not, how could you rephrase it differently so it's loving and truthful?

The best friend strategy takes time and patience—but it works effectively when given the chance.

Thoughts and Feelings

Feelings are always logical—but often the thought that leads to them is illogical. Never downplay or minimize the feelings of your teens, but gently challenge the thoughts that lead to those negative feelings.

Strategy # 4: Encourage Goals and Dreams

Jack and his teen son, Jeremy, came to see me because of Jack's concerns that his son was unmotivated and not applying himself in school. Within minutes of sitting down in my office, Jack announced, "You know I'm very upset because we only got a B on our science project." The word "we" caught my attention. Jack was taking responsibility for his son's school work. He went on to say that he had been phoning all of his son's teachers each week, regularly trying to make sure all of the assignments were in, and yet his son did not appear to be worried at all. Later in the session, when Jeremy had left us, I explained to Jack that I liked to compare raising teens to riding a bike. When children are little, they ride along with their mom or dad in a baby seat in the back. As they get older, they ride their own bike with training wheels. Soon, they're able to pedal the bike themselves while the parent is holding the back of the seat. But eventually, hopefully, the parent lets go of the bike and walks beside it. By the time your children are teens, of course, they should be riding on their own. But in Jack and Jeremy's case, I pointed out, it was as if Jeremy was still in that little seat behind his dad, enjoying the ride. No wonder he wasn't worried.

Jack desperately wanted his son to succeed. His heart was in the right place but his strategy was completely ineffective. He was overfunctioning, and if he persisted, Jeremy would develop into a dependent, insecure teen. Jack was raising a child, not an adult.

But Jack was worried about what to do next. "If I jump off the bike," he pointed out, "Jeremy will fall flat on his face." I acknowledged that Jack would have to get off the bike slowly, gradually passing more and more responsibilities over to his son.

We want our kids to own their own lives, but by overfunctioning, we rob them of opportunities to become independent and mature adults. We need to let them set their own goals, nurture their own dreams and develop the courage and ambition to strive towards those dreams. Setting goals is actually one of the best ways for kids to build their self-esteem because setting and achieving realistic goals (the trick is making sure they're realistic) is an awesome feeling. And that boost in self-esteem encourages teens to set more goals.

When teens set their own goals and reach them, they learn that they can have control over how their lives turn out. Learning about control and choices is one of the best ways to reach emotional maturity. Also by setting realistic goals, teens learn what gifts they have (e.g., athletic ability, compassion, creativity, leadership skills) or what gifts they want to develop. If we don't try anything new, we don't learn what we are good at. Healthy parenting is like coaching. Coaches don't run out onto the field to play the game; they stand at the sidelines to encourage and teach strategies so that kids score their own goals.

In order to "get off the bike" and help your kids set goals, I suggest parents take the following four steps.

1. Acknowledge What You Do

Make a list of all of the things that you do for your teens that they could do for themselves. Your list might include things like

- I wake him up in the morning
- I remind her what books to take to school and what classes she has that day
- I make her lunch for her
- I remind him to do his homework
- I pick up and put away her clothes

The first step is to be honest and acknowledge what you do. Now you know what you need to do differently.

2. Encourage Your Teens' Dreams

I've learned from working with teens that many of them don't like the expression "setting goals." It sounds too much like a school activity. I use the word "dream" instead. To get kids thinking about dreams, I ask them to write for two or three minutes on each of the following questions:

- What is the dream you have for your life?
- What job or career interests you?
- Who has a cool job that you would like to learn more about?
- What places would you like to visit?
- What activities would you like to do someday?

Writing is an important part of this exercise. It allows teens to focus on their paper instead of on me (or you), and the reduced eye contact tends to lessen anxiety for many teens, which helps them think better. Writing also allows young people to record whatever comes to mind, without the embarrassment or self-editing that sometimes happens when things are said aloud.

Having your teen write down his dreams can give you real insight into who he is and what he wants to do in his life, but more importantly, the exercise encourages him to consider what he could be striving towards. Many young people are unmotivated because they don't know what they want to be doing. They see school as a waste of time instead of as a stepping stone towards their next goal.

3. Be a Partner (Don't Take Over)

The next step is for parents to partner, which means finding ways to support your teen, without taking over. (Remember, coaches are not supposed playing the game.) Tell your teens that you want to help them reach their dreams or goals, and ask them what you can do or say that would be helpful. "Helping" to one teen might mean asking them about their homework. Another teen, however, might call this nagging. To one teen, "helpful" is having a parent tutor her in math. For other teens, this might be their worst nightmare. I can't tell you what your teens find helpful because I don't know them. You might also come at it a different way by asking, "What's not helpful?"

4. Encourage Your Teens!

When you see your teens making efforts to do things on their own and striving towards goals, that's your cue to encourage and praise them. It can be scary for teens who have had so many things done for them to start taking responsibility. We need to praise them, love them and encourage them for being courageous.

When you allow your teens the freedom to set their own goals and dreams, they experience a new level of trust from you, and it empowers them to set their own goals in life. And setting and owning their own goals is simply the best way for them to start building their self-esteem.

In this chapter, I have emphasized the importance of building our teens' self-esteem and therefore their character. The best way to do this is by being an inside-out parent, focusing on your teens' efforts, not just their end results. By praising our teens' efforts, we are encouraging them to be courageous at trying new things.

Most adults know that, in the short term, it is often safer to avoid setting any goals that are outside our comfort zone. But in the long term, the cost of this is never developing our skills, strengths and our character. I have spoken with many teens who are afraid to make mistakes, because they are afraid of failure. Some of them are such perfectionists that they often don't hand in assignments, even if they are almost complete, because they are not quite perfect. Others don't even try because they think, "What's the point; I'm probably going to fail anyway." When teens have developed this kind of attitude, it's critical for parents to help teach and redefine success for them. Making mistakes is part of life. Failure is often just part of the process. The goal should always be to try their best, and to strive for excellence, whatever that is for them. It's important for you to let them know how proud of them you are, even just for trying something new. This gives them courage to step outside their comfort zone, enabling them to discover their gifts.

My own story is a perfect example of this. When I was 13 years old, I was diagnosed with a learning disability. The psychologist told me I would be lucky to finish high school. I was hurt and angry and absolutely devastated. When I reached high school I found the work very difficult. I went for extra help and had a couple of different tutors. It quickly became apparent that I needed to be extremely motivated if I was going to pass. But my parents never, and I mean *never*, asked to see my report card. It wasn't that they didn't care. They simply knew that if they pushed me and overfunctioned, I would have rebelled (and probably never gone to university). So instead, they adopted the inside-out attitude, asking me if I had tried my best. They also asked me what they could do that would be helpful (which eventually led to finding tutors and learning more about my disability). But they focused more on my character development than my marks. They made it clear that I was responsible for doing my best, not for a grade on my report card. As a result, I felt I owned my school work; I became intrinsically motivated, highly disciplined and hard working. As I learned more about my disability and practised techniques, my marks climbed until I was a straight-A student.

I wouldn't necessarily recommend that every parent *not* look at their teen's report card, but my parents' trust gave me an incredible boost in self-esteem. They helped me redefine what success is, and taught me that failure is not the end but rather an important step in becoming successful (however you define it). Failure is not something to be feared; instead, we need to learn from it to help us become stronger.

I am sometimes asked if too much praise will create false self-esteem in kids. False self-esteem is a cover up for low self-esteem. Teens need encouragement. What's more, praising your teen doesn't mean that you are ignoring or avoiding areas that your teen needs to work on. Your teens need to know that you are proud of them.

Many parents tell me, "I think we have put too much emphasis on self-esteem. My kid doesn't lack self-esteem—just the opposite. He has such an attitude of entitlement." Over the years many people have wondered if we, as a culture, have gone too much "the other way"—focusing too much on building kids' self-esteem (e.g., not using red markers to emphasize errors on tests; not penalizing for late assignments; not having any "winners" on sports teams). The problem is not that we've focused too much on self-esteem; the problem is that it's imbalanced. A critical part of developing a healthy self-esteem is understanding our strengths but also acknowledging the areas that we need to work on. So it's critical for parents to understand that helping our kids develop a healthy self-esteem means not only praising them for their effort, but also challenging them regarding the areas that need work in a loving way. (See Chapter 5, "Communication.") If parents are prasing kids while allowing them to walk all over them—yes, the kids will develop a major attitude of entitlement, and this is not healthy self-esteem.

Some parents mention that they have read that praise can make young people dependent on what other people think. This school of thought recommends acknowledging effort with a phrase like, "So you tried out for soccer," instead of saying that you are proud of the fact that your child tried out. I agree that we don't want our teens to become dependent on what we or anyone else thinks of them. But all teens desperately want the approval of their parents, even if they don't admit it. And I've seen the positive effects of genuine parental praise on hundreds of kids. But since it is *their* self-esteem we want to develop, it is a good idea to move from praise to a question about how they feel about themselves. Usually when I'm praising a teen I'll say something like, "Susan—I'm so proud of you for having the courage to try that. I'm proud of you—but more importantly are *you* proud of you?" By asking that question, I'm trying to see if Susan has internalized the praise for herself. Healthy self-esteem, after all, results not in arrogance but in confidence. We should be able to acknowledge what we are good at or what we are proud of (as well as what we need to work on).

Tips for Affirming and Encouraging

> **Don't compare.** Be extremely careful about how you talk about any of your teens. Most parents are aware that comparing your teens to others can be devastating to their self-esteem. Nobody wants to be compared to brother, sister, cousin or neighbour. Affirm your teen and leave other people out of the conversation. **Affirm effort, not marks.** Remember to affirm your teens' efforts and character development, not just their achievement of a mark, award or honour.

Building our children's self-esteem is the cornerstone of inside-out parenting. And raising teens with healthy self-esteem all comes down to respect. We need to respect ourselves, and in doing so model strong self-esteem. We must also respect our teens' ability to take on responsibilities in their lives and gently challenge them to think of themselves in respectful ways. As parents, our respect for their goals and dreams is a powerful influence. And perhaps most importantly we need to show respect and love for them through our generous use of praise and encouragement.

"I like how my mom encourages me to do better. I like when she builds up my self-esteem and reassures me I can do things that I may normally doubt myself on."   **— Danielle, age 13**

Focus on Dating, Sex and Sexuality

Dating

One of the questions I get asked most often by parents of teens and preteens is when kids should be allowed to start dating.

I usually say that most teens are not ready to date until high school age—15 or 16 at the earliest. But it's difficult to make any hard and fast rules about when kids should or shouldn't be dating. So much depends on the individual teens involved—their level of maturity, judgment, self-esteem and values. Dating and romantic relationships are part of growing up, but they can be the source of emotional confusion, and, of course, the start of sexual activity. How ready your teen is to navigate all of these things depends on a number of factors. When I am talking with teens about dating, I ask the following questions to understand their readiness.

How Confident Do You Feel About Yourself?

If teens struggle with low self-esteem there is a good possibility that they will be attracted to a partner who has low or false self-esteem, which can create an unhealthy relationship. If teens do not feel confident about who they are, they are not ready to date, whether they are 15 or 25. You can't force your teens not to date, but you can encourage them to take the time to become more self-aware and self-confident before they jump into a relationship. If they are having any sort of emotional difficulty or are feeling confused about what they want and how they feel, assure them that waiting until they are in a better place emotionally will ensure better dating experiences. When teens feel great about themselves, they are likely to choose great partners who treat them well.

What Qualities Do You Want in a Partner?

For any romantic relationship to be healthy and successful, we must love our partners for who they are, rather than for how they make us feel. But this kind of selfless love takes a great degree of maturity. One way to get your teens to move in this direction is to encourage them to think about the qualities they are looking for in another person. When I asked one teen to make a list about what she looked for in a guy, she wrote down, "He must be hot, gorgeous, drive a nice car, have a good smile, dress nicely and if he's got money to pay for stuff that would be great." When I asked her to look over her list and identify any patterns she saw, she quickly noticed that they were all about appearances. She was surprised at herself, saying that she didn't realize that she was being so shallow. "Maybe I'm not really ready to date," she admitted.

Suggest to your teen that she write out a Top 10 List of qualities she'd like in a dating partner. Encourage her to focus on a person's character rather than appearance. Suggest that your teen study her list, evaluating and challenging it. It's also a good idea for her to put a star beside the qualities that are non-negotiable for her. (One girl I coached, for example, told me that her non-negotiable quality in a guy was that he not do drugs.)

You might also introduce your teen to what I call the "Heart and Head Rule." Your heart immediately knows if someone is attractive to you. But your head knows what values you hold. When dating, it's important that both the head and heart give us a thumbs-up. Listening to the heart alone is likely to lead us to bad decisions.

If teens have spent some time thinking about the type of person they are interested in, they are less likely to make choices that they will regret later or less likely to say yes the moment someone asks them out.

What Values Do You Put on Physical Intimacy?

Physical intimacy can become an issue even on a very first date. One teen told me that she had agreed to go to a movie with a guy she just met because she thought it was the kind of date where physical contact would be limited and they would be able to get to know each other a little (the guy's mother even dropped them off and picked them up, thus limiting the time they spent alone). Once they got into the movie theatre, however, it became very clear that the boy had no intention of watching the movie and was dead set on making out, despite the fact that they were surrounded by people. The girl was very clear that this was not acceptable to her, and that was the last time she dated the guy. If, however, she had been less confident in her thoughts and feelings, she might have found herself in a relationship that moved her into physical intimacy long before she was ready. Before teens begin to date, therefore, they need to have thought about how they feel about physical intimacy. They should make some decisions about what they might be comfortable doing and when. At what point would they feel it was okay to hold hands or to kiss? What about genital sex or oral sex? Of course, it is not realistic to develop strict rules about physical intimacy, but if teens examine how they feel about it on a regular basis, they are less likely to make decisions that they later regret or to get hurt in the relationship. (See "Focus on Sex and Sexuality" later in this chapter for more discussion of this topic.)

Safety in Numbers

When I speak with parents about dating, we are usually talking about the kind of dating the parents remember from their first encounters: two people alone for dinner, going to a movie or at a club. But today, many teens spend more time in groups than in isolated couples. Sometimes, members of the group have linked up as couples, even if they rarely see each other alone. "Group dating" can be a great way for teens to try out romantic relationships in the safety of a crowd. Going on dates with a group of friends can keep the relationships from becoming intense and intimate too quickly. If your preteen or teen is adamant about dating at a time when you feel he or she is too young, you might want to encourage outings that necessarily involve other friends.

How Will Dating or a Relationship Fit In with the Rest of Your Life?

When teens start to date, it's also important that they understand what impact dating or a relationship will have on the time they have to spend with friends and family, or on school work and other activities. For teens with busy schedules, dating may mean that sacrifices have to be made in other areas. Before dating, teens need to ask themselves how they will manage their time. As parents, you can impose boundaries around school work and contributions to the family—and let teens know that they still need to continue to meet the expectations that have been set out. You may want to establish a boundary around how many nights a week your teen can be out with friends. They may choose to spend this time with a boyfriend or girlfriend but remind your teens about the importance of their friendships—any relationship that isolates teens from their peers, or even from the other activities that they love, is not a healthy one.

The one thing you don't want to do when your teen has expressed interest in dating (or has started to date without your expressed consent) is to create a "Romeo and Juliet" situation by declaring all dating off limits or telling your teen that you don't like his partner. (See "Focus on Friends and Peer Pressure" in Chapter 1 for a discussion of what to do if you don't like your teen's friends.) A total ban on dating before a certain age is likely to incite rebellion from your teen and to make the object of his or her desire just that much more desirable. Instead, you can create some boundaries around dating—including times, frequency, curfews and so on. You may want to have rules about where your teens spend time with their dates. Are bedrooms off limits, or can they be in there if the door is open? Are they allowed to be at home alone? You should ask to meet your teens' dates, particularly if a relationship seems to be ongoing. You may also want to meet the parents of the other teen.

But remember, the key to making sure your teens are ready to date is to make sure they have really thought about the issues involved in dating. Ask what they are thinking. Ask them why they feel the way they do. What's shaped their opinions? Have they seen certain bad or good

Dating Violence

Studies of violence in dating have shown that it is much more common than most of us might have thought. Dating violence can be physical, emotional or sexual. It may involve pushing, kicking or hitting, verbal abuse, constant criticism or belittling, name calling, excessive jealousy, possessiveness, lewd or embarrassing comments, sexual coercion or sexual assault, amongst other things. But sadly these very adult-sounding problems are not confined to adult relationships. The Public Health Agency of Canada reports that dating violence can begin as early as grade school. In a survey of approximately 1,700 grade seven, nine and eleven students, 29 percent of the girls and 13 percent of the boys said that they had experienced dating violence. As well, 19 percent of girls and 4 percent of boys said that they had been subjected to sexual coercion. Those with low self-esteem appear to be particularly vulnerable to dating violence.

Parents whose teens are dating or in relationships need to encourage their children to talk with them whenever they are concerned about something that happens on a date. Parents should also watch for warning signs that their children may be the victims of dating violence, including:

- any unexplained cuts, burns, bruises or other physical injuries
- not socializing with other friends
- no longer participating in activities they used to enjoy
- little interest in family activities
- a drop in grades
- nervousness, withdrawal, difficulty sleeping or depression

If you suspect that your teens have experienced dating violence and they are not opening up to you about it, counselling may be the best option.

FOCUS ON *Dating, Sex and Sexuality*

experiences with their friends? Providing an open dialogue with your teens about dating will help them decide whether or not they are ready, instead of making you determine a specific age when dating is allowed.

Sex and Sexuality

While sex can be a happy, healthy part of adult life, it is an activity nevertheless fraught with some very sobering consequences: being sexually active may lead to unwanted pregnancy, sexually transmitted diseases and emotional pain. It's not surprising then that many parents want to protect their teens by making rules about sex. But as discussed in "Boundaries and Structure" in Chapter 6, parents need to avoid creating boundaries around things they can't control, and there is no way a parent can control whether a teen becomes sexually active or not.

What a parent can and should do, however, is ensure that their teens have accurate information, healthy self-esteem and enough self-knowledge that they are able to make decisions that are right for them. Where sex is concerned, an inside-out approach is the most important parenting tool anyone can have.

Most public schools these days cover sex education as part of their curriculum. But keep in mind that your child may not have been paying attention in class! Despite the ample information in schools, for example, many teens are still unaware that people can contract STDs during oral sex. Ask your teens about what they have been taught and what they know (you may have to educate yourself first). Information about contraception and sexually transmitted diseases and infections are available from schools, community health centres and a number of public and private agencies, including many provincial health ministries, the Public Health Agency of Canada (www.phac-aspc.gc.ca), Health Canada (www.hc-sc.gc.ca), and Planned Parenthood (www. plannedparenthood.org).

Once you know that your teens have all of the information they need about sex, contraception and STDs, make sure they know that they have to be prepared to put this knowledge into *action* if they want to be sexually active. Are they prepared to see their pediatrician or family doctor about contraception? Are they willing to walk into a drugstore and buy their own condoms so they can always practise safe sex? Point out to your teens that while they have a right to make decisions regarding their own bodies, they also have a responsibility to keep themselves healthy and safe, and to prevent an unwanted pregnancy.

While schools might provide sex education curriculums, what they can't cover adequately are the emotional effects of sexual activity and any moral views people may have about sex. As mentioned in the dating discussion above, it's important to encourage your teens to think about how they feel about physical intimacy.

There has been a lot written in the past few years about a seemingly new and more casual approach to sex in the teen world. Indeed, many teens talk about being "friends with benefits" to describe an agreement between friends that they can be physically intimate, no strings attached. Teens also use the phrase "hooking up" to describe getting together with someone they've just met or don't really know, in order to have sex. There have also been reports about increasing frequency of oral sex among teens. Many teens consider oral sex to be a less intimate or serious act than intercourse because it cannot result in pregnancy, carries a lower (although still present) risk of STDs and does not involve full nudity. Regardless of their oral sexual activity, many teens consider themselves virgins as long as they have not engaged in intercourse.

But even if teens seem to have a more casual attitude towards sex than previous generations, their motives for sex are strikingly similar. Besides physical pleasure, most sexually active teens are looking for emotional intimacy or social status. Those looking for emotional intimacy may well be hurt if their partners in sex want to divorce physical from emotional intimacy. And even those who are looking for social validation by being sexually active may find that sex leaves them feeling vulnerable or emotionally fragile.

FOCUS ON *Dating, Sex and Sexuality*

157

No matter what terms they use to describe their activities, or how they differentiate between various sex acts, the vast majority of teens I talk with find sex to be emotionally powerful. It's important, therefore, for parents to urge teens to explore their thoughts and feelings in regards to sex. Encourage them to ask themselves how they would feel if their boyfriend or girlfriend broke up with them after they'd been intimate. How would they feel if their partners told other people that they had been physically intimate? In a year's time, do they think they will look back on their decision and be okay with it? Is peer pressure or coercion playing any part in their interest in having sex? Is simple curiosity overshadowing their values in any way?

Remind your teens that not all young people are sexually active, and if they want to wait until they are older, they are certainly not alone—no matter what their friends say. Many teens want to wait until they are in a committed relationship or are married for good reasons: waiting means no physical consequences to deal with and being in a committed relationship will make them feel more secure emotionally. If your teens have decided that they are going to be sexually active, however, keep in mind that you can't control this. You can voice your opinion and your values in ways that are not condescending, controlling or manipulative. You may choose to give your approval or withhold it. But whatever you do, make sure that your feelings do not interfere with your relationship with your teens. If they need your support or your guidance, they should still feel that they can come to you. Being an inside-out parent means understanding, listening to and loving your teens, even when their opinions and choices are not ones that you would make for them.

Sexual Orientation

The teen years are a time of discovering who we are intellectually, emotionally and sexually. For some teens this means a realization that they are gay, lesbian or bisexual.

Even if they don't have a problem with homosexuality, parents who find out that their teens are gay or lesbian often find the discovery difficult. As members of a minority, homosexuals often experience prejudice and face challenges in their personal and professional lives. As parents, you may worry that your child will now become a victim of prejudice and homophobia. You may worry that you won't have grandchildren (although many gay and lesbian couples are now having children or adopting). And if you are heterosexual yourself, you might find it difficult to accept that your children will be living a life that is in some ways contrary to yours: while you may have felt able to answer their questions and give them advice about their love lives before, you may worry that your differing sexual orientation makes your experience and point of view irrelevant. For some parents, homosexuality conflicts with their religious beliefs or values.

What causes people to be heterosexual, homosexual or bisexual is still not fully understood, but current research suggests that sexual orientation is not a choice but part of our genetic code. It has nothing to do with how parents raise their children. Homosexuality is not a mental disorder. Any counselling that purports to cure or change homosexuality can cause emotional confusion and harm Your children are who they are—and being an inside-out parent means that you need to support their discovery of themselves and accept them.

Adolescence is the time when most people begin to discover sexual identity. While some may have known for as long as they can remember that they were attracted only to the same sex, others may have a great deal of confusion or conflicting feelings. Just because teens have thoughts and fantasies about or even physical experiences with people of the same sex, it doesn't necessarily mean that they are gay or lesbian. For many people, it takes time to recognize their sexual orientation, so teens should not feel in a rush to label themselves. They should also realize that sexual orientation is a continuum. While some people feel strictly homosexual or heterosexual, many others fall somewhere between those two extremes, or experience

FOCUS ON *Dating, Sex and Sexuality*

varying degrees of bisexuality. If your teens are struggling with their sexual orientation, counselling may help them work through it.

Being different from the majority of people can be very difficult and stressful, particularly for young teens, who tend to have a strong need for conformity. Gay teens often become isolated, withdraw from friends, experience a drop in their self-esteem and may become depressed. Some reports suggest that homosexual teens account for a significant proportion of teen suicides. If teens are having difficulty coping with their sexual orientation, they may well need some counselling to help them through it.

For gay teens, parental advice, guidance, support and love are still relevant and important. Approach their dating just as you would with heterosexual teens. If their self-esteem is low because of their concerns about their sexuality, encourage them to postpone dating until they feel good about themselves. Set the same boundaries for dating as you would for your straight children. Treat your teen's homosexual friends and romantic partners with the same open-mindedness and respect that you would treat all your teens' friends.

If homosexuality conflicts with your religious beliefs or your values, it is important that you think about your "big picture," as I explained in Chapter 1. If your primary goal is to raise happy, healthy, well-adjusted teens (and I hope it is), focus on accepting, respecting and loving them. This may not be an easy task. If you are having difficulty dealing with your teen's homosexuality—for any reason—get help for yourself so that you can be supportive of and emotionally available for your teen. Check out www.pflagcanada.ca (Parents, Families and Friends of Lesbians and Gays) for a group in your area.

Focus on Bullying and Violence

Bullying is, unfortunately, a common occurrence in childhood and often continues on into the teen years (some studies suggest that it peaks in early adolescence—grades eight and nine). But bullying should never be seen as "just part of growing up." It can cause serious physical and mental pain for its victims and long-term problems for victims and bullies alike. In extreme cases, the victims sometimes lash out violently against those who bully them (as in the high school shootings in Littleton, Colorado and Taber, Alberta) or turn their pain, anger and frustration inward by committing suicide. What's more, frequent bullying creates a world for our children where violence and cruelty appear to be socially acceptable. Even those children who simply witness bullying are going to be affected by this poisonous environment.

What Is Bullying?

Physical bullying is hitting, punching, tripping, shoving, unwanted sexual touching, stealing or forcing a person to give up his or her belongings. **Verbal bullying** is name calling, taunting, intimidating, humiliating, sexually harassing or spreading rumours or gossip about someone. **Social bullying** is excluding, swarming or mobbing someone, or writing graffiti about him or her. **Cyberbullying** is threatening, spreading gossip or rumours, posting humiliating pictures or videos, or making fun of someone via the Internet or text messaging.

Boys are more likely to be physical bullies; girls tend to be social and verbal bullies. Cyberbullying is prevalent among both boys and girls. But almost every child is going to get into a fight with someone or say something cruel to a friend at one time or another. What specifically makes these actions bullying rather than the outcomes of arguments or conflicts of some kind?

- Bullying always involves an imbalance of power—a bully holds more power than his victim. Bullying is often a way for the attacker to gain more power over those he attacks by controlling them and controlling how others react to them.
- Bullying is a sustained attack—generally the hurtful words and

actions occur over a significant period of time and are not an isolated incident. Much of the destructive power of bullying is the promise that it will happen again.

- The goal of bullying is to wound or cause pain. (Friends may get upset with each other and say insensitive things. But in these types of conflicts, when it has become clear that someone's feelings have been hurt, the attacker will apologize.) The bully who has hurt someone's feelings has achieved his goal and will continue.
- Bullies generally attempt to isolate their victims—not only do they target individuals, but they will also try to get others to target them as well.

Who Is Likely to Be a Target of Bullies?

Bullies are not looking to take on a crowd. They generally target kids whom they feel other children will not defend—those who have few friends and are not members of a group. Bullies often target kids who have low self-esteem and are therefore likely to be easily intimidated and wounded by the bully's words and actions. Children and teens who are different in any way, whether physically, racially, in religious background, or even in choice of hobbies and interests, may become the target of a bully.

Bullies are not likely to pick on someone who will generate a lot of sympathy in others or who is popular or well liked by their peers. The bullies want to be liked and admired, so they will target someone who they think they can get others to turn on as well.

How Can You Tell If Your Teen Is Being Bullied?

If your teen is being bullied, he or she may exhibit

- a drop in grades
- reluctance to go to school or to other activities
- sudden changes in behaviour, or uncharacteristic behaviour
- sad or sullen behaviour after receiving a phone call or an email
- depression
- frequent stomach aches and headaches
- problems sleeping
- loneliness
- frequent incidents of lost or missing money or belongings, without a reasonable explanation
- torn clothing, unexplained bruises or injuries

Teens Protecting Themselves

If you suspect that your teen is being bullied and is in danger of physical harm, you will need to get involved. But parents also need to guard against overfunctioning, and rushing in before the teen has had a chance to deal with the situation himself. While teens should not think that it is their *responsibility* to stop the bullying, they may be able to minimize it, stop it from escalating or even avoid it altogether, by employing some of the following strategies:

- Teens who are being bullied should try not to cower or act afraid. Bullies are looking to frighten and intimidate—if they don't think that they are having this effect, they may look elsewhere for a victim or give up. But, of course, teens need to use their own judgment about appropriate actions. Sometimes it is much safer to hand over money or a jacket than risk getting hurt.
- Teens need to be assertive when approached by a bully. They should hold their heads up, look people in the eye and use their body language to convey confidence. When they walk

away from the bully, they should try to do so in a calm, self-assured manner.

- Teens who are being bullied should not go on the offensive or try to be cruel and aggressive in response. The bully is almost certainly better at this kind of tactic than the victim is.

- Bullying victims should ask their friends for support. Simply seeing her intended target with another person may be enough to make a bully abandon her plans. If teens are able, they should join a group a friends. (They should not, however, allow their friends to confront the bully or otherwise escalate the confrontation or violence.)

- Teens should make a log of all incidents and keep copies of emails, notes, web postings or phone calls, if possible. If and when they do report the bullying to school staff or another adult, they will have a clear record of what has been happening.

- Teens who are bullied should not put themselves down or think that the bullying is their fault.

- Teens should not accept bullying as part of growing up.

- Teens who are bullied should tell a trusted adult about it. If talking to an adult is too difficult, the teens might write a note documenting what has been going on. Reporting abuse is not tattling on someone—it is sometimes the only way to start to solve a difficult problem. What's more, by drawing attention to bullying behaviour, teens are not only protecting themselves but other victims as well. (Recognizing this may make it easier for them to come forward.)

- Bullied teens should work with a trusted adult on an action plan.

What Parents of a Bullied Teen Can Do

First and foremost, parents of bullied teens need to be inside-out parents, who listen to and support their teens. Your teens should believe that you are a safe person to come to if they are being bullied in any way. (You can only help your teens if you know about their problems.) Inside-out parenting also means that you are committed to building and supporting your child's healthy self-esteem. If your teen is being targeted by a bully, it is important to recognize that his self-esteem has been dealt a harsh blow. He will need extra support and understanding, and may benefit from counselling as well.

Children need to know that others can and will come to their defence. Don't ever minimize bullying or tell your teens to toughen up.

Don't approach a bully or bully's parents yourself, unless you know the parents and feel confident that you can talk with them calmly and reasonably. Keep in mind that your emotions may be difficult to control, and if you don't know the other parents, you won't be able to predict how they will respond—they may be defensive (their kid did nothing wrong), see nothing wrong with what their teen is doing, or be bullies themselves. Try to appeal to a third party for help. Usually the best place to go is to the school principal or one of the teachers. If the school is unresponsive and/or your child is in danger of being seriously hurt, you many need to involve the police. Insist that the problem be taken seriously by the teachers and the school.

Be aware that conflict resolution, while an extremely important skill, is really not the solution in the case of bullying. Even if your child has struck back at the bully, the situation is not the same as two equals who get into a fight over a misunderstanding or disagreement. Here, the bully has no interest in resolving conflict—and generally the only thing the victim wants from the bully is to be left alone. If teachers and school administrators suggest some sort of conflict resolution as the *only* solution, point out to them that this may not be sufficient.

Schools are most effective at addressing bullying problems if they implement school-wide policies and awareness campaigns to combat anti-social behaviour (rather than addressing problems as isolated incidents). Volunteer to get involved in anti-bullying initiatives at the school.

In her excellent book, *The Bully, the Bullied, and the Bystander*, Barbara Coloroso identifies four key ways for a child to protect himself from bullying: a strong sense of self, being a friend, having at least one good friend who will stand by him and belonging to a group. Social skills are so important in both preventing your child from becoming a victim of bullying and in giving her the tools to deal with bullying. Try to facilitate your teens' friendships when you can—perhaps by making your home a welcoming place for other teens, including your children's friends in family functions or teaching your teen to maintain their friendships (by calling or emailing, seeing each other after school, being considerate of others' feelings, helping out friends when they can and so on). If you sense that your teen is still isolated socially, or if his friends are also being bullied (and are unable to protect him), you may want to arrange counselling for your teen.

What If Your Teen Has Been Bullying Someone?

As painful as it is to hear that your child has been a victim of bullies, it can be just as difficult to accept that your child may be victimizing others. While you should never excuse your child's behaviour or fail to give adequate consequences for it, you must also take a close look at how your attitudes and parenting style may have contributed to the problem. You must accept that you will have to work with your children to prevent bullying from happening again in the future.

Many bullies have low self-esteem. Your child may feel bullying is the only way to gain the approval and respect of her peers. In some cases, bullies' victims may inadvertently make them feel insecure. For example, if the victim is a gifted student, his abilities may have made your teen feel self-conscious about his academic performance. Your child may see bullying as a way to level the playing field.

Or has your teen been bullied by someone else? Perhaps a sibling? Or are you or your spouse bullying your teen? Is bullying behaviour being modelled in your home—with one spouse bullying the other?

Many bullies are raised by parents who are not providing adequate emotional support. It's essential that you work to become a fully plugged-in parent if your teen has been bullying others. Being plugged in will also help you become aware of your children's activities—something often missing in the lives of bullies. Bullies also tend to have parents who are either very permissive or very rigid. Reviewing the parenting styles outlined in Chapter 2 may help you reexamine and improve your parenting style.

While most often violent or aggressive behaviour stems from self-esteem issues, it's important to recognize that this does not hold true for all bullies. But even if low self-esteem is not at the heart of your teen's need to inflict pain or humiliation on someone else, a lack of empathy certainly is. Try to help your teen understand the gravity of his actions and the degree of pain he is causing. At the same time, make sure that there are appropriate and adequate boundaries and structure in his life. Bullying and aggressive behaviour should never be allowed at home.

Bullying is a very serious matter and I suggest that you attend counselling with your teen to resolve whatever issues are contributing to your child's behaviour as quickly as possible. Letting your child get away with bullying isn't only unfair to the other children around him. When children and teens become accustomed to being violent or abusive to others, they carry these habits with them into the future. They often have difficulty in personal relationships and may have trouble in the workforce. Bullies are also four times more likely than non-bullies to be convicted of crimes by the age of 24. And a study in Norway and Sweden by Professor Dan Olweus reported that 60 percent of men who engaged in bullying in grades six through nine were convicted of crimes in their adult lives.

Prosocial Teens and Bullying

As Barbara Coloroso points out in *The Bully, the Bullied, and the*

FOCUS ON *Bullying and Violence*

Bystander, the most powerful way to defuse bullying is to create an environment that simply doesn't support it. If teens who are not directly involved in attempts to bully—the bystanders or witnesses in other words—step in to show their disapproval of the bully's words and actions, the bully will likely abandon her actions. Bullies want to be admired, not criticized or shunned by their peers.

Talk to your teens about what they might do if they see bullying happening. Remind them that bullying has a negative effect on everyone. Witnesses who do nothing or who join the bully as a way of avoiding being a target themselves or to win the bully's favour often have intense feelings of guilt and shame. Encourage your teens to let a trusted adult know what is going if they see someone being hurt. Get them to brainstorm about how they and their friends might defuse a potential bullying situation themselves. Is there a way the bully might be distracted? How might your teens come to the defence of the bullied? Often the best protectors of potential victims are reformed bullies themselves (who may find they get more attention and positive reinforcement in this new role). Is there a way to show the bully that he will be more popular or well liked by not bullying?

One teen I knew decided that she and her friends would have a policy of inclusion at the end-of-the-year party. They made sure they invited everyone, including the teens who were usually left out of social events. Then she appealed to the boys who were likely to pick on the outsiders to be the peacekeepers at the party. She asked them to tell her about anyone who was bothering or teasing others or generally causing trouble so she could ask them to leave. As she expected, the only kids who were likely to cause problems were busy making sure that everyone was getting along, and everyone enjoyed themselves.

Encourage your teens to acknowledge their own power and to accept their responsibility for positively affecting their social environment. "If you're not part of the solution, you're part of the problem" is a cliché but it holds a powerful truth when it comes to bullying.

Communication

"I wish my parents would simply listen more and talk less. They would learn so much more about who I am."

—Aurora, age 17

"How can I get my teen to listen to me?"

"How can I get my teen to talk and open up with me?"

These questions are easily the most common ones I get asked by parents of teenaged children. Communication is one of the biggest challenges for parents as their children enter the teen years. While children may have had no problems talking with their parents when they were small, suddenly the after-school chats, the dinner table conversations, the free exchange of thoughts, feelings and information can dry up to a meagre trickle as adolescence takes hold. Our teens' growing independence and need for privacy, as well as the emotional and physical changes they are undergoing, often make it difficult for them to share with their parents as easily as they once did. And unfortunately many parents react to this new reluctance to talk in a way that only makes the situation more strained and difficult.

But there's good news! There are simple things that parents can say and do that may have an enormous positive impact on their communication with their teens. In this chapter, I discuss a number of problems or stumbling blocks to good communication and six strategies to overcome these problems so you can connect and communicate effectively with your children (or with anyone—spouse, family, friends and co-workers). But first, I need to say a few things about how we communicate.

There are two components of communication—non-verbal and verbal expression. Verbal communication is the words that we use. Non-verbal communication is everything that we do (e.g., facial expressions, timing, tone of voice, etc.). Verbal communication is the "what" and non-verbal communication is the "how." And that how is *so* important. It is now widely understood that 93 percent of communication is non-verbal! So the old saying, "It's not what you say, it's how you say it," turns out to be very true. While we may think that we've chosen our words well enough for our feelings and ideas to come across, our actions may be undercutting our message. In the following pages, keep in mind that none of the strategies I discuss below are going to do you much good if you don't master Strategy #6: Know What You Are Saying Non-verbally.

Six Strategies to Communicate Effectively with Your Teen

Strategy #1: Be Aware

Be aware of your parenting style and parenting attitudes. Blamer, sergeant, babbler, weather reporter and teacher are all attitudes that make real communication with your teen very difficult. If you've identified yourself as having any of these attitudes, be on your toes when talking with your children. Conversational habits are often very hard to break—it only takes a few words to fall into old patterns. And remember, you can work on communication strategies with great effort, but you won't see results if you are still operating with an outside-in parenting style.

Strategy #2: Don't React, Respond

Once we've become aware of the parenting attitudes or style that we want to change, we need to put that change into action. The challenge, as mentioned above, is not to revert to old habits. The way we talk with our children often falls into a predictable pattern—the responses of parents and teens alike tend to be reactive, happening so fast that no one thinks about the effect. But the great news is that we can train ourselves to respond differently and adopt new habits. It only takes one person to alter the course of a conversation, so even if the parent is the only one focusing on change, the potential improvement can still be dramatic.

The key to improved communication is to *respond*, not *react*. Responding requires you to think in advance about how you want to address a situation. What do you want to say? What don't you want to say? How do you want to voice it? When? What words do you want to use? What you want to communicate is planned out carefully, thoughtfully and critically. But even if you know what you want to say in a conversation, how do you avoid simply reacting to what the other person says—letting the conversation fall into the pattern you are trying to avoid? There are three techniques that I have always found helpful: the "'I' technique," the "Hamburger technique" and the "Parking technique."

The "I" Technique

"You're not making any sense."

"I don't understand what you are saying."

Which statement would you rather hear? Which sentence would make you lash out in self-defence and which would encourage you to explain your point of view calmly and thoughtfully? Using the word "I" in conversation can be a powerful tool in keeping the discussion going in a positive and productive manner.

When people are in conflict, you can often tell what kind of self-esteem attitude they have based on the first word that comes out of their mouths. People with false self-esteem are often aggressive during disagreements, starting their statements with the word "you": "You're wrong," "You make me mad," "You are so frustrating." This approach immediately makes the listener feel defensive and sets the stage for conflict. People with low self-esteem, however, are likely to try to avoid conflict by being passive and not responding, or being passive-aggressive. The passive-aggressive person will not talk with the person they are having the disagreement with, but with a third party. Their conversation, therefore, often starts with "he" or "she"—"She is so irritating," "He's such a jerk." Obviously, avoiding a discussion with the person in question does nothing to further communication. But people with healthy self-esteem tend to use the word "I" most often when they are in discussion with someone else.

Using the word "I" in a conversation does not mean that the speaker is being self-centred. Rather, it indicates that the speaker is choosing to respect himself and others. The word "I" makes it clear that it is the speaker's opinion or point of view that is being offered. Think of the difference between "I'm worried about your attitude towards school" and "Your attitude towards school is lousy." Statements that start with "I" can express thoughts and feelings without attacking the other person or claiming to be objective truth. Using the word "I" can also be an excellent way of encouraging someone else to speak. "You need to tell me about this party" is a demand and sounds threatening. "I think we need to talk about the party" is an invitation to a conversation. "I" statements can also make it clear that you are ready and willing to listen to the other person's response—"I think we need to talk" or "I'd like to understand how you feel about this."

So, using the word "I" in conversations is a great way to get responses rather than reactions from the person you are talking to. And making yourself use the word "I" instead of "you" or "she" can help you avoid reactive statements and keep you on track as well.

The Hamburger Technique

Falling into old reactive habits and tired, ineffectual arguments is easy to do when we try to talk about difficult or contentious topics with our teen children. The hamburger technique is my favourite way to avoid this trap and move towards thoughtful responses on both sides of the conversation.

What do beautiful, juicy hamburgers look like? Well they have a nice big bun on top, some meat in the middle and another bun on the bottom. I like to think about an effective conversation as a delicious hamburger. The meat represents the problem or issue that you want to address. The top bun represents a positive statement from you. And the bottom bun represents another positive observation. The key to resolving any conflict is to use this model: bun–meat–bun.

What do most of us do in conflict? We jump right into the meat section and start telling the other person what they've done wrong. What's the typical response? The other person gets defensive, tunes out and the situation remains unresolved. You need to place some bun on both sides of the meat to make the whole thing go down easier.

But my description might make the tecnique sound easier than it is. At one of my seminars for parents, I attempted to model it with a volunteer father from the audience. I pretended I was his daughter. He started with one brief positive statement and then launched into the meat of his problem. But that problem reminded him of another and another. After the third layer of meat, I began to zone out, just as his daughter would have.

Here are a number of tips to make the hamburger technique work for you. (Many of these are also great ways to improve communication whether or not you are using the hamburger technique.)

Focus on only one or two problems. One of the biggest mistakes I see parents make with this technique is that they stuff too much in between the two buns. It's overwhelming for even the most receptive teenager. Children and teens often have short attention spans (especially when it comes to discussing conflicts), so you want to keep your hamburger talk short and to the point. Don't drag it out. Don't give multiple examples for the same situation or get sidetracked with other issues. It will only cause your teen to tune out.

Make sure the buns are authentic. If you are just using positive statements simply to get your teen to listen, the technique won't work. Your teen will sense that your words don't come from your heart. So, before you begin, ask yourself, what do you appreciate about what your teen has done lately? What are some positives you could affirm? What is your positive intent in bringing this conflict up? Great beginning phrases include:

"I appreciate that you . . ."

"I love the fact that you . . ."

"I'm so proud that you . . ."

"I'm bringing this up because I love you and I really want to strengthen our relationship."

Use Authentic Language

When my editor, Brad, read a first draft of this manuscript, he drew my attention to one of the suggested buns. It started with the word "sweetheart." "If I called my son 'sweetheart,'" he said, "he'd roll his eyes." Brad had a good point. Every family has its own language of intimacy. Some use many terms of endearment. Others, while being loving and positive to one another, don't use words like "sweetheart" or "darling." When providing love, support and encouragement to your child make sure you use language that is authentic to your family. If you don't, your child is likely to question your sincerity or ask what book you've been reading!

Make sure the buns are positive, not double negatives. When one father I worked with made what was supposed to be his first positive comment, he said, "We'll you're not as negative as you used to be." What kind of positive remark was that? We want to make sure our bun comments are truly positive, not double negatives. If you have to use the word "not," think again.

Use lots of buns—all the time. After one of my talks with parents, a 16-year-old guy who was in the audience suggested to me that I should really encourage parents to use lots of buns, all the time. He said, "If I hear positive comments only just before the meat, I'm going to get really worried every time I hear a positive comment." Great point—parents take note!

Use the word "I." As I mentioned earlier, when we use the word "I" we are respecting ourselves while respecting others. "I" statements tend to help us avoid blaming others ("I'm feeling angry about this situation" instead of "You make me so angry"), and they also invite the other person to comment rather than pushing her to defend herself.

Focus on feelings; thoughts are up for debate. Feelings are not debatable, but thoughts are. When it comes to tackling a problem or issue, it is important that we distinguish between our feelings and our thoughts and that we acknowledge that our thoughts or observations are always going to be our subjective perceptions—not unquestionable truths. When I encouraged one father to focus on his feelings, he said to his daughter, "I'm frustrated because you are not helping out around the house as much as the rest of us." Unfortunately, the second part of his sentence moved from his feelings to his perception of reality. His daughter was very likely to have a different point of view of the situation. People see things differently, so I recommend that when parents do share their thoughts or opinions, they preface these with statements like:

"In my opinion . . ."

"The way I see it . . ."

"I'm not sure if this is how you see it, but this is how it's coming across to me . . ."

When you acknowledge that you are simply sharing your opinion, teens will be more willing to listen and respond rather than react. (For example, if the father had said, "I'm frustrated because it seems to me that you're not helping out as much as much as we need you to. That's how it appears to me. What do you think?" he probably would have received a better response.)

Remember to add a bottom bun. I can't tell you how many parents I've coached to use this technique who then forgot to use the bottom bun. They got so focused on the meat and what they *really* wanted to talk about that they forgot to affirm their child at the end. You don't want to be fake or redundant. So think of other ways you can voice your appreciation to your teen. Once more, let them know why you want to bring the conflict up. Here's an example:

> "Again, I just want to say how much I love you. And I know this must be tough to hear, but I really want to work on building a great relationship with you and to help you understand what I'm thinking."

Ask for feedback. The point of raising any problem is to resolve it. So once you've had a chance to voice your concerns to your teens, the last sentence should be to ask their opinion. Some good lines include:

> "What do you think about what I have just said?"
> "Do you agree with it? Disagree with it?"
> "What can we do to resolve this?"
> "What are your suggestions?"

Be sure to invite their feedback. Get their perspective. Listen to what they are saying. Brainstorm *together* for solutions.

Use the hamburger technique for special situations. Often parents ask me if they should we use this hamburger technique for every situation. No—that would be overkill and the technique would lose its effectiveness (never mind become absolutely exhausting). I encourage parents to use this technique for more serious conflicts. That being said, you can use the various steps individually and regularly. For example, you don't need to wait to use the hamburger technique before you voice your opinions with "The way I see it . . ." or "From my perception . . ." and so on. And don't forget to spread those buns around beforehand.

Strategy #3: Choose or Create Good Timing

Timing can make or break a great conversation. To see the truth of this, try the following. Think back over the last few years to an amazing connection you made with one of your teens. Ask yourself these questions:

- Where was I?
- Who was with me?
- What time of the day was it?
- How was I feeling?
- How was he or she feeling?

I ask thousands of parents those questions, and it is amazing how similar the answers always are. Before I talk about the most common locations for the best conversations, let's take a look at the answers to those other questions.

Ninety percent of parents say that there is no one else with them when they make great connections with their teens. The same percentage of parents report that the conversations happen after school or in the evening. And the vast majority report that both they and their teens were feeling relaxed and comfortable.

From these answers, it's clear that one-on-ones work best. It would also seem that the end of the day works better than the beginning. It's hard to concentrate when you have a full day of school or work or other activities ahead of you. The end of the day may also be when you are most likely to wind down and therefore feel most relaxed.

So what about the best times and locations for great talks? The ones most commonly mentioned are

- the car
- the family room
- the kitchen
- the teen's bedroom
- a restaurant
- on a walk
- during a family vacation

The car might be a surprise to you, but it makes a lot of sense, especially for guys. Male teens often find that making eye contact when talking about personal matters or difficult subjects raises their level of anxiety. In a car, of course, it is tough to look each other straight in eye. Girls may also find this type of sideways talk lessens the intensity of heart-to-hearts and makes them feel less vulnerable, less exposed. The other liberating thing about talking in the car is that most of the time (with the exceptions of road trips or long-distance travel), everyone knows that the conversation is going to be relatively short. Teens might feel willing to express a thought or feeling if they know that the conversation will be forced to conclude when they reach their destination. (But keep in mind that some car trips may be better for talking than others. During one of my workshops in which we were talking about timing and communication, one mother told me that she often had amazing conversations with her son in the car—but not always. She wanted to know why this was. After we talked a little more, a pattern revealed itself. When the mom was driving her son to some event for which they had to be on time, her anxiety was high. She and her son seldom had satisfying conversations then. It was during the car ride back home that they often had their best conversations, because she wasn't anxious about getting somewhere on time.)

If you find that your teen responds well to sideways conversations, you may try to talk at times and in places where eye contact is reduced: on a walk or hike, in the kitchen while cooking or baking together or while doing some other kind of sport or activity that demands your visual attention. (Kitchens are great conversation spots, according to many parents I talked with. I suspect that this is because people are almost always doing something in the kitchen, which reduces their eye contact.)

Restaurants are also a good place to have conversations because there are no distractions. There are no phones ringing (if everyone's cellphone is turned off), no doorbells buzzing, and no one needs to get up to get anything. Family vacations are a time when many parents and teens manage to talk because there are no strict deadlines, the family often has more time to spend with each other and everyone is relaxed.

Another common time when parents and teens talk is at night as everyone is going to bed. Many parents tell me that some of the best conversations they have with their children occur when they go into their bedrooms to say goodnight. It's the end of the day. Everyone is

Eye Contact between Mothers and Sons, Fathers and Daughters

Research suggests that gender differences in how a person responds to eye contact can be seen in boys and girls as young as three to four years old. Most girls prefer eye contact when they speak with someone. The majority of boys do not. This is important to keep in mind when you are talking with your opposite-sex child. Mothers who are talking with their sons about sensitive subjects might be best to find ways to talk sideways to reduce their sons' anxiety. But fathers talking to their daughters will have to remind themselves to make eye contact so their girls will be reassured that their dads are listening to them.

winding down. The quietness gives teens and parents time to think; the dim lights reduce eye contact and are relaxing.

So many parents tell me that they've tried to have deep conversations with their teen but it hasn't worked. It's often because they were on a forced timeline in an environment that was not effective. If we want our conversations to be effective, these elements ensure the best chance of success:

- a good location (the car, the bedroom, the kitchen, a restaurant or vacation spot)
- a good time (after school or in the evening)
- being alone together
- being (both you and your teen) relaxed

Get solution-focused and start looking for those golden opportunities. Seize the moments, or better yet, create them!

The Parking It Technique

Obviously we don't live in a perfect world. I'm often asked what parents should do if important conversations start and those five variables are not in place (e.g., parents are stressed, kids are stressed and so on). In those situations I recommend that you use a technique I call "Parking It." to park it, say to your teen something like "Clearly, neither of us is at a good place to discuss this right now. Let's park this conversation until later tonight or tomorrow when we are in a better place."

After hearing me describe this technique, one parent wrote to tell me of how she used it: "Last weekend, my daughter was late for her curfew. In the past, we would have just yelled and argued because we were so angry. But it was never effective, nor did we find a better solution. So the next time it happened, my husband and I took your advice and parked it till the next day. When we were all calm, we were able to discuss her curfew and negotiate a time and fair consequences for if she was late. It made such a difference."

This technique requires a lot of self-discipline. Many people want to deal with conflicts right away, no matter where they are, who is around or how anyone is feeling. They do not think about whether or not the timing will be effective, but rather about getting everything out as soon as possible (sometimes because they can't control their emotions, and sometimes under the mistaken belief that anything not dealt with immediately will be forgotten). But people do not *effectively* deal with conflict when they are really angry or stressed because all of their energy is poured into their emotions, and their ability to think rationally goes out the window. We need to be able to think to resolve conflicts.

Other people can't stand conflict, so rather than address the problems immediately or later, they try to ignore the trouble, hoping that it will go away. Of course, nothing gets resolved this way, problems pile up and resentment and bitterness build.

"Parking it" is not avoiding a problem or sweeping it under the rug.

Full Parking Lot

During one of my speaking engagements, a mother raised her hand and said, "But what do you do if your parking lot is full? I feel like I don't even know where to begin."

Great question! First, I'm talking about a parking space not a parking lot. A parking space should only ever have two or three conflicts in it at any one time. If someone has a parking lot filled with dozens of conflicts, chances are that they have really been sweeping things under the carpet rather than parking them. Second, if you're just starting this technique and there are many different issues you haven't discussed with your teen, start with one conflict that you want to resolve first. Don't try to work on all the conflicts at once. That would be too overwhelming for both you and your teen. Take the issues one at time, as you are able to handle them.

It's dealing with the issue at a time when a resolution is most likely to be reached. I usually recommend that conflicts be discussed within a 24-hour period (depending on how serious or time-sensitive the issue is) to avoid forgetting about the conflict. For discussions that have no urgency, some parents have waited one or two weeks for an optimum time so that they increase their odds of the conversation going well.

The following tips can make the Parking It technique work for you.

Teach your kids the technique. To park a conflict for a specific time instead of getting angry and saying or doing things that are hurtful is one of the best anger management techniques for children to learn (no matter what their age). If parents are allowed to park conflicts, so should children. It requires a lot of self-discipline, so if they can do it, encourage them.

Save the Parking It technique for tough conflicts, not petty situations. I wouldn't want families to use this technique for every little disagreement that comes up. If they do the technique gets overused and loses its effectiveness.

Keep no more than two to three parking spaces at any one time. You don't want to create a parking lot and have a backlog of unresolved conflicts. Try having a maximum of two or three spaces.

Agree on a time to discuss the parked issue. Instead of just jumping into a conversation with your teens, wait for great timing and then ask them if they've got a few minutes to talk with you about something. Asking them shows that you respect their time and the conversation will likely go better.

Avoid bad timing. Creating or choosing good timing for a conversation with your teen also means avoiding the worst times to talk. You can ask yourself the same questions I list at the beginning of Strategy #3, but focus on when you last had a bad conversation. Most of the worst talks happen in the morning, when parents are stressed, anxious or rushed and when teens are tired, hungry, or stressed or rushed themselves. And if you want to make a bad situation a lot worse, just start involving other people. Avoid bad timing, and park it when conflicts come up during these times. Most importantly, maximize your opportunities when great timing presents itself. It only makes sense.

Strategy #4: Learn to Ask the Right Questions

I've learned that one of the most important skills in communication and getting our teens to talk is learning how to ask the right questions. If we don't ask the right questions, we don't learn who our children are, how they think, how they make decisions, what drives them, what stresses them and how we can be most helpful to them.

A few years ago, Pauline and her 16-year-old son, Frank, came to see me. Frank had just been caught smoking pot on school property. Pauline had a very distant relationship with her son and was struggling with how to connect with him. Pauline was extremely angry about her son's pot smoking, but instead of bringing the topic up at home, she decided to bring it up in my office.

Her first question to Frank went like this: "What the heck were you thinking? Do you realize that if this happens again you will be expelled and that it goes on your transcript and that you might not be able to get into the university of your choice!"

I stopped Pauline and asked her if she was trying to find out why Frank made the decision to smoke pot or was she just trying to give him a lecture. Pauline tried again: "Okay—so Frank, what's with the pot?" But what kind of a question is that? It's so vague, and far too open-ended for a teen who already has difficulty talking to his parents. Pauline had never learned how to ask the right questions. As a result her son wasn't talking with her in a meaningful way.

The poor choices our kids make (e.g., skipping school, doing drugs, being promiscuous, stealing, lying, choosing unhealthy friends or partners) are never the primary problem. Of course these things turn into problems of their own but they are symptoms of deeper trouble. Inside-out parenting requires us to discover what is causing our teens to make poor decisions. (Setting consequences for the behaviour can follow, as I discuss in Chapter 6.) And the only way we can do this is if we learn to ask the right questions.

Here are some of my favourite questions to get teens talking. Remember to use only a few at a time, otherwise teens will feel they're being interrogated.

"Getting the Information" Questions

"I heard that you _____. Is this true?"

"When was this happening?"

"Who was this happening with?"

"How often?"

"What time of the day?"

"Yesterday I heard you say _____. Did you really mean that?

Feeling Questions

"How do you feel about _____?"

"How long have you felt that way? What else was happening in your life during that time?"

"What's your own theory about why you feel that way?"

"When do you feel this way the most?"

"On a scale of 1 to 10, how _____ do you feel?" (choose an emotion)

Going Deeper Questions

"You mentioned that you feel _____. Can you help me understand why?"

"You said that you feel _____. Can you describe that for me?"

"What's the most difficult part of this for you?"

"What is the one thing you think I most don't understand about you?"

"Finish this line. 'If you really knew me you'd know that I _____.'"

Impact Questions

"Why do you think you've made that choice?"

"What are you gaining from that choice? How does it help you?"

"What are the costs of that choice? How is it hurting you?"

Ownership Questions

"What do you think is your responsibility in this?"

"What do you think is my responsibility in this?"

"If you could rewind the clock, what would you do differently?"

"What do you think I should have done differently?

"What percentage would you say is your responsibility?

Clarifying Questions

"I heard you say _____. Is that what you meant?"

"Are you saying this: _____?"

"Okay, help me get what you're saying because clearly I'm not getting it."

"In this situation, how do you think I'm not understanding you?"

Solution Questions

"If you had a best friend just like you, what would you tell her to do in this situation?"

"What are your various choices in this situation?"

"What are the pros and cons of each of your choices?"

"What do you think is the best choice to make, even if it is not the easiest?"

"What is your head saying about this? What is your heart saying?"

"What has worked for you in the past? How can you use the same solution now?"

Other Helpful Lines

"I appreciate . . ."

"I need . . ."

"I'm proud of . . ."

"I love the fact that you are . . ."

"I'm curious about . . ."

"The way I see it, and correct me if I'm wrong . . ."

"Can you help me understand . . ."

Ask Specific Questions

Part of asking the right questions is also tailoring the questions to your teen. If you've got a teen who has always had difficulty expressing himself or putting feelings into words, it's much better to ask specific questions rather than open-ended questions. For example, with Frank, I encouraged Pauline to ask, "When you smoke pot, what feeling does it give you? Relaxed? Calm?" instead of simply, "So, how do you feel, Frank?" It's okay to give suggestions when you ask questions, as long as you aren't looking for a specific answer, but are truly listening to your teen's responses. This is often also helpful for teens who don't actually know how they feel.

Ask for More Information; Leave Solutions to the End

Another way to make sure you are asking the right questions is to continue asking questions when a teen begins to share. If your child offers a little information, ask for a bit more. In my session with Frank and his mother, I eventually got Pauline asking specific questions that focused on Frank's feelings when he smoked pot. Frank admitted that the pot helped him feel calm. Pauline pushed a little further. "So, Frank, why do you think you're smoking pot?" she asked. Frank responded, "It just helps me. I feel so depressed and confused all the time and it just puts my mind at ease." That's when Pauline missed a golden opportunity. Her response was "Well, do you think there might be a better way to deal with that?" Frank had just let his mom in, sharing his feelings and hinting at the root of the problem. Pauline, however, had jumped to solution mode.

Solutions need to happen at the *end* of a conversation, once we have a clear idea of what the problem is. We have to understand what is broken before we can fix it, and it was still far too early for Pauline to be talking about solutions. If Pauline had asked another question on the same subject like, "Can you help me understand why you are feeling anxious?" Frank might have continued to move towards identifying the real problem. Don't be afraid to keep asking questions when teens are sharing.

The two lines I use most of the time in my practice are, "Can you help me understand . . ." and "I'm curious . . ." The first question works because teens are more likely to share once they are assured that my intent is to understand. All humans have a need to be understood—it

I Don't Know

"I don't know" are easily the three words I hear most frequently in my office. Some teens respond this way to my questions about their thoughts and feelings because they really don't know. Others use these words because they don't want to share the answers with me and are trying to end the conversation. I've noticed that if I ask someone a question, and they look away from me for one or two seconds before looking back and answering, "I don't know," there is a high probability that they are trying to figure the answer out, but are honestly unable to. If, however, the person's gaze doesn't break from mine, there is a good chance that they simply don't want to share their thoughts. When talking with your teens, if you get the first type of "I don't know," be patient. Most of us are not very self-aware. It often takes time to figure out how we feel about things. Getting comfortable with silence is one of my greatest tools as a coach, and it can serve parents well too. Parents need to raise questions about a teen's feelings and perspectives without being in a rush for answers or feedback. We need to give our teens time and silence to figure things out.

makes us feel valued, heard and respected. The second question is an effective way to get teens to talk because curious is a neutral statement—not positive or negative. When teens sense that the intent of my questions is not to preach or lecture at them but simply to "get" them and genuinely understand them, they are usually willing to talk.

Are Solutions Always Necessary?

During one of my workshops a father pulled me aside and said, "I don't understand something you said about listening. I've got three daughters, and they are always telling me to stop giving them solutions. But to be honest I don't feel that I'm being helpful unless I give them a solution. If I just listen, I think I'm not helping."

He's not alone. It's often hard for parents to listen to their children's troubles without feeling the need to jump into problem-solver mode. But if we want to be truly helpful to our children, we need to understand how *they* define helpful. In this case, the girls needed someone to listen to them, so clearly having their father listen, and just listen, would have done them the most good. There may be times when they want a solution too, so I encouraged the father to ask them whenever he wasn't sure. When I tell parents that, they often say, "That sounds nice, but practically speaking, what should I say?" I recommend being blunt, "I want to be helpful right now but I'm not sure what that is for you. Would you like me to just listen or would you like me to share my ideas?" If our intent is to be helpful to our children, we have to respect that sometimes that means listening instead of providing solutions.

Strategy #5: Understand the Difference Between Facts and Perception

As I mentioned earlier on, everyone sees the same events in a different way. For effective communication with anyone, but especially with teens, it's essential that we keep this in mind, accepting other people's points of view and clearly acknowledging that our own thoughts are just that—opinions and individual perceptions. Until we accept this we will get stuck arguing about opinions and treating them like facts.

At one of my workshops, I met a mother, Anne, who told me that in a recent argument, Trevor, one of her three teenaged sons, had claimed that she loved her other two boys more than him. To her mind, this was a ridiculous notion. I encouraged her not to dismiss his point of view, or tell him he was wrong, but to return to the subject later when they were alone. So Anne waited for a good time to talk—when they would both be relaxed and would have some privacy. Anne went into Trevor's bedroom in the evening several weeks later, and asked him if that was really how he felt. When he said yes, she felt defensive but reminded herself to get curious, not defensive. Instead she responded, "Can you help me understand what am I doing that is giving you that impression?"

Trevor went on to explain how it was little things his mom was doing that made him feel that way. He thought she showed more affection to his other brothers, gave them more freedom, said "I love you" to them more often and was more lenient. Anne decided to get curious notdefensive. She asked him to tell her more, encouraging him to describe examples of her behaviour. The more she just listened

Statements That Sound Like Facts	Statements That Voice Your Perception
<ul><li>"You are not motivated."</li><li>"You're angry all the time."</li><li>"You feel bad about yourself."</li></ul>	<ul><li>"From my perspective, it seems that your motivation has gone down. Would you agree?"</li><li>"It seems to me that you're angry. Is this true?"</li><li>"I'm concerned about how you feel about yourself. It seems to me that you often put yourself down. Is this true?"</li></ul>

and asked specific questions, the more he talked and shared. After listening to Trevor for over an hour, Anne could understand how he had come to his point of view. Despite the fact that Anne felt she loved and treated her sons equally, it was very small differences on her part that had sent a loud message to Trevor. At the end of the conversation, Anne thanked Trevor and asked for his forgiveness. She told me in an email that since that conversation she had noticed a huge decrease in his anger towards her.

As Trevor and Anne's story points out, two people can hold very different points of view about the same situation. By acknowledging that your teen's perception might hold some validity and by working to understand that point of view, parents can both open communication with their kids and go a long way to resolving differences and conflicts.

In the Heat of the Moment

We often say things we don't mean in the heat of an argument. Emotions get the better of us, and we make unfair accusations or say things to hurt or shock. But it is important to realize that we sometimes also give honest but critical feedback when we are upset. This is especially true for teens who are having difficulty talking with their parents. If they have been bottling up emotions, these feelings are most likely to spill out during an argument. Listen to what your teens say when they are angry, frustrated or upset. Don't assume that everything that is blurted out during a fight is not sincere. But remember that during an argument, when people are angry, is *not* the best time to discuss feelings. Come back to those feelings later, when you find a great time to talk.

Whenever any of us are sharing our opinion (especially if it is something more negative in nature), it's imperative to communicate that this is our perception, not a fact. Using the "I" technique from Strategy #2 is an excellent way to signal that we are expressing a point of view, rather than the truth. And as I mentioned in my discussion of the hamburger technique, simple phrases are good ways to introduce opinions.

Strategy #6: Know What You're Saying Non-verbally

For three years I was the executive producer and host of a national music TV talk-show, and one of the things that really hit me when I first started watching myself on TV was my own body language. In some interviews I looked nervous. In others I looked confident and prepared. In still others I looked as if I were talking to my best friend. In all of these cases it wasn't what I was saying but it was how I was saying it that made the difference. My tone, my facial expression, what I was doing with my arms and my hands—all of these little cues conveyed a powerful message. I decided that I would start studying myself on camera regularly so I could see what I liked and also what I wanted to change.

Most of us don't have the opportunity to videotape our body language. But the truth is that in communication, 93 percent of the message is conveyed by our body language. That means that you could apply everything I've been talking about up to this point, but if you're not aware of your body language, you could unintentionally be sending a powerful negative message.

Non-verbal communication includes both physical actions or body language and the tone or expression you use when talking (*how* you say things). To analyze your non-verbal communication, here are some questions to think about.

- Do you make eye contact or do you look distracted when your kids are talking to you?
- What tone of voice do you use? Is it loud and authoritative or is it calm?

- Do you demand your teens to do things, or do you ask them politely?
- Do you cross your arms or put your hands on your hips?
- Do you roll your eyes?
- Do you tap your fingers, jiggle your foot or fidget in any way?
- Do you turn your back when people are talking?
- Do you sigh or groan in response to what people are saying?
- Do you look serious?
- Do you laugh or smile inappropriately (e.g., during serious or emotional discussions)?
- Do you cut people off or interrupt them?
- Do you give people enough time to answer a question or do you jump in?
- Do you allow people to speak for themselves or do you speak for them?
- Do you listen enough?
- Do you smile?
- Do you nod when people are talking to show that you are listening?

So often it's those subtle little things we do that will send messages different than the ones we intend to send. I see this all the time with the parents and teens in my practice.

- Maxie's father had come into my office with his daughter because he was frustrated that she was not talking to him. We worked together for a while, and eventually Maxie started sharing some of her feelings. Even though Maxie's dad had said that he wanted to understand his daughter, as soon as she started to express a point of view her father didn't like, he rolled his eyes and starting looking out the window. He hadn't said anything, but Maxie noticed his body language and closed up.
- Patty and her son had not been getting along well when they

came to see me. As we attempted to get to the root of their problems, I noticed that whenever Connor started to talk—no matter what it was about—Patty's arms were crossed and her expression was stony. No wonder Connor was having so much trouble opening up.

- Brianne's mother wondered why her daughter was so closed. I watched them interact and noticed that whenever Brianne started talking, her mother would cut her off.

While all of these parents came into my office hoping to improve their communication and relationship with their teens, and while the words they were saying to the teens might have been effective, their body language and actions sent the opposite message. The rolling eyes, the crossed arms and the interruptions all suggested that they weren't interested in listening, were not open to understanding their children's thoughts and feelings or felt that what they had to say was more important than their teens' responses.

Congruent Communication and Mixed Messages

In healthy communication, our verbal and non-verbal messages have to be congruent. As Brianne's story suggests, non-verbal communication goes beyond body language. Our words *and* our actions need to match. When parents say one thing but do another, they are sending mixed messages, which is confusing. When children receive mixed messages, they are more likely to model their behaviour after what their parents are doing, rather than what they are saying. What's more, children won't trust parents who say one thing but do another.

In my family, we children learned at a very young age that the highest value in our home was honesty. It was not about being perfect, having excellent school marks or being the best on sports teams. The importance of honesty was verbalized repeatedly, and my parents told us that they would do their best not to get angry as long as we were honest with them. But more important than talking about honesty was the way in which my parents modelled their beliefs. Whenever we shopped in the U.S., my parents always (and I mean always) were honest about declaring their purchases at the border. They never told lies, not even little white lies. When one of my friends called and I didn't want to talk to her, my mother would not fabricate an excuse for me—she made me take the phone. If someone told either of my parents something in confidence, they never repeated the story.

"Don't worry that teens never listen to you; worry that they are always watching you."   **—Robert Fulghum**

It was hundreds of small non-verbal messages that sent a very powerful message to us about honesty. But parents send many other types of non-verbal messages to their children through their actions. If you are always late, your child will assume that punctuality is not important, even if you stress that it is. If you say that people should always keep their promises, but your child sees you break the commitments you've made, they aren't likely to believe your words. If you claim that good sportsmanship is more important than winning, but you spend the game shouting at the referee from the stands, guess what you're really saying! And most importantly, if you say that your teens' thoughts and feelings are important to you, but you don't listen to them or spend the time to find out who they are and what is happening in their world, they aren't likely to trust your sincerity enough to talk honestly and openly.

Honesty and Non-verbal Communication

Non-verbal communication and honesty are strongly connected. I'm often asked:

- How can I get my teens to be honest?
- How can I get them to trust me?
- How can I get my teens not to lie?

Honesty is one of those magical things that teens learn from our non-verbal communication. Sure, we can tell our teens to be honest, but if we are showing dishonesty through our actions (non-verbal communication), we are teaching them indirectly that it is okay. So ask yourself:

Just How Honest and Trustworthy Are You?

- Do you read your teen's emails without him knowing it?
- Do you read your teen's diary without her permission?
- If someone calls and your child doesn't want to talk to him, would you tell the caller that your child is not home when in fact he is?
- Would you lie to a teacher or school administrator so that your child doesn't have to suffer a penalty?
- Do you tell your children that you will keep something confidential but break that confidence to tell your partner or friend?
- If your child asks you something, do you say "I don't know" when you simply don't want to tell the truth?
- When you make a commitment to your children, do you stand by it or do you often change the rules?
- If you are shopping in another country, do you lie at the border about how much money you have spent?
- If you have been undercharged at a restaurant and you notice, do you say something to the waiter?
- Do you lie to your children to avoid conflicts or to keep from upsetting them?
- If someone tells you something in confidence, do you keep that secret or do you tell your children?
- If a child shares something in confidence, would you use that secret against her at a later time?
- Do you make promises you can't keep?
- Do you break promises?

Addressing the Mixed Message

No one is perfect. What do we do if we've engaged in behaviour that we wouldn't want our teens to repeat or to consider acceptable? One father approached me because his relationship with his 16-year-old daughter had fallen apart when she had discovered that he had had an extramarital affair. He wanted to know what he should do.

If there is one action that really blows up a parent's trustworthiness, it's cheating on his or her spouse. Often parents rationalize that an affair should have no effect on their children because they didn't cheat on them, but this thinking is distorted. By betraying and hurting their spouses they've proven that they can't be trusted. And their behaviour has expressed a disregard for honesty, loyalty and compassion.

Whenever parents do something that contradicts the ideals they want to share with their kids (even transgressions as serious as an affair), they should address the mixed message directly.

Take responsibility for your actions by acknowledging your mistakes
Don't ignore what you've done hoping your teens will forget. Chances are they won't, and avoiding the subject will only imply that you think your bad behaviour was acceptable or unimportant.

Apologize and really mean it
It's important that you express regret, but often when I hear parents apologize for their behaviour, they are quietly defending it. They say things like, "I know what I did was wrong but . . ." Justifying is not apologizing. If your behaviour has hurt your child, ask for forgiveness as well.

Give your teens time
If your transgression is something that has caused your teens serious pain or discomfort, it will probably take time for them to work through it. Don't rush the process.

Ask what you can do to rebuild their trust
When your teens' trust in you has been damaged, ask them how you can rebuild it. You might be surprised by what they have to say.

Tips for Getting Your Teens to Talk

Listen more, talk less

I asked 1,200 teenagers, "If your parent did one thing differently that would make the greatest positive difference in your relationship, what would it be?" The most common answer for both genders, ages 13 to 19, was, "Listen more, talk less."

Ask specific questions

If teens are having trouble with open-ended questions (particularly about feelings), be specific and provide suggestions. For example, "How do you feel about ____? Angry? Frustrated? Sad?" instead of just "How do you feel?"

Make eye contact

Remember that generally guys will feel less anxiety while talking sideways while girls often prefer eye contact. But base your technique on your own experience with your teen. There are always exceptions.

Soften your voice

Be aware of your voice. Does it sound too loud? Demanding? Make sure you soften your voice when you ask questions.

Ask for more information

When they share a little information with you, ask for more. For example, if they mention that they feel anxious, ask, "Can you help me understand why you are feeling anxious?"

Get curious, not defensive

If they share something that is negative about you, don't get defensive. Get curious. Say to them, "Tell me more. I want to understand you but to be honest I'm not sure I do yet."

Empathize with how they are feeling

If they share a vulnerable emotion with you, give them feedback to let them know you're listening (e.g., "I can understand you feeling that way," or "That must be so painful," or "I'm so sorry that you've been feeling that way."). Don't challenge how they feel. Be understanding.

Offer empathetic body language

If they become emotional, use body language to let them know you are there. Offer them a tissue. Put your hand on their shoulder or knee. Make sympathetic sounds or nod your head. All of these subtle cues let teens know you are listening to them.

Don't attach your own meanings to their words

Don't put words in their mouths or attach your own meaning to what they are saying. For example, if your teen says, "Dad, you seem so angry all the time," don't respond with "Well, sure, tell me I'm a terrible parent." Instead, ask them what you've been doing to make you seem angry.

Get comfortable with silence

Give teens time to figure out their answers. Don't rush them or start talking again if there's a pause.

Restate what you are hearing

Repeat what you have heard them say. Ask if you've got what they were saying right.

Ask them if they feel understood

Before you talk solutions, ask them if they feel heard and understood (e.g., "Do you feel like I have heard what you said? If not, help me understand what you think I'm missing here.").

Once they feel understood, let them know how you are feeling

It's important that teens understand how we think and feel about situations. Share this with them, but only *after* they feel fully understood.

Make sure you share your opinions in an assertive way—not in an aggressive way. If you are sharing a debatable opinion, ask them if they agree or disagree—you want them to be engaged in what you are saying and not tuned out.

Thank them

After they have shared with you, thank them for being open and vulnerable. Acknowledge how much courage it took to share. Affirming their courage will make them want to share with you again.

Show affection

After a heart-to-heart conversation, give them a hug. Let them know how much you love them.

Talk solutions (This is the LAST Step!)

Ask how you can be helpful to them. Encourage them to suggest ways to resolve any problems. Possibly negotiate a boundary with them. As parents you always have veto power but you want your teens as involved as possible in developing solutions to their problems.

Focus on Separation and Divorce

For previous generations, separation and divorce were rare occurrences. These days, however, it is estimated that roughly 36 percent of Canadian marriages will end in divorce. And perhaps because it is so common these days, as parents, we often underestimate the impact that separation and divorce will have on our children.

But while parents are going through emotional turmoil themselves, they have to be concerned with their children's feelings and emotional adjustment.

Parents are often well aware of the difficulty that young children will have understanding and coping with the separation of their parents, but the growing independence and maturity of teen children may prevent parents from fully understanding the effect that a marriage break-up has on them. Teens, however, rely very heavily on the security, familiarity, structure and routine of their families while they are moving towards a new life on their own. (One teen I know mentioned that no longer hearing his father's favourite music in the house had a profoundly unsettling affect on him.) Being forced into unknown waters at home, just as they are venturing into new territory outside of home life, can be very upsetting. What's more, witnessing the failure of the most influential romantic relationship they know, just as they are beginning to explore this aspect of adult life themselves, can create tremendous anxiety and confusion. Teens who have witnessed their parents' separation or divorce (particularly if an infidelity has led to the split) may find it difficult to trust future partners. So despite teens' independence and maturity, parents need to be sensitive to the emotional impact their separation will have on the older children in the family. Teens may experience a host of difficult feelings.

Feelings Teens May Experience About Separation and Divorce

Shock

Even if they realize that their parents have not been getting along, it is often difficult to accept that the family they grew up in is going to change so drastically.

Anxiety

Teens are likely to be worried about a number of things. They may ask, What will happen to us? Where will I live? Will I have to change schools? How will we manage financially? Will the same thing happen to my future relationships?

Sadness

A divorce is not only the end of a marriage. It's also the loss of the earlier family structure. Before teens can embrace their new family model, they may need to grieve.

Guilt

Teens may worry that something they have done has contributed to the problems in the marriage. Or they may feel guilty if they realize they are relieved that the marriage—and the fighting—is over.

Hope

Some teens may cling to the hope that the break-up is not permanent and that their parents will get back together.

Embarrassment

The intensity of their emotions may make teens embarrassed, or they may find themselves worried about what others will think.

Anger

Teens may also feel intense anger that their parents are separating. They may think their parents didn't try hard enough. They may ask why their parents are putting them through this and feel that their parents are letting them down.

How to Tell Your Children About a Marriage Break-Up

There is no doubt about it—separation and divorce will be a difficult time for all involved. But how you tell your children about the marriage break-up and how you and your ex-spouse handle parenting after a separation can have an enormous impact on how quickly everyone can heal.

Choose a good time to tell your kids about the separation. (See the six strategies outlined earlier in this chapter for tips about talking with your teens, including timing.) Keep in mind that when introducing something as emotional and difficult as the break-up of a marriage to your kids, you will want to have plenty of time to talk and answer questions. Also be aware that your teens may *not* want to talk or ask questions right away. They may find the news too overwhelming to process on the spot. They may not know what questions they want to ask. Follow their lead. If they want to end the conversation, let them know that both parents will make the time to talk with them again about the separation whenever they are ready and as often as they want. You may want to have follow-up conversations with children separately so they each can ask their own questions, and your answers can be tailored to their age and their concerns.

If possible and appropriate, it's best that you and your spouse are both there when you break the news to your children. Sitting with the other parent and talking to your children calmly and compassionately about what is happening will go a long way in reassuring your children that both parents will still be in their lives and will work together as parents.

- Assure your children that they still have two parents who love them.
- Reassure them that they have in no way contributed to the family break-up (even teens need to hear this). Emphasize that the problem is between the parents, not between the parents and kids.
- Tell teens that it is okay to be sad or angry about the break-up. Allow them to mourn the loss or express their frustration, anger or confusion.
- Be sensitive to teens' concerns for their future—they may be worried about where they will live, the financial repercussions of separation, about their new responsibilities (they may need to be helping out more, etc.) now that there is only one parent at home. Answer questions as honestly as you can, but avoid burdening your teen with worry or with more information than they want or need.
- Give your teens lots of time to acknowledge and accept what is going on.

After the initial discussion, there are a number of ways to ease the transition and help the separated family function as smoothly as possible.

Parents should come to an agreement that all parental decisions need be addressed by both of you. Your marriage may have ended, but your parenting partnership must still continue. Keep the lines of communication open—it is never acceptable to make the children the messengers between their parents.

As you adjust to your new life, be open about what is happening, but don't cry on your teens' shoulders or ask for their emotional support. As a parent, you shouldn't add to their pain or burden them with your anxieties or fears.

Don't criticize, blame or badmouth your ex-spouse. Teens need to be able to have an independent relationship with both their parents,

FOCUS ON *Separation and Divorce*

and should never have to defend one parent to another, or feel guilty about loving a parent, even if that parent has caused the other pain. Never ask or encourage your kids to take sides. Putting kids in the middle of a parenting disagreement is unfair and harmful.

If you notice your teen behaving in a troubling manner during or after the separation (skipping school, doing drugs, breaking boundaries), be an inside-out parent and try to find out what thoughts and feelings are behind the actions. Recognize that your teen may need professional help to work through their grief, hurt and anger.

As with establishing all boundaries, it's important that teens be involved in setting up the new living arrangements and routines. They should be consulted about where they want to live and how shared custody might be scheduled. Try to sit down with your ex-spouse, the children, and a calendar to figure out in advance what everyone's schedule is like and how their activities and needs can be accommodated. Sometimes finding a third party (like a counsellor or a family mediator) can be helpful in working out the new family structure and routines. A written plan, covering as many details as possible, may help avoid confusion, misunderstandings and conflict.

Maintain as much of the former family structure and routine as possible. This will provide security and comfort for your children. Try to avoid moving your children to new schools or moving far from their neighbourhood and friends.

Teens who are now living in two different homes will be comforted by familiar items (perhaps photos, bedding or childhood toys) in both places. Try to make moving between the two homes as easy as possible for your teen by having duplicate personal items at each house.

Even more important are familiar and consistent boundaries and routines. Work with your ex-spouse to try to make the rules as similar as possible between the two homes. If there are new spouses in the picture, leave them out of these discussions initially. It's important the parenting is

Staying Neutral

I have to be honest—not criticizing your ex-spouse may be a lot more difficult than it sounds. What if he or she is saying inappropriate things about you to your children? What if your ex-spouse is actually telling lies about you? Don't you have a right to tell your side of the story, defend yourself or set the record straight?

In one family I coached, the father, Bob, had vowed not to talk negatively about his ex-wife. But each time his kids came back from their mother's house, they told him all of the things she had said about him. Most were unflattering, many were untrue, and they all seemed aimed at undermining his children's affection for him. For example, Bob's ex-wife told the kids that Bob was not paying child support or providing money for his kids. Rather than firing back at her, however, Bob refused to get into the details with his kids. Instead, he said things like, "Well, there are always two sides to every story and that's her opinion. I have a very different opinion and perhaps when you're older I'll share it with you." He always kept his statements neutral. He refused to add to his kids' burden by involving them any further in his conflicts with his ex-wife. Rather than worrying that the things the kids heard from their mother would damage his relationship with them, he realized that they were telling him these things because they felt safe to do so—it was a sign that his relationship with his children had remained strong. Bob did, however, ask his ex-wife directly not to talk about their relationship to the kids, pointing out that it was unfair and damaging to them. And he brought his kids to a counsellor (me) so that they would have a safe place to unload what they were hearing from their mother.

If you think your ex-spouse is sharing inappropriate information with your kids or running you down in front of them, you can certainly ask him or her not to. But don't involve your children. How you behave with your children will have a far greater impact on their relationship with you than anything they are likely to hear from their other parent. When the going gets tough, try a few of the following lines to keep the conversation with your kids neutral:

"Well, that's your dad's opinion."

"I'm sorry you heard that. I have a very different opinion, but this is between your mom and me. It's not your problem and I don't want you to feel burdened."

"There are always two sides to a story. When you're older I'll share more with you."

"I'm sorry you feel that way."

"I'm glad that you feel safe enough to tell me."

"I am always here to listen to you."

"What can I do to help you?"

"I don't blame you for feeling really frustrated."

And what if you are tempted to say negative things about your spouse? What if your spouse isn't providing child support, and you are forced to deny your child things as a result? What if your spouse constantly breaks promises to your child? Do you commiserate with your child's hurt and anger? Do you let them know that you think your ex-spouse is behaving badly? Again, the most important thing you can do is to love and support your child, and lessen their burden and pain, rather than add to it. Telling them that their other parent is being selfish, irresponsible or a jerk is not going to make them feel better—and it may make them feel foolish or guilty if they want to continue to have a relationship with that parent. Let your child know that you understand their frustration and pain, but allow them to work out how they feel for themselves. If they need to talk about how they feel about their other parent, it may be best to find a neutral third party, like a coach or a therapist, with whom they can talk.

done by the biological parents and that it is done together, in the interests of the children.

Holidays, celebrations and special days can be difficult after a separation. Both parents and teens should brainstorm about how to observe special days and events. Some families opt for two birthday celebrations, for example, while others choose to alternate homes for celebrations and holidays. Parents and children can help to ease the pain of lost traditions by creating new ones in each home. Make sure that your teens can keep up with their extended family on both sides—even if being in contact with your ex's family is uncomfortable for you.

If one parent moves away, parents and teens need to work together to figure out ways for everyone to stay in touch. Some families find it helpful to set up regular times for phone calls, emails or instant messaging. Regular visits with the non-custodial parents (perhaps over holiday periods, for example) can be arranged.

Take care of yourself. Newly separated parents often struggle with depression, anger and anxiety, and so may find it difficult to be emotionally available for their children. But during this difficult time, it is especially important that parents stay "plugged in" with their kids. If you feel too overwhelmed with your own emotions to be of help to your children, seek counselling for yourself or for the whole family. If you are feeling overworked and overwhelmed by your new life and responsibilities, reach out to family and friends for help, and work out ways to make time for yourself. Parents who are stressed, unhappy and overworked cannot do their best parenting.

Research suggests that parents' success in coping with a separation and divorce and adjusting to their new lives has a huge impact on their children's ability to do the same. After a separation, try to model fairness, healing, resilience and a positive outlook for the future. Your behaviour during these challenging times can be an enormously positive life lesson for your children.

Separation and divorce are never easy, but they can be handled well. I have met numerous separated families who have created happy, healthy new family structures by putting their children's welfare first—in other words, by always keeping the big picture in mind.

When Parents Date

When single parents begin dating, the effect on their children must always be taken into account. This is especially true if a parent has started to see people after the death of a spouse or a divorce. Young children and teenagers alike may feel that any parent who starts a new relationship is betraying the other parent. Children may worry that a parent's affection for a new person may interfere with his or her affection for them. And while it is not surprising that small children may be jealous of any time a parent spends with another adult, it's important to realize that teens may feel this way too. Remember—it's one thing for them to want to spend to time with their friends instead of you; it's an entirely different thing for them to feel that *you* want to spend time with others.

If a parent begins a relationship after a divorce, teens may also feel angry that after all the adjustments they have just undergone, they are being asked to accept another change in their in their lives. They may not want to spend any time getting to know new partners. They may feel a loss of privacy with a new person in their home on a regular basis.

Teens may also be uncomfortable being faced with the fact that their parents have romantic and sexual lives. While it is easy for kids to overlook the fact that their parents are sexual beings, it's hard for teens to ignore this once their parents are dating, especially as teens may now be dating too.

To complicate matters, teens may have a hard time with their parents' romantic lives if they perceive that there are different rules for parents and teens, for example, curfews, sleepovers, and so on. Remember that you are modelling behaviour—and your teens will notice every nuance of your new relationship. But you should also be clear with your teen that there are differences between adult dating and teen dating— including maturity, self-knowledge, judgment and so on.

Because children and teens can harbour such complex and complicated emotions about their parents' dating, I always recommend that parents don't start a new relationship until at least a full year after a separation or divorce. Many parents said they didn't feel ready to date for two to three years. But waiting to date has great benefits for parents as well. It takes time to grieve the loss of the marriage. It takes time to process the split and learn what went wrong. What can parents learn about themselves as they reflect on the breakdown? How can they take that knowledge to help them in their next relationship? What would they do differently? How did they contribute to the breakdown? Often the temptation is to blame the breakdown completely on the other person. But as I discussed in Chapter 3, emotional maturity means taking responsibility for ourselves. This process takes time, and if people jump too quickly into their next relationship, often it's because they feel they need a partner (as I described in the section on self-esteem), which is not healthy.

I also suggest that parents don't bring their dates home initially—meeting too many new people can be confusing and anxiety-producing for children and teens. Wait until you are certain the relationship is serious before introducing a new person to your children—I usually recommend six months or a year after seeing each other regularly. But keep in mind that, even if you are serious about this new person, when you have kids, you are a "package deal." If your new partner doesn't like kids or has a poor rapport with your children, I strongly encourage you think about whether or not you should continue dating. This is the reality of being a single inside-out parent.

The good news is that given adequate time, children and teens are often very happy to have their parents begin dating. I've worked with many families in which the kids have actively encouraged their parents to get back out there. And when parents and teens are emotionally ready to invite a new person into their lives, the chances for a happy future together are much higher.

Lidija, age 17, was furious when her father, Peter, started dating after only a few months of being separated from her mother. She was, in her own words, "pissed" at her dad for dating too soon and she was extremely rude to him and Maggie, his new girlfriend, especially when they announced they would be getting married as soon as the divorce was legal. After months of this emotional distance and rudeness, the three ended up in my office. Peter felt caught in the middle—he loved his new partner and he also loved his daughter. I asked Lidija what would be the number one thing that her father and Maggie could do to make the situation easier for her. She blurted out, "Stop making out in front of me!" Of course, Peter and Maggie were not "making out," but seeing any physical affection between them was extremely difficult for Lidija to handle. I've heard this same complaint from hundreds of teens whose parents begin dating after a separation. Although Maggie and Peter wanted to be more affectionate, they decided to respect Lidija's wish. This one simple action helped move this family from a place of conflict to a more neutral place. Maggie and Lidija did not become closer, but they weren't fighting as much, which was an improvement. And when I coach families, it becomes clear that this phase is often transitional. Things move from "conflict," to "neutral" to "resolution." By respecting Lidija's wish, Maggie and Peter made an act of "truce." And over the years, each birthday, Christmas and family holiday slowly started to get easier. Lidija later told me it took her over five years before she stopped being angry at her father and actually started "liking" Maggie. Before this, she had felt that to like Maggie was to be disloyal to her mother (who desperately wished she was still married to Peter). Getting biological and step-parents to ask, "What is the number one thing I can do to make this transition easier for you?" is simple and practical, and it will help you to move in the right direction.

Focus on Step-Parents and Blended Families

When parents remarry, they are introducing a new person into a pre-existing family, which is a significant adjustment for everyone. While the new couple are in love with and committed to one another, it's unrealistic to expect that children, and especially teens, will feel the same way about the newcomer. Relationships between step-parents and stepchildren take time. If both partners have children who will be living in the same household (a "blended family"), the same will hold true for step-siblings. In fact, most families I've coached tell me it takes around five years for the new family to feel like a "real" family. So what can families do to make the transition as smooth as possible?

Once a new partner has been introduced to your children, give your kids time to get to know him or her before you begin to live together or marry.

Discuss the wedding and new living arrangements with your kids. Involve your children and teens in the wedding planning and ceremony.

Step-Parents

With adolescents, the hope that step-parents will develop the closeness and the love that the parents and their children share is not necessarily realistic. Bonding and love take a great deal of time, and a step-parent is entering a teen's life at a time when the teen is in the process of separating from his parents and gaining independence. The goal, therefore, of step-parents, should be to form a healthy, happy relationship—like a friend or a trusted aunt or uncle—with their stepchildren. But realize that even this won't happen overnight.

Step-parents should not take it personally if teens rebuff or challenge them. It's easier for teens to take their conflicted feelings out on a step-parent than on a parent. Parents, however, should always address these behaviours and encourage their teens to talk with them about how they are feeling.

Just because your teens may be spending less time with you, and seem to need you less as they grow older, don't think that they won't

Step-Parent as Support

In one family I coached, there was a lot of conflict because the step-dad, Lou, did not approve of how the mom, Diane, was disciplining her teenage daughter. When he felt that Diane was not being strict enough, he would take over. The more involved he got, the more Diane's daughter would fight back. Lou was trying to be helpful, but he had married Diane when her daughter was already in her teens—so his stepdaughter was not going to accept his attempts at parenting. Rather than focusing on disciplining his stepdaughter, Lou should have been concentrating on supporting his wife and being more of an uncle figure to her daughter.

But the truth was that Lou had some good ideas around boundaries. So I encouraged Diane to learn from him—to listen to his ideas and perspectives, and to ask him, questions like: "What do you think I'm doing well?"; "What do you think I need to work on?"; and "What ideas do you have for boundaries/discipline?" I also insisted that Diane and her daughter's biological dad come to see me together for coaching. After the parents had been working together for several months, Lou began to feel that the situation was under control and was better able to pull back.

be affected if you start spending a lot of time with a romantic partner. They need to know that you are still there for them, that they are still a priority in your life. Make sure you spend some time alone with each of your children so they don't always have to share your attention.

Step-parents should not try to compete with or replace their partner's ex-spouse. They should never denigrate their stepchildren's other parent.

Step-parents should leave all discipline and consequences to the biological parent. They should only step in if the biological parent is away or unavailable—and only if this is an agreement that has already been made between the biological parent and the step-parent. During absences, biological parents need to give their authority to the caregiver and let their kids know that they are doing this.

A step-parent's main role should be to support his or her spouse. If children are very young, the biological parent may ask the step-parent to take a more active role in parenting, but with teens, it is best that step-parents not try to be the authority figure in the family—teens are not likely to accept this, and their resentment will harm their relationship with their step-parent.

Blended Families

Don't expect step-siblings to form relationships with each other quickly or easily. Give them time.

Make sure that you have a single consistent set of boundaries for all children living together. Conflict and jealousies are sure to arise if one set of kids have limits on watching television, for example, and the others don't. To avoid having differing sets of rules, parents will need to sit down with children and work out new household guidelines. This will likely take a number of compromises and plenty of negotiating. Parents will also need to work with their ex-spouses if there are significant changes in family boundaries. Complete consistency between the two households may not be possible, but support and respect for the new structure and routines from the ex-spouse will make the adjustments easier for the kids.

Give step-siblings some independence from each other. For example, teens and older children shouldn't be expected to babysit their younger step-siblings all the time. Children of similar ages shouldn't be expected to do everything together. If at all possible, step-siblings should have their own rooms, or some space with privacy. Don't force step-siblings to share all of their possessions.

When starting a blended family, sit down with all of the kids and brainstorm some new family traditions. Make the new family arrangement positive by finding some fresh and exciting ways to spend time together.

Avoiding the War Zone

I'll never forget coaching the blended family of Marcia and Tony. The conflict between the step-siblings and the step-parents was non-stop—they fought about chores, about using the car, about what TV shows to watch, about going out at night, about spending money—about everything. It turned out that Marcia was extremely strict with her teens. Tony, however, was very lenient. Combining the two parenting styles and children who had been raised in very different ways had turned the family home into a war zone. While we were able to work out some compromises and establish some routines and boundaries that everyone could live with, I couldn't help thinking that Marcia and Tony could have avoided a great deal of the pain, chaos and confusion if they had talked about their parenting attitudes and expectations much earlier in their relationship.

When parents enter new relationships with partners who also have kids, it's essential that they discuss their parenting values, approaches and routines as early as possible. Waiting to work out these differences until everyone is living under one roof is unfair and potentially damaging to the children involved.

FOCUS ON *Step-Parents and Blended Families*

6 Boundaries and Structure

"The two most important things every child and teen needs are
lots of love and lots of discipline."

—Margaret Gordon, my mother

There are some people (I recently heard about a daycare that operated on this philosophy) who believe they should never say the word "no" to children or teens. This doesn't make any sense if parents think about the big picture. If children are never told "no," they never learn about boundaries and discipline. And if they don't learn about boundaries from others, they are likely to struggle learning to how set boundaries for themselves, which can lead to all kinds of problems from overeating to overspending to overscheduling, and so on. The key is learning how to say "no" in a loving and assertive way, so that children still feel respected while learning about boundaries and structure.

When I talk about inside-out parenting and keeping the big picture in mind, some parents wonder if I'm being impractical. It's all well and good to talk with my teen about how he is feeling when he smokes pot, they might say, but surely it's also important to get him to stop doing drugs. Of course it is. But as I have mentioned earlier, the point of inside-out parenting is to start at the inside (feelings and character) and work outwards to changes in behaviour. Once we have honestly evaluated our goals and our own attitudes, once we have committed to building our teens' self-esteem, and once we have learned to communicate with our teens effectively, we are ready to help guide their behaviour. And the best way to do this is to provide boundaries and structure in our teens' lives.

Boundaries and structure (or rules) provide a sense of security and safety for all of us, regardless of age. Within a well-established structure, we can make decisions and exert some control over our lives because we know what is expected of us, what we can expect of others, which actions and behaviours are acceptable and which are not. If we don't meet expectations, we can predict the outcome of our actions. Let me give you an example.

Imagine that you've started a new job in an office. There are no established office hours—people come and go as they please. (Some days when you arrive, the office manager hasn't shown up, so the door is locked and you have to wait.) No one's responsibilities are spelled out—some times the mail clerk brings your mail; other days you have to go get it yourself. You never know the time frame in which you must finish any of your tasks. You might be expected to complete a job in a week but next month your boss will be furious that you didn't get it done in a day. Senior staff steal office supplies on a regular basis, but your fellow worker is fired for bringing a pen home. Some weeks you will get paid for your work, some weeks not. In an environment like this, what do you think would happen? No doubt staff morale would be terrible, and tension, conflicts, inefficiencies and general chaos would rule the day!

No one would expect an office to be run like this, but many parents don't realize the extent to which family life also benefits from clearly defined expectations and consequences, schedules and rules—in other words, boundaries and structure.

Of course, the importance of boundaries and structure is most obvious when our children are very small. Most parents provide some consistent daily structure for their toddlers and preschool children— regular meal times and bedtimes for example. And a number of firm boundaries are established, whether it is teaching our small children that there are words they can't use or that they must not bite when angry or frustrated. If we continue to provide appropriate structure as our children grow older and their abilities and needs change, and if we develop boundaries as the circumstances arise, then we may find that the teen years are easy sailing. But so often, as children become more capable and independent, parents fail to establish new boundaries and abandon structure. Yet rules, routine (with flexibility), responsibilities and predictable outcomes and consequences reduce confusion and conflict over such things as privacy, school work, help around the house, and spending. Clearly outlined boundaries—expected actions and behaviour—will also teach self-discipline and responsibility.

Drawing Boundaries

I mentioned earlier that many parents have boundaries or rules for their young children. Often these boundaries are quite specific—as in "no candy before supper"—and sometimes they are more wide-reaching, like "no lying." But where do we need to draw boundaries when we are living with teenagers? Take a look at the following list of boundary areas that come up in parent-teen relationships to see what boundaries you already have in place and which you might want to establish.

Physical Boundaries
- Do family members need to knock before entering each other's bedrooms?
- Are family members allowed to look through each other's belongings or correspondences?
- Can family members borrow each other's things without asking?
- Do you, as parents, have the right to inspect your children's rooms or read their email or diaries?

Financial Boundaries
- What do your teens have to pay for?
- What do you have to pay for?
- Do your teens get an allowance? If so, how much? Do they need to earn it? How do they earn it? What are they responsible for?

- Do your teens have to have their own bank accounts?
- Will you lend money to your children or are they expected to save up for their purchases? If you lend them money, what is the family policy about paying it back?

Communication Boundaries

- If your teens tell you something in confidence, will you tell other people? Will you tell your spouse?
- Do you allow for your teens to swear? If not, and they do anyway, what is the consequence?
- What words do you allow and what words are off limits?
- If your teen puts someone down or engages in verbal abuse what action would you take?
- What tones of voice are acceptable?
- Is your teen allowed to interrupt when someone is speaking? If so, when and how?

Responsibility Boundaries

- Are your teens expected to wake up by themselves in the morning?
- Are your teens responsible for any household chores? Which ones?
- Are your teens expected to prepare any meals for the family?
- Are your teens expected to make their own lunches?
- Are your teens expected to do their own laundry?

Social and Dating Boundaries

- At what age do you allow your teens to begin dating?
- How many nights per week are they allowed to go out?
- Do they have a curfew? If so, what time do they need to be home on weeknights? Weekends?
- Are teens allowed to have sleepovers with a girlfriend or boyfriend?

- Would you buy birth control pills or give your teens condoms if you knew that they were sexually active?

Media Boundaries

- Do you limit the amount of time your teens can spend on TV, MSN, Facebook or other computer activities that are not homework?
- What is the family policy about answering the phone? Are there times when the phone should not be answered (e.g., dinnertime)?
- Is there a family policy about listening to music on headphones?
- Is there a family policy about answering cellphones? (e.g., not at dinnertime or past 11 p.m.?)

School/Homework Boundaries

- Are there designated times and places for doing school work?
- Whose responsibility is it to make sure school work is complete? Are there consequences outside of school if homework is not done?
- Are there limits to the amount of parental help given with homework?

Driving Boundaries

- How often you drive your teen places? Is there a limit?
- If your teen wants a ride somewhere, when and how must he ask?
- If your teens are licensed to drive, who pays for their insurance and gas? Who pays if they get a ticket?
- What do your teens have to do to maintain the privilege of using the family car?

Blended-Family Boundaries
- Who is in charge of discipline?
- If the biological parent is in charge, under what circumstances can the step-parent provide discipline or impose consequences?

Bedtime Boundaries
- Is there a set bedtime for your teenage children? Are there any other expectations for nighttime routines (e.g., computer or music off at a certain hour)?

Smoking/Alcohol/Drug Boundaries
- Is smoking, underage alcohol consumption or drug use allowed on your property?
- If not, what would the consequence be if you found out your teens were consuming these things in your home?
- What would the consequence be if you found out your teens were consuming these things outside of the home?

Emotional Boundaries
- Do you allow your teens to voice their anger? Depression? Sadness?
- Are there any emotions you don't allow your teens to express?
- Do you consider it acceptable to cry on your teen's shoulder?
- Do you consider it acceptable to go to your teens for support?

Eating Boundaries
- Do you require everyone to eat together as a family? For all meals, or just some?
- Is eating in front of the TV allowed?
- Are there limits to how much junk food your teens are allowed to eat or what kind of food they can bring into the house?

Attitudes and Boundaries

The Overfunctioning and Underfunctioning Attitude and Boundaries

As you read through the sample list above, you may have realized that you do have many clearly defined boundaries in your family life—or that you have very few. If in Chapter 2 you identified yourself as an overfunctioner, a mother bear/rescuer, a basket case, an underfunctioner, a friend or a doormat, then it is very likely that you live in a family in which many of the boundary issues listed above have not been addressed.

Overfunctioning parents often have no personal and emotional boundaries between their children and themselves: they may feel responsible *for* their teen or take on their teens' triumphs and problems as their own. They sometimes use "we" when talking about their teens, such as, "We only got a B on our science project." They may also get their sense of self-worth from the successes of their children or might blame themselves when their teens make poor choices or do badly in school. Overfunctioning parents also create a lot of anxiety for themselves because they spend a great deal of time worrying about things that they have no control over. For example, an overfunctioning parent might try to convince their teens not to hang out with other teens who are smokers, rather than focusing on establishing consequences for their own teens if they begin smoking too. (Parents with a basket case or friend attitude also may have no boundaries between their children and themselves, but in these cases, parents may also share their personal problems with their kids.) But over- and underfunctioning parents may also create environments where conflict and confusion arise because of relatively simple everyday habits—family members talking over one another in conversations, teens taking money from a parent's wallet without permission, family members walking into bedrooms unannounced, siblings borrowing each other's clothes without asking.

Also, in families without adequate boundaries, it's usually unclear who is responsible for what—expectations and consequences aren't spelled out or agreed upon (and sometimes change, seemingly at random). In this kind of environment, it's easy to play the blame game, as there are plenty of opportunities for frustration, resentment and anxiety, on everyone's part. But parents who don't establish boundaries also fail to teach teens to take responsibility in their lives. If there aren't clear expectations about behaviour and contributions to the work of family life for teens, they may remain immature in their outlook and behaviour, and stay dependent on their parents for far too long. And any teen who is catered to and overindulged is likely to develop a sense of entitlement.

Parental Peer Pressure

The reasons that parents don't establish boundaries within a family are much like the reasons they overfunction: guilt, fear, exhaustion and the misguided desire to be a dream parent. Establishing and following through with boundaries is a lot of work—fatigue often plays a big role in a lax attitude towards rules and routine. Another factor in many parents' reluctance to establish boundaries is what I call "parental peer pressure." Some parents are not only afraid of what there teens will think about family rules but are also afraid of what other parents will think. Parents who compare their parenting with that of others, sometimes make poor decisions by following what other people are doing or not doing.

The Sergeant Attitude and Boundaries

Perhaps, while you read the list of boundary topics, you were reassured that you have many rules in your family. It's important to recognize, however, that while structure and boundaries are necessary, parents who operate with the sergeant attitude (or even the teacher attitude) and impose rules and routines with a rigid, authoritarian approach are not likely to get the results they want. Sergeant parents are very controlling, telling their children what to do and how to think. Their consequences for any broken rules are tough. Teens are not allowed to have their own opinions and are not involved with developing family rules or negotiating consequences. As a result of their exclusion from the process, teens may rebel against the boundaries, overtly or covertly. But even if family rules are followed, the results will often be far from what the parents had hoped for. Teens in these types of families often do not learn to make decisions or think for themselves, and are often attracted to friends and mates who are controlling. Also, they often struggle with low self-esteem. It's essential, therefore, to fashion family boundaries with the inside-out attitude.

The Inside-Out Attitude and Boundaries
Part of being an inside-out parent is providing adequate and appropriate structure and boundaries for your teen children. Inside-out parents

- believe they are responsible *to* their teen, not *for* their teen
- establish reasonable and flexible boundaries
- impose fair consequences, which are known in advance whenever possible
- allow teens to negotiate the consequences (whenever possible)
- allow their teens to have opinions different from their own
- model the kind of behaviour they are expecting from their teens
- respect their teens' space and belongings

There are hundreds of different situations to which boundaries can be applied in parent-teen relationships. To be prepared, parents need to think *in advance* about what they want their boundaries to be. Always ask yourself:

- What's fair?
- What's reasonable?

- What terms are negotiable?
- What terms are non-negotiable?
- What is a fair reward?
- What is a fair consequence if a teen oversteps a boundary?

Once parents have answered these questions for themselves, they need to discuss these expectations with their teens, explaining why the boundaries are necessary and how the rules will work. For example,

- "In our home, I want one of our boundaries to be knocking on closed doors before entering. So when you come into our room, you must knock before coming in. And when I come into your room I will do the same and knock before entering. This demonstrates respect on both our parts for each other's space."
- "If you want to borrow something of mine, I'll do my best to share things with you, but I expect you to always ask my permission instead of just taking something. And I promise I will do the same."

When these boundaries or expectations are *not* discussed it creates chaos, conflict and confusion.

Tips for Establishing and Following Through with Boundaries

Often parents will tell me that they *have* set boundaries but they are still in conflict with their teens or have a rocky relationship. Usually when I talk more with these parents, it becomes clear that they have tried to establish boundaries, but have not done it effectively. Here are a number of tips to establishing and following through with boundaries that work.

Prioritize

Brainstorm about all the areas of your teen's behaviour that concern you. School? Swearing? Curfews? Chores? Make a list. Then pick three or four things that are the most important to you. I do not recommend that parents make long lists of changes to discuss with their teens. It will be too overwhelming for everyone.

Choose Things You Can Control

Often when parents bring their lists to show me, I am concerned about what they have chosen to focus on. Problematic boundaries include such rules as

- no smoking
- no sex
- no drugs
- no underage drinking
- no hanging out with certain friends
- always following the family's religion

What is the problem with these restrictions? These are all values and behaviours that parents cannot see or monitor. You may have worked out a suitable consequence for underage drinking, but that will be beside the point if your teen is successful in hiding his drinking. It's also important to keep your boundaries concrete and measurable, and to define any behaviour you are referring to. For example, if you want to make a no-swearing rule, keep in mind that what any two people consider swearing may be very different.

What's more, parents can't control what their teens' values are—you may have strong beliefs about premarital sex or your faith, but dictating or lecturing about these issues may very well push your teen into rebellion. The key with values is to talk with your teens about *their* values. Get them to do their own thinking.

Parents can't control teens' behaviours; however, they *can* create a structure that reflects their values with appropriate rewards or consequences.

For example, you cannot control whether you teens smoke, but you can do the following:

- Model wise choices by not smoking yourselves (as I have mentioned previously, role-modelling is very powerful).
- Establish a "no smoking" policy in your home or on your property, and set a reasonable consequence if your teens break this rule.
- Throw out cigarettes you find lying around the house.
- Refuse to buy cigarettes for your teens.
- Focus on building a great relationship with your teens and on accepting who they are, even if you don't approve of their choices.

Choose the Right Time

In Chapter 5, I talked about the importance of choosing a good time to talk about problems. The same holds true for establishing boundaries. Make sure you are in a good emotional place when you approach your teens about new boundaries. If you're too angry, wait. Try to make sure that your timing also works for your teens. Let them know that you want to discuss something, and ask when they will have time to talk.

Choose the Right Language

Review the six communication strategies in Chapter 5 before you sit down with your teens to discuss boundaries. Use the "I" technique. Rather than saying, "Your mother and I have talked and we're sick of what we are seeing! We're going to take control and show you we mean business," try something like: "Your mother and I were talking, and we realized we've done a poor job at communicating what we expect. We've been vague and inconsistent and that is really unfair to you and we apologize. We want to make a plan with you that will make both your life and ours much better. We don't want to make the plan by ourselves. We want to get your input and listen to what you have to say so we can make a plan that makes sense for both of us. Are you willing to discuss this with us? If not, that's fine, but it just means we need to do it by ourselves, and it's to your advantage to share your input with us."

Focus on how you feel, and apologize for any of your mistakes.

Don't Fight It

I'm often asked what parents should do if their teens are not interested in discussing boundary plans. I say, "Don't fight it." Be very clear with your teens that it is to their benefit to discuss this with you. But if they still are resistant, don't get worked up about it. Simply focus on what you can control—the plan. Let your teens know that you are going to continue on it without them. Then follow the tips that I have outlined, adding one extra step: write a letter to your teen using the hamburger technique. Let your teen know all the positives, why you love her, what you appreciate about her. When you get to the meat, be short but sweet, explaining the boundaries you are now going to enforce (a chart of the rules and consequences can be useful for visual learners). Finish the letter with lots of positives.

Keep a copy of the letter so you know exactly what you said and how you said it. If your teen refuses to read it, or throws it out, that's her problem, not yours, and I'd suggest that you still follow through with the consequences that are stated. For tough situations like this, I strongly recommend parents see a professional counsellor or family therapist to coach them through it. It's also helpful to get a professional counsellor to read the letter in advance to make sure it's loving, kind and respectful but also clear and reasonable regarding the boundaries being discussed. I've coached hundreds of parents through this type of process and in every instance (when the parents were willing to do their part), we saw positive changes. The key is to be loving and respectful while remaining firm with your boundaries.

Use Lots of Positive Statements

The first thing to do before embarking on a discussion of boundaries is to let your teens know how much you love them. Tell them how much you want to build a great relationship with them. Discuss any positive choices or behaviours you have seen them make or do recently. (Don't talk about when they were young children—talk about recent positive actions). Think of all of this *in advance* so you can build them up and get them ready for the changes.

Discuss and Negotiate Boundaries

When discussing boundaries with your teens it is important to negotiate with them. Always ask for their input. After you've shared what you think, ask what they are thinking. Do these new plans seem reasonable? Can they think of alternate ways to address the situation? In many cases, there may be some room for compromise. For example, you might suggest a curfew of 11 p.m., but they want 11:30. You might agree that if they manage to get in on time at 11 for the next three weeks, the curfew can be extended to 11:30. If boundaries are to be effective, it's essential that you invite your teens into the discussion, listen to their input and involve them in the process in a genuine way.

Use Specific Time Frames

Time frames are extremely important when it comes to setting up boundaries. Many parents overlook time frames, and this can lead to problems. Each and every boundary must have a time frame assigned to it. For a no inappropriate language rule, for example, the time frame is likely ongoing. But for other things like chores, the time frame will need to be more specific. Often parents will say, "You have to do your chore every week," but when is the deadline for the week? Does the week start on Sunday or Saturday or Monday? What about the time of day? Do you mind if your teen is doing his laundry at 11 p.m. and putting his wet clothes into the dryer before going to bed?

For teens your spelling out the timing expectation of a new rule is often the most helpful part of the plan. They usually don't react well to the demand to do something "right now." (You may have noticed that if you say this they are almost always busy). But they do tend to respond when they are given a window in which to work. For example, if you know you want your teens to clean their rooms once a week, let them know they can do it anytime from Wednesday to Saturday (or whatever window works best for the family). When they get a window and a deadline, teens can organize their time and feel in control of their schedules.

When you are establishing boundaries be very clear about the amount of time in which you want things done, if there is day you are expecting things to be completed, and if there are times of day when tasks should or should not be undertaken.

Discuss and Negotiate Currency

Time-outs often work extremely well with young children, but good luck trying to get a 15-year-old on a time-out chair! The principle, however, is the same for children or teens: inappropriate behaviour results in a consequence. For teens, the key is for parents to identify the right currency. Every teen has a currency—something that is very important to them. It can be anything from money, computer use, MSN, socializing, cellphones or video games. The best way to come up with appropriate and effective consequences is to encourage teens to think of their own consequences and rewards. When I tell parents this, many of them think I'm crazy. After all, wouldn't teens just choose really easy consequences? Not usually. In fact, I find that teens are often more hard on themselves than parents.

The key to effective consequences is that they cause enough of a "pinch" that they motivate but are not so overwhelming that they discourage teens. One 13-year-old teen I coached suggested that his parents deduct five dollars off his allowance each time he said an inappropriate word. I could see that a penalty this heavy might backfire by making the teen resent and rebel against the new rule. I advised a smaller monetary consequence instead.

As you negotiate consequences and rewards, ask yourself, "Can I follow through with this?" Don't agree to anything that you don't think you can follow through on.

Teen Involvement and Parental Authority

Often parents think that by asking their teen for input, they are giving away authority. Not true! By asking teens, parents are not agreeing to do what their teens say, but instead are simply inviting their opinion, listening to it, evaluating it and negotiating something that both can agree on. And parents always have veto power.

For teens, the toughest part of boundaries is sticking to them.

For parents, the toughest part of boundaries is following through with the consequences.

Write It Down

I recommend that all boundary plans be in writing for several reasons. First, people will remember different details of conversations. It's important for the sake of everyone involved that anything that is agreed upon is written down so that it is completely clear to all.

Second, simply talking things out might be fine for auditory learners, but is not effective for visual or hands-on learners. They need to *see* the plan and to *do* something in order for the boundaries to sink in. If possible, get your teens to do the writing. This gets them on board and makes this more their plan, rather than your plan for them. (Remember, the goal is for parents to function less in order for teens to function more, so get them to do the work.)

Your plan in total should not be more than one page (longer than that will look far too confusing and overwhelming). Keep it simple, organized and to the point. The form I have found helpful is this:

Expectation	Time	Reward	Consequence

Follow Through

After you're finished your first round of discussions and put your boundaries in writing comes the tough part—following through.

No one said this was going to be easy. But it is essential that your words and your actions match. If parents don't follow through, here is what will often happen:

- Teens will learn not to trust what you say.
- Teens will be very reluctant to create any more plans with you.
- You will see no positive changes in your teen's behaviour.

It is the parent's responsibility to do as he or she says. It's not being mean; it's being fair and trustworthy.

Following Through and Modelling Self-Discipline

The very skill that most parents want their teens to develop is the very skill that many of them struggle with themselves: self-discipline. Creating a boundary plan is the tool to help parents teach their teens about self-discipline. Following through with consequences is an ideal way for parents to model self-discipline for their teens.

Common Mistakes with Boundaries, Discipline and Teaching Responsibility

Parents Have Expectations for Their Teens That They Are Not Modelling

Nothing makes teens angrier than seeing hypocrisy in their parents. If parents expect their teens to knock before entering their room but then barge into their teen's room , or interrupt when they've told their teens not to, teens simply won't follow the rules themselves, and parents will lose the children's respect.

Parents Have Not Thought Through Their Expectations

Let's face it. Most of us are very busy. We can barely make it through the day with a moment to spare. Many parents are "reactive" to inappropriate behaviour. They've never really thought through their expectations. It's critical that parents be "proactive, " thinking in advance about what they expect.

Give It Time

When establishing new boundaries, remember that change won't happen overnight. It takes three weeks to break a habit and three weeks to make a habit. For this reason, the first six weeks, while everyone is getting into the new routine, are usually the most difficult. Review your plan after two weeks and revise it if necessary, but give everyone time to break old patterns of behaviour and develop new and better ones.

It's important to let your teen know that this plan is not set in stone. Otherwise your teen may be reluctant to make a change. Most families I work with have to revisit and renegotiate between three to five times before they find the plan that works, with the currency (reward or consequence) being the aspect that is adjusted the most often. So be patient. Manage your expectations and keep revisiting the issues until you find the right plan.

Parents Are Not on the Same Page

If parents do not show a unified front when it comes to structure, boundaries and discipline, teens, consciously and sometimes unconsciously will "divide and conquer" to get the result they want.

The Boundaries Are Too Vague

Teens can be brilliant at finding grey areas. If you make a rule that there is no swearing, for example, you may find that your definition of swearing is very different from your teens'. You must define what you mean by swearing and identify specifically what language is inappropriate. Remember, boundaries must be clear, measurable and focused on behaviour, rather than concepts.

The Rewards or Consequences Are Not Clear

What if it were against the law to speed, but the police never gave out tickets? How many people would speed? Without a clearly defined consequence that teens know in advance, boundaries have no power.

Teens Are Not Involved in the Process

If parents overfunction, teens will underfunction. When it comes to boundaries, that may mean not following the rules. Only if teens are completely resistant to helping formulate boundaries should parents put a plan together without discussing and getting their children's input.

Parents Don't Follow Through with the Consequences

When parents say one thing but do another it sends mixed messages. Teens get confused and they learn that they can't trust what their parents say.

The Plans Are Too Long and Confusing

For a new boundary plan to work, it must be short, simple and to the point. Remember: teens for the most part have short attention spans (especially when talking about boundaries, so you want to get right into it. Charts are great for visual learners or hands-on learners while for auditory learners writing down the boundaries and consequences works well.

Parents Believe That Discipline Is Cruel or Unloving

So many adults, having experienced the sergeant attitude from their own parents, grew up thinking that discipline is cruel, strict, unfair or unloving. But there is a *big* difference between a rigid and unyielding approach to rules and the inside-out approach. Children and teens desperately need discipline. I believe it is more cruel for parents to allow their teens to be undisciplined and irresponsible than to set up clear and fair boundaries and consequences so that they can learn how to be responsible and independent.

Parents Believe They Are Responsible for *Their Teen Instead of* to *Their Teen*

If parents feel responsible for their teen, they tend to experience intense anger or anxiety if they see their teen making a poor choice. Teens often find this reaction very annoying. In response, teens are likely to do exactly the opposite of what the parent wants.

Modelling Boundaries: The Walters Family

When the Walters family came to me, the parents were concerned about some of their children's habits, in particular their swearing. As we began to negotiate an inappropriate language policy for the family, one source of the kids' frustration became clear. They were being asked not to swear, while their father regularly used the "S" word and dropped the "F" bomb all of the time. The parents agreed that the new rule would apply to everyone in the family. (They also agreed to their kids' request that the slang word "friggin'" be considered acceptable.) Then they brainstormed consequences. The family decided that each time someone used inappropriate language, they would have to put one dollar in the "swear jar." At the end of each month, the Walters would donate this money to a favourite charity. After three weeks, they'd collected a considerable amount for charity, the swearing was down, and the teens were so encouraged by their parents' participation that they asked if there were other boundaries that they might establish for the whole family. Mr. and Mrs. Walters admitted that they were not great at putting away their things and keeping their bedroom tidy, even though they were asking their teens to do these tasks themselves. They agreed that these would now be family boundaries. The Walters teens, once extremely reluctant to accept the idea of a boundary plan, were now wholeheartedly on board.

Dr. Karyn's Recommended Teen Boundaries

People often ask me what basic rules and expectations I would recommend for teens and their families. Obviously the needs of each family are different, but here are some boundaries that I've seen be very helpful. (Remember: most of these can be established with your children well before the teen years.)

Communication Boundaries
Be Honest

Make honesty the number-one value in your home. Honour this value. Model this value.

Don't Interrupt

Make interrupting unacceptable. Too often I see children or teens interrupt their parents. When parents respond to their teens after an interruption, they are indirectly teaching, "It's okay to interrupt people." Instead, I suggest you say in a loving way, "Sweetheart, you've just interrupted me. I'll talk with you when I'm done." Also tell your teen that if you interrupt them, they can say to you, "Mom, you just interrupted me."

Cindy's Story

Cindy, age 17, came to see me because she wanted to become more disciplined with her school work. But as we talked it became clear that she lacked discipline and the ability to set boundaries in almost every area of her life:

- She was sexually active with her boyfriend even though she felt too young
- She was not doing school work
- She was regularly overeating
- She was spending her entire paycheque within two days of receiving it

During one of our sessions I asked her about what kind of rules her parents had set for her. She admitted that they hadn't established any, but she clearly needed them. "Can we bring them in here for you to help them set some up for me? I think it would really help," she said. Her parents were shocked that their teen daughter was asking for them to set up boundaries. But Cindy knew she needed her parents' help to develop her own self-discipline. Over a number of months, addressing one issue at a time, we set up boundaries; Cindy stopped having sex with her boyfriend, improved her school marks and began to save money. Cindy's story was not entirely typical—she was extremely motivated to change—but it does illustrate how desperately teens need boundaries, and also how they will thrive with them, given the right approach.

Honour Confidentiality

Both teens and parents should always keep their word. If you say you won't tell anyone, you should honour the secret unless the person confiding is going to hurt themselves or someone else.

Apologize

If they have hurt another person, parents and teens should apologize. You can teach children this skill at a very young age. But just saying sorry is not enough. Make it mandatory to say *why* you are sorry: "I'm sorry because . . ."

Don't Call Names

Often parents ask me if name calling is normal among siblings. Would most parents tolerate physical abuse among their teens? Of course not! So raise the bar and apply the same non-negotiable boundary to verbal abuse or name calling. I've talked with many teens who struggle with low self-esteem because their siblings called them "fat," "ugly," or "stupid." Verbal abuse is damaging and as parents it is our responsibility to make sure our family provides a safe and respectful environment for each member of the family.

Say Please and Thank You

It's best to start teaching this basic tenet of good manners to children when they are very young. And it's easy to let this boundary lapse when the kids grow old. But don't! Teens and parents should always say please and thank you.

Say "I"

Children, preteens and teens, like their parents, should use the "I" technique. Rather than saying, "You make me mad," encourage them to say "I feel mad."

School Boundaries

Be Responsible for Getting Up

By grade five or six, preteens can be fully responsible for getting themselves up in the morning, setting their alarms and, if necessary, getting their things ready the night before. Think about getting your preteen an alarm clock for his or her birthday to mark the new responsibility.

Develop a Homework Routine

By grade seven, most preteens are capable of developing a homework routine for themselves. They should be able to delay gratification, get their homework done on time and keep a schedule. Their parents should be moving from managing to partnering with them. It's a good habit for preteens and teens to do their school work first, then enjoy their free time in the evening.

Money Boundaries

Set Up Bank Accounts

I recommend that by grades four to six children have their own bank accounts for their spending money. It should be in their own name and they should manage it, rather than have their parents take control of it. Parents should show them how to make deposits, how to make withdrawals and even how to balance a chequebook. This money should be *their* money to do with as they please. They should also be responsible for buying gifts for other people, as well as anything that they want for themselves. Parents can offer to teach teens how to start saving a percentage, but I do not recommend that parents make this mandatory. Sometimes teens need to learn the hard way: if they spend all their money quickly, they might find themselves wishing they hadn't. Children and teens need to learn the value of money as early as possible. Once they have a limit (see below) and their own money, they often start learning very quickly.

Set Limits

Parents should talk with their preteens and teens about who is paying for what. Will parents pay for all of the teens' clothes or just what is needed (with teens paying for the extras)? Is there a dollar limit to be spent by the parents on individual items, with teens chipping in if they want a more expensive article? How will entertainment spending be handled? Car expenses for young drivers? Will an allowance be provided? Discuss, brainstorm and figure out clear spending boundaries, then put all decisions in writing.

Physical Boundaries

I think privacy is extremely important in families. Teens should not snoop in their parents' room or through their parents' belongings. Nor should they take things from their siblings' rooms without asking. Parents also need to follow this privacy boundary as it relates to their teens' rooms and possessions. If parents do decide that they may need to "break privacy," perhaps as a consequence for certain teen behaviours, they should let their teens know in advance under what circumstances their privacy privilege might be taken away. Everyone in the family should knock and *wait* for a welcoming response before entering a room.

Contributing Boundaries

I feel strongly that children, preteens and teens should have responsibilities that benefit the whole family. Parents often tell me that the chores their teen is doing are things like cleaning his bedroom, but this only benefits the child himself. I recommend that parents make a list of all the things that need to get done in the house and have the kids sign up for the jobs. Be clear on how long you anticipate each task taking and when it needs to be completed.

As children get older, they can handle more responsibility. For example, an eight-year-old should not be cutting the grass but she could help water the plants or feed the dog. I recommend that by grade nine, teens should help out with laundry. They can be responsible for getting dirty clothes to the laundry room. They can be taught how to use the washer and dryer and how to clean their clothes that need special care (like handwashing). You may want to make them responsible for doing some of the family laundry, or folding and delivering it to bedrooms. By grades eight or nine, teens should be learning how to cook and possibly even making one meal a week for the family.

Media Boundaries

Families should establish reasonable limits around television. While every family will have a different limit, if there are no limits at all, we tend to get lazy and watch whatever comes on TV. Having limits forces us to prioritize what we do with our time.

While the Internet is an amazing tool and resource, it does hold dangers. For that reason, I suggest we treat using it the same way we treat driving a car—as a privilege, not a right. All privileges come with responsibilities. Family members using the Internet should not be

- giving out personal information (pictures, addresses, etc.)
- talking to strangers
- online beyond a predetermined amount of time per day or per week
- online after a certain time in the evening
- viewing certain types of material (e.g., pornography, violence, etc.)

I also suggest that the computer be left in a central part of the home (most experts advise not allowing teens to have computers in their rooms).

Emotional Boundaries

Expression

All members of a family should be encouraged to express their anger or other emotions in words (e.g., "I'm angry" or "I'm sad") rather than acting it out (e.g., slamming doors, screaming, etc.). All family members should feel free to cry or voice their pain so that they don't feel burdened to keep it inside.

Parking

Parents, children and teens should all use the park it technique if they are not in a good emotional place (i.e., too angry) to talk. This is healthy anger management.

Sexual Boundaries

Encourage your teens to think about what qualities they are looking for in a partner and what their values are concerning physical intimacy. You can't determine sexual boundaries for them, but you can ask them to establish some for themselves.

While you can't control whether your child becomes sexually active or not, you can put limits on what happens in your home.

Eating Boundaries

Research done by the National Center on Addiction and Substance Abuse (CASA) in 2005 at Columbia University tells us that the more often families eat together (rather than alone or in front of the TV), the less likely kids are to

- smoke
- drink
- do drugs
- get depressed
- develop eating disorders
- consider suicide
- say there is tension in their family

The research also tells us that children who eat meals with their families are more likely to

- delay gratification
- delay having sex
- eat their vegetables
- have stronger vocabularies
- know which fork to use
- think their parents are proud of them
- get A's and B's in school

I definitely recommend eating at the family table. If, however, your teens resist, preferring to eat alone or in their rooms, find out why. Are they being excluded from dinner table conversation? Do they get cut off? Do they not like the food being served? Be an inside-out parent and get your teens to help you create a family dinner experience that everyone can enjoy.

I also suggest that only a limited amount of junk food be available. If it's in the house, it is tempting for teens and adults to eat more of it than they should.

Relational Boundaries

And perhaps the most important rule of all—be responsible to your children. I encourage parents to adopt the thinking, "I am responsible *to* my teen." When parents think this way, they focus on what they can control and are motivated to learn new skills by reading books, going to seminars and so on. Their anxiety about parenting is reduced and their sense of empowerment goes up.

Providing Structure vs. Scheduling

As I mentioned at the beginning of the chapter, teens, just like all of us, benefit from a life that has structure with flexibility. In my list of recommended boundaries, I've included a number of things that help to provide structure for teens—family meals, chores, laundry, meal preparation, media boundaries, homework expectations and morning routines. The Focus sections "Teen Sleep and Nighttime Routines," "Money Management, Allowance and Work" and "Eating and Eating Disorders" also discuss in detail how boundaries can provide necessary structure for teens. Many of us, however, confuse schedules and planned itineraries for structure. Routines, expectations and boundaries help keep us organized, focused and responsible. They provide security and predictable outcomes for our behaviour and actions. Scheduling, however, just keeps us busy. And if the scheduling is done for us, the way it is for many children and teens by their parents, we learn nothing about

Driving and Boundaries

When a teen gets his driver's license, it's a big move towards independence. No longer does he need mom or dad to pick him up, although he
may still need to borrow the family car. Yet all teens are different. Some
can't wait to get their licence when they turn 16, others put off driving
for years, or may never learn to drive. I recommend that parents let their
teens move at their own pace. But when teens are ready to drive, there
are a number of issues that should be discussed and resolved:

- Who pays for the driving lessons? The driving test?
- Who pays for the insurance?
- Who pays for gas? How is it calculated?
- Can they use the family car?
- If they get a speeding or parking ticket, who pays for this?
- How often can they use the car in a week? And when?
- Do they need to do anything to earn the use of the car? Run
  errands? Pick up siblings?
- Can they have friends in the car? How many?
- Are there certain locations they cannot go? Highways? City?
- What happens if they show signs of irresponsible or
  dangerous driving?

When I got my licence as a teen, I had to pay for the driving test, my
gas use, and any speeding or parking tickets that I got. My parents
offered to pay for the insurance (since we were on a family plan). After
a couple of bad accidents (I was not a strong driver at first), my father
sat me down and said, "Honey, I know that you're a good driver but at
times you've been careless and other times you've had very bad luck
with weather. I just want you to know that if you get one more speeding
ticket or accident, you'll have to be taken off our family insurance plan
and get your own insurance because our rates are going up too much
because of your accidents." He said this lovingly but also set a clear
boundary. I realized that if I was taken off the family insurance plan, I

wouldn't be able to afford my own policy and therefore would not be able to drive. Since that conversation all those years ago, I've had a perfect driving record!

If your teens decide not to get their licence, make sure that you nevertheless establish rules about their transportation. Set a limit on how much driving you will do for them, how much notice you need and when they need to take a bus. If they are going to take taxis, be clear who will be paying for them.

Boundaries Instead of Anger

When parents feel intense anger or anxiety, it's usually because a boundary has been crossed, whether they realize it or not. I often tell parents, "Acknowledge your anger but don't focus on it because you can't control it." Instead, examine what has made you angry. If there is no boundary in the family about the behaviour in question, or if there has been no reasonable consequence set out for breaking the boundary, work on establishing a boundary and a reasonable consequence. Reserve your energy for discussing the boundary and following through with it in the future. Setting boundaries is simply the best way to manage your anger and anxiety.

how to manage our time and our responsibilities.

When I ask parents to think about the big picture or to identify their primary goal as parents, one of the most common responses I get is, "I want my teen to be balanced; to lead a balanced life." But statistics suggest that this is one goal that North American parents are failing to achieve—for themselves and for their children. In the last 20 years, the time families spend together during weekdays has decreased by 45 minutes a day. Children's participation in structured sports has increased by 50 percent and time spent on unstructured children's activities has dropped by the same rate.

It's important to note that there are good reasons why parents have encouraged kids to be involved in organized sports and other extracurricular activities. A 1998/99 Statistics Canada report noted that, on average, 87 percent of Canadian children ages four to 15 participated in organized sports or activities outside of school. Younger children who were involved in extracurricular activities showed fewer difficulties in math or reading and stronger social skills than those who did not participate. For preteens and teens between the ages of 12 and 15, those involved in organized activities reported higher self-esteem, had fewer difficulties with friends and were less likely to smoke than those teens who did not participate. (The report pointed out, however, that more research is needed to determine if there is any cause-and-effect relationship between activities and outcomes.) And of course, parents' concern for their children's physical health has led many to involve their kids in organized sports.

But the downside of all these planned activities is that for many middle- and upper-middle-class families, spare time is almost nonexistent, with every waking hour planned and scheduled. An overly structured or unbalanced life can be stressful for anyone, but it is particularly tough for teens who are struggling to gain some independence, and discover what they want from life.

Fiona came to see me with her mother. She was in grade nine, and from the outside she seemed like the perfect teen. She had straight A's in school, was well liked, had many friends and was highly involved in her school. But what people didn't know was that Fiona struggled with anxiety and panic attacks. During attacks she found it difficult to breathe, became dizzy and would shake. She had trouble sleeping and concentrating. She bottled up most of her feelings and worked hard to maintain her picture-perfect image. As I got to know Fiona, I learned some very important facts. She was involved in four different extracurricular activities, some of which required two to three meetings each week. When I asked her mom how many hours of extracurricular activities Fiona had per week, she said "only 10 or 12." But Fiona and her Mom weren't accounting for the time it took to get ready, to drive to and from the activities or to unwind when Fiona got home. When we added it all up, Fiona's extracurricular activities took more like 20 or 25 hours—all on top of a full-time school schedule. No wonder Fiona was suffering from anxiety! She was completely maxed out. What Fiona and her mother had failed to do was to provide a margin in her schedule.

Building Margin into Our Daily Lives

In his book *Margin: Restoring Emotional, Physical, Financial and Time Reserves to Overloaded Lives*, Dr. Richard Swenson introduces an extremely useful tool to help people establish more balance in their busy lives. Imagine a piece of ordinary lined writing paper. On the left side of the sheet is the margin, separated from the rest of the paper by a thin red line. This area is not meant for writing in but if we're running out of space, it's okay to use it. The margin is for emergencies—it's a reserve, an extra. In life, we need a margin as well. Unfortunately, most people live their lives without it, filling in every day from one edge to the next, with no reserves left over.

Let me give you an example. If I asked several close neighbours how long it would take to drive from our homes in Toronto to the airport, some might say 30 minutes; others might say 40. But I'd say one hour. Why? Because it would take only 30 minutes if:

- I hit every green light
- traffic was moving really well
- I didn't get stuck behind a truck
- I was able to find parking right away

In other words, if everything went perfectly, I *might* get there in 30 minutes. But let's be honest—how often does that happen? That extra

30 minutes is the margin, the extra, and it makes a big difference, especially over an entire day. Most of us indulge in too many activities, packing our schedules, buying too much stuff, spending more than we earn and eating more than we need. When we create spending, eating and financial habits without margin, our bodies and emotions pay the price.

We need to build margin into our daily lives. In Fiona's case, I had her complete the following "Five-Step Action Plan." If your teens are feeling overscheduled and overwhelmed, I recommend they do the same. (This strategy works for parents too!)

The Five-Step Action Plan for a Balanced Life

1. **Make a list.** Write out all of the activities you are engaged in or are thinking about signing up for.
2. **Prioritize.** Rank these activities from 1 to 10, based on how important they are to you.
3. **Estimate.** Divide all activities into two categories: optional and non-negotiable. Optional items include such things as sports, student council, drama club and volunteering. Non-negotiable activities include sleeping, eating, school attendance, homework and studying. Estimate the time commitment of all potential activities. Make sure that the time includes a margin—for example, travel to and from the dance lesson or the soccer game.
4. **Create a time chart.** Fill in the slots with the non-negotiable items first. Take a look at how much time is left. (This is usually an "aha!" moment for most people.)
5. **Cut back.** Now comes the tough part. If your goal is emotional and physical health and balance, you may need to cut back on some of your optional activities. Look at how you prioritized your optional activities, how much time each will take and make some choices. You can use the Yes and No technique that I discuss later in this chapter to help you decide what to keep and what to cut.

In Fiona's case, I insisted she see her doctor about the physical aspects of her anxiety. But she was also able to help herself by following the action plan. She decided to drop two of her four commitments. While her mother had reservations about quitting these activities mid-year (and I fully understand the importance of keeping commitments), we all agreed that Fiona's emotional and physical health had to come first.

Keep Some Nights Unscheduled

Too many of us these days are addicted to doing. But we all need time to relax, unwind and just enjoy being. Most children and teens (and adults for that matter) need at least one or two nights a week that are unscheduled (no activities planned). And we have to be careful not to be judgmental about what relaxing looks like. When I worked with Frank, he expressed frustration with his parents because they would yell at him to stop being lazy whenever they found him watching TV. Yet Frank was involved in two different extracurricular activities and worked very hard at school. Television was what he found relaxing, and so I communicated to his parents that I thought it was okay in moderation. As parents, we need to encourage a sense of balance in our kids and that means allowing and even encouraging our teens to take time for themselves. To be honest, this is often a skill that teens don't have difficulty with, so perhaps parents need to learn from them.

The Yes and No Coin

Sometimes it can be very difficult to say no. When someone asks us to volunteer on a project, we may feel guilty if we don't agree to help out. If the school coach approaches us to play on a sports team, we may feel awkward or ungrateful in turning down the invitation. Or we may find it hard to say no to interesting opportunities—recreational, educational or social events—that come our way. For teens who find themselves with too many activities and commitments, I like to introduce them to the "Yes and No Coin" technique. I get them to imagine that yes and no are the words on either side of a coin. Whenever they are saying yes to some-

Time Chart

How do you want to spend your time? Try mapping in your non-negotiable commitments to find out how much time you really have.

	Sun	Mon	Tues	Wed	Thurs	Fri	Sat
1 a.m.							
2 a.m.							
3 a.m.							
4 a.m.							
5 a.m.							
6 a.m.							
7 a.m.							
8 a.m.							
9 a.m.							
10 a.m.							
11 a.m.							
12 noon							
1 p.m.							
2 p.m.							
3 p.m.							
4 p.m.							
5 p.m.							
6 p.m.							
7 p.m.							
8 p.m.							
9 p.m.							
10 p.m.							
11 p.m.							
12 a.m.							

You may want to use colours to give you a good visual. For example:

Orange   school/commuting
Pink   part-time job
Red   miscellaneous errands
Green   volunteer work/school committees
Yellow   exercising
Purple   sleeping
Blue   relaxing (unscheduled)
White   socializing

thing, there is a no "attached" on the other side of the coin—in other words, they are saying no to something else. We are always saying both yes and no when we make choices. I encourage them to look at some of the decisions they have to make using the yes and no model. If they say yes to the school play, what are they saying no to? Maybe it's time for homework or babysitting or free time with friends. Is this okay with them? If they say no to playing in the city hockey league, maybe they can say yes to playing on a school team. Would this be a better option for them?

Once teens realize that they are saying yes and no whenever they make choices, they are able to make better choices for themselves. The Yes and No Coin technique can also be used for decisions concerning spending, eating and other actions.

Teen Routines

Many of the teens I work with are *not* struggling with an overscheduled life, but rather are having trouble completing tasks (like homework) in the ample time they actually have. Some, while appearing to have plenty of time for leisure and sleep, do not seem to be getting the rest and relaxation they need. (See "Focus on Teen Sleep and Nighttime Routines" in this chapter). For many, their problems arise from the routine they have set for themselves.

When I ask teens to break down how they spend their time on an average school day, this is often what I hear:

A Typical Daily Teen Schedule

Up	7 a.m.
School	8 a.m. to 3:30 p.m.
Home	4 p.m.
Nap	4 to 6 p.m.
TV/MSN	6 to 7 p.m.
Dinner	7 to 7:30 p.m.
TV/MSN	7:30 to 9 p.m.
Homework/MSN	9 to 11 p.m.
Bed	11 p.m.

(And sometimes they get up again in the middle of the night for an hour to talk with friends, go online or complete homework.)

There are a number of problems with this schedule.

- Homework time is not focused—they've got the computer, MSN, TV, cellphone, etc. on, which makes it difficult to concentrate. While it might work for some, for many it's an inefficient work habit.
- The majority of teens say they are the most efficient (most alert, most productive) shortly after they get home from school (after a break), usually around 5 p.m. to 7 p.m. But according to this schedule, this is the time they are sleeping or watching TV, rather than doing school work.
- Teens who nap often struggle with falling asleep at night. Unless there is a physical reason to sleep or they are sick, it's far better to get to bed at a good time and have a night of unbroken sleep. We need to take care of our bodies in order to concentrate and work well.
- Doing homework late at night usually doesn't work well for a

number of reasons. First, teens are getting tired so they are not at their most alert or efficient. Also, many teens find it difficult to fall asleep quickly after they've been thinking for the previous few hours. The intellectual effort winds them up, rather than allowing them to unwind. And, of course, late nights mean teens will likely be tired the next morning when they have to get up.

Healthier Schedule

Over the last few years, I've coached hundreds of teens to develop new and better daily habits. I don't dictate any plan (and I would not advise you to either) but rather ask questions to help teens to come up with a routine that achieves the goals of feeling rested, feeling relaxed (feeling that they've got some free time and downtime) and feeling prepared (with all their homework done well).

Here is the most common routine that teens themselves suggest when I'm working with them to set up a better schedule:

Up	7 a.m.
School	8 a.m. to 3:30 p.m.
Home	4 p.m.
Relax	4 to 5 p.m.
Focused Homework Time (media-free)★	5 to 7 p.m.
Dinner	7 to 7:30 p.m.
Free time	7:30 to 10 p.m.
Bed	10 to 11 p.m.

★ media-free requirements:
- no computer (otherwise MSN automatically comes on)
- no cellphone (not even on vibrate)
- no land-line phone calls (other family members can take messages)

I don't suggest that you make your teens adopt this plan. As I've said many times, it's important that you don't overfunction for your children. Instead suggest that they develop a schedule for themselves. You can show them the routine above to get them thinking about their own schedules and what might help them feel rested, relaxed and prepared. Or you can ask them if they'd like to try this routine to see how it feels after a few days. When schedules are presented as a "trial period," teens are often more willing to try them.

Media-Free Time

If teens struggle with being self-disciplined and focused, I sometimes recommend this strategy. As parents, you can't make your child be a motivated student, but you can help to create a school-friendly environment. One of the ways to do this is to make homework easier to complete by making media-free time in the home. Find out how much time your children think they will need to do their homework on an average night. I find that most teens say between one to three hours. Then establish that amount of time each evening or after school as media free. During that time there should be no phone use (cell or otherwise), no television or radio, no music and no MSN or other computer chat networks. If teens are having trouble observing the media-free boundary, brainstorm with them about possible consequences if they break the rule. In my practice, many teens have suggested that their parents take their cellphones away from them until the media-free period is over. When they are used to the new routine, they will likely have the self-discipline to turn off their phones without their parents' interference.

The Benefits of Boundaries and Structure

A family that operates with clear boundaries and structures, with expectations and consequences that are understood and accepted by all members, and with schedules and routines that support everyone's physical and mental health, enjoys many benefits. Conflict, confusion and anxiety are reduced because everyone knows what is expected of them. Boundaries also allow parents to focus on what they can control and accept what they cannot control. Once clear rules are in place, parents tend to feel less anxiety (even when their teen is making poor choices) because they know that they have provided appropriate guidance, even if their teen is not following it (they are responsible to their teen not for their teen). What's more, if the process for establishing the boundaries is a collaborative process with parents and teens, parents can improve parenting skills and their teens feel safe to give them feedback.

Teens benefit from the process too. They learn how to stand up for themselves and voice their opinion. They recognize that they are allowed to believe different things than others, including their parents. As a result, they have no problem voicing what they value and believe to their friends. Teens also feel invested in the boundary plan and are more likely to follow it (and less likely to lie about their actions and behaviour) because they believe it is reasonable and fair. And when teens are contributing to the work of maintaining family life, they often have stronger self-esteem as a result. In addition, the family feels united as a team and there is a strong sense of belonging because everyone is helping out. (And a sense of belonging is one of the core variables of a healthy self-esteem.) I firmly believe that establishing boundaries and providing structure is essential to creating harmonious family life that makes everyone, both parents and teens, feel happy and respected.

Sample Boundary Plans
Plan A: Jason, 15 Years Old
Jason was a motivated student and had some great friends. But he was constantly asking his parents for money, swearing when he got angry (which was often) and did little to contribute to the family. His parents' response was to nag him (in other words, overfunction), which

only made him angry and avoid his parents. Here are boundaries that they negotiated with Jason:

EXPECTATIONS	WHEN	REWARD	CONSEQUENCE
CHORES			
Bedroom Every day I need to make my bed and put away all my clothes.	Everyday before school	$ 20/per week allowance	$ 2/per day that my room is not organized
Bathrooms Clean toilets, sink, mirrors, bathtub	Weekly. Anytime on Saturday or Sunday.		$5 if not done, done late or not completed
Garbage Collect garbage in bathrooms, kitchen, living room, family room, bedrooms.	Must be collected by 10 p.m. Tuesday and put at the curb by 8 a.m. Wednesday		$5 if not done, done late or not completed
MONEY			
Clothes My parents will pay for my clothes but I am responsible for all my spending money (e.g., gifts, fast food, enter- tainment, movies, etc.)	Ongoing	Same as above	
Cellphone My parents will pay for my basic cellphone package ($30/month) but I need to pay for anything beyond that.			If I don't have enough money to pay the overtime on my cell phone, my parents will take my cellphone until I can pay them back
Allowance It will be given weekly by 7 p.m. Friday			

EXPECTATIONS	WHEN	REWARD	CONSEQUENCE
LANGUAGE			
I must not swear or use offensive language, including the "s" and "f" words, "ugly" and "stupid."	Ongoing	Same as above	$ 1/ for every off-limit word

Here are the results of Jason's first three weeks working with the new boundaries:

Week 1:   Jason received $5 of his allowance.
Week 2:   Jason received $12 of his allowance.
Week 3:   Jason received $18 of his allowance.

Not only did this plan radically reduce the conflict between Jason and his parents—also, his parents functioned less and nagged less, Jason functioned more and contributed more, stopped swearing almost completely and started managing his money.

Plan B: Michelle, 16 Years Old

Michelle's mother described her as "angry, unappreciative and irresponsible," while Michelle described her mother as "controlling and annoying, constantly treating me like a child." All of their issues, however, stemmed from a lack of boundaries around friends, cellphones, motivation and curfew. Instead of establishing boundaries, Michelle's mother was micromanaging her daughter, which was making Michelle angry and causing her to feel suffocated. The boundary plan they came up with addressed the things that her mother could control. (See "Friends and Peer Pressure" in Chapter 1 for advice I gave Michelle's mom about how to respond to Michelle's choice of friends.)

EXPECTATIONS	WHEN	REWARD	CONSEQUENCE
Media-Free Time			
Every day I will have media-free time to encourage me do my homework. During this time I am not allowed to have a cellphone, music, TV or Internet.	Sunday–Thursday, 7–9 p.m.	Use of Cellphone	No cellphone until the full 2 hours of media-free time is completed.
Cellphone			
Mom bought the cellphone and will pay for the $25 basic plan. But I am responsible for anything over $25 per month	Monthly	Use of cellphone	I need to pay for anything over $25 per month. If I can't pay, my phone will be taken away until I have it.
Curfew			
I will arrive home no later than 1 a.m.	Friday and Saturday	Freedom to stay out until 1 a.m.	For every minute that I'm late I will have double that amount deducted my curfew the following Friday or Saturday. So if I'm 15 minutes late, I need to come home 30 minutes earlier than usual.

Here are the results for Michelle's first three weeks of working with the new boundaries:

Week #1:   Michelle lost her cellphone privilege for two days. She read during most of her media-free time rather than doing her homework. She had to come home two hours early on Saturday evening.

Week #2:   Michelle started dabbling into her homework during media-free time. She lost her cellphone privileges for only one day.

Week #3:   Michelle started actually doing more of her homework during media-free time. She said, "After all, I might as well."

Note. Because Michelle had a long history of being extremely late for her curfew, her mom decided to make the curfew boundary more strict. However, after Michelle showed tremendous improvement over the next few months, her mom loosened this boundary.

The conflict immediately started to decrease once Michelle and her mother began discussing boundaries. Michelle's mom stopped much of her controlling behaviour and talked with Michelle instead, asking questions and listening. Michelle said that her relationship with her mom became positive and encouraging. Over a six-month period, as this plan became second nature for Michelle, her academic average went from the low 60s to the high 70s, and most importantly, her effort went from a C/D to a B.

Focus on Money Management, Allowance and Work

In a world in which consumer bankruptcies are on the rise, easy credit proliferates and personal savings are at a low, one of the most important lessons any parents can teach their teen is how to manage money. But how do we do that? There are a number ways to help our children develop financial responsibility but at the heart of all them is this simple truth: *Teens don't learn money management unless they are actually the ones managing the money.*

I met Matthew when he was 17 and in grade twelve. He explained to me that his parents were nagging him to save for university, but he admitted that he spent all his money on electronic gadgets and fast food. Matthew's mother had therefore insisted that he give her all his paycheques. This rule was causing an enormous amount of conflict between them. Matthew felt his parents were controlling, annoying and unfair, while his parents thought Matthew was irresponsible, unappreciative and disrespectful.

When I asked Matthew's mother about the rule, she expressed concern about his university savings, and also said that by handing over his paycheque, Matthew was learning money management. But of course, Matthew was learning nothing, except that his mother wanted to take control. I recommended that Matthew be responsible for his own money, but that his parents be clear about what they would pay for and what he would need to pay for. They decided that they would pay for his room and tuition at university but he would be responsible for all his spending money, books and the $2,000 deposit due in the middle of the summer. I advised Matthew's parents to put this all in writing, and to point out that if Matthew didn't have the $2,000 saved, he would not be able to go to university that year. I suggested that if teens cannot show enough responsibility to save a small percentage towards their tuition, then they are probably not ready or responsible enough to be at university.

By setting this boundary, the parents were able to pull back, the conflict was reduced and the mom no longer felt as anxious (although she was concerned about whether or not he would save the money).

To the surprise of both of his parents by the due date of August 1, Matthew had his $2,000.

Matthew's story is a perfect example of the kind of financial responsibility most teens can take when they are given the chance. And many teens can master this skill much earlier. I recommend five basic strategies that allow teens to learn about money by handling their own financial affairs.

Give an Allowance

But what if your child isn't ready to earn money outside the home? How do they learn money management skills? An allowance is the answer.

I suggest that by the time children are between nine and 11 years old, they be given an allowance. The size of the allowance might depend on what you can afford, what you are expecting them to pay for, what you expect them to save, the work they are expected to do for the money and their age. There is a lot of disagreement among parenting experts and parents themselves about whether that money needs to be earned or not, but I don't recommend that parents give an allowance if their children don't have to do anything for it. Most adults I know don't get cheques in the mail for doing nothing, so giving kids money they don't earn doesn't prepare them for the real world.

As I outlined earlier in this chapter, all boundaries, including those that have to do with money, should be discussed in advance by parents and teens. It's important for parents to listen to their teens' input and then figure out together a plan that's reasonable and makes sense for everyone.

Here are a few allowance guidelines:

Be Clear About What Chores Teens Need To Do

As well as identifying the chore, outline how you want it done. Establish what kind of deduction teens can expect from their allowance (the consequence) if the chore isn't completed.

Make Sure the Deadline Is Clear

Clear time expectations are extremely helpful for teens, as they don't like to be told that they have to do something *right now*. Give them a time window and a final time deadline for all chores.

Make Sure That the Allowance Is Reasonable Given What Your Teen Is Doing To Earn It

I coached a family whose daughter was receiving $100 a week allowance for cleaning her room, which took her about two hours. Her parents wondered why she wasn't motivated to get a part-time job, but since she was making $50 an hour, their daughter didn't have a lot of interest in working for minimum wage. It's wise to make the allowance relative to how much work your teens are doing so that they get a good understanding of the value of a dollar.

Make Sure That Your Teens' Chores Do Not Just Benefit Them

If the only chore teens have is to clean their room or their bathroom, then the benefit is just for them. Since parents do many things that help their kids, it's important that parents get their teens to do chores that benefit the entire family (e.g., cooking a family meal, putting out garbage, vacuuming, etc.). I usually recommend that parents make up a list of all the tasks that need to get done in a week or a month and then have their kids take turns picking which job they are going to be responsible for.

Make Sure That Each Chore Is Solely the Teen's Responsibility

When teens share jobs it can create a lot of conflict. For example, if Susan and Adam do dishes on alternate nights, there is plenty of opportunity to fight about whose turn it is (especially if there has been any disruption to the weekly schedule). There is less chance of confusion and disagreement if teens fully own their jobs (e.g., Adam does the dishes and Susan collects garbage).

Make Sure You Put Everything In Writing

All boundaries work better if you outline the details in writing (see sample boundary plans in this chapter). This step is extremely important if you've got a teen who learns visually or is a hands-on learner.

Be Clear About When Teens Receive Their Allowance

Pick a payday and stick to it; you want to create a routine. In choosing the day, you may want to consider which days of the week you know both you and your teen will be home, and which days you can most easily get to the bank or cash machine. Many families find Friday works well as teens then have money for the weekend. Sometimes the calmer atmosphere of Sunday works best. (In extreme cases, when teens claim they have not received their allowance or there is a history of confusion about payments, I've actually suggested that parents pay by cheque so it can be tracked, or that teens sign some sort of receipt when they get paid.)

Keep a Record of How Teens Are Doing with Their Responsibilities

You'll probably find that you need to do this only at the beginning. Once families get into the routine, the written plan will not be nearly as crucial. (Remember: It takes three weeks to break a habit and three weeks to make a habit. So usually the first six weeks are the most difficult until everyone gets into their new routine.)

Be Positive and Affirming

If you constantly tell your teens that they are not doing a good enough job at their chores, you are going to discourage them. If they have not done a chore to your standard, use the hamburger technique. Start positive. Show them the parts that they missed. End positive. Give them 30 minutes (a time frame) to improve their effort so that they can get their full allowance. You want to encourage, empower and step back. A critical spirit will destroy this process.

Be Clear About What Their Allowance Is Supposed To Pay For

Should your teens pay for their own clothes? For birthday gifts? Is their allowance intended to be their spending money for movies and other social expenses? Do they pay for their own cellphones? If parents are paying for everything, there is a good chance teens won't be motivated to do their chores because they don't really need the money.

Revisit the Plan

I recommend that, after two weeks or so, families take some time to figure out what's working and what's not. Again, use the hamburger technique to discuss any problems. Listen to what your teens think is working and what they think needs to be changed. On average, it takes three tries before families find the right plan.

There are some parents who don't like the idea of paying their teen to do jobs that help the family. I can also understand the belief that the running of the household should be a group effort, and that no one should be paid. But too often when I coach families like these, parents are the bank, paying for an endless number of items and activities for their kids (and then wondering why their children are irresponsible with money). The point is that for children and teens to learn money management, they need to have the opportunity to earn money as well as manage it. Until kids have jobs outside the home, an allowance given for doing chores provides a good way for teens to have some money of their own.

Set Up Bank Accounts

Having and using a bank account is a great way for kids to start honing their money management skills. There is nothing like seeing a record of deposits and withdrawals to show how you are saving and how you are spending. I recommend that by grades four to six children have their own bank account in their name for their spending money. (But if you haven't started your teens with bank accounts when they were this young, it's not too late to start.) This bank account should in no way be managed by the parents—your kids should be able to use the money in whatever way they want (keeping in mind my earlier advice that you need to establish what things you expect your children to buy for themselves). If you've got financial investments for your children, keep those in a separate account. Only by allowing teens to be fully responsible for their own money, can we help them to develop their financial skills.

I also encourage parents to offer to teach teens how to start saving a percentage of their allowance or earnings, but I do not recommend that parents make this mandatory. Sometimes kids need to learn the hard way that when they spend all their money quickly, they may wish they hadn't. But you can ask them if they would like two accounts— one for spending money and one for savings. If the kids choose to have a separate savings account, show them which type of account can offer the most interest, explain the different rules and requirements of the different accounts (e.g., many savings accounts limit the number of withdrawals each month) and encourage them to check their balances to see how their money grows.

Talk About How Much Things Cost

Chris had grown up in a privileged family, with private schools, trips around the world, and a large allowance for doing nothing. His parents, although they loved him very much, were constantly providing the easy way out for him. If he did poorly on a project, his mother would complain to the teacher. If he was late doing an assignment, one of his parents would often finish it to make sure he didn't lose marks. As a result, Chris suffered from low self-esteem (see Chapter 2 for a discussion of overfunctioning and low self-esteem), had absolutely no discipline or drive and was in constant conflict with his parents.

At 18, Chris quit school and moved out of the house. Shortly after that, I started to work with him and I learned that he wanted to finish school. When I asked him what kind of life he wanted for himself, he said, "I want a lifestyle like the one I grew up in." So I asked him if he knew how much money it took to have that kind of life. He had no

One Parent's Account of a Successful Financial Plan

"When our daughters started high school, we sat down with them and negotiated what we would pay for (all school-related expenses, a flat-rate clothing allowance, family trips) and what they were responsible for (all spending money). We wanted them to make school their priority and, therefore, didn't want them to get part-time jobs during the school year. So we had them make a list of the jobs they would like to be responsible for around the home. We negotiated an allowance. If they did their task by the deadline and by the standard we requested, they would get their full allowance. This allowance not only helped them contribute around the home but also helped them be fully responsible for how they spent their own money. Now since our girls had a limited amount of money, they were very careful about finding the best deal. Although it was difficult at times sticking to this boundary and saying no, I really see how it has helped my daughters in the big picture."

idea. I asked him if he knew how his parents provided that kind of life-style. He had no idea. And then he said, "To be honest, money is a taboo word in my family. I have no idea how much my parents make or how much most things cost." Chris had very little sense of money reality. I recommended that he make a list of questions to ask his parents.

Chris was surprised by how open his mother was to talking about money. She discussed the financial struggles she and Chris's father had had when they first got married. She explained how they had to budget, and how she and his dad both climbed the corporate ladder. And she shared with him how much money they needed to pay for their current lifestyle. Chris later said to me, "It's weird. My parents always preached at me about how important education was but I've always heard of those high school dropouts that are millionaires and I just figured that would be me. But now I realize my parents got ahead by working really hard and getting higher education." Chris remained to living on his own, but continued to work on his relationship with his parents, and the following year he finally graduated from high school and applied to several college and universities.

Money can be one of those interesting topics in families. Some families talk too much about money—for example, parents who repeatedly complain about a lack of money, stress and burden their children and teens. In other families, any talk about money is taboo. I encourage parents to talk about money in healthy ways that are age-appropriate. You don't have to disclose the details of your financial situation but rather help your children understand the cost range of both the necessities and luxuries of modern life. You can make a game out of it to see how much they already know. Ask them how much they think these things cost per month: mortgage, car, insurance, gas, food, cellphones, holidays, cable, Internet access. When teens have a sense of the amount of money it takes to run a household, they are more likely to understand the kind of financial decisions that get made in the family and are better prepared for their own money management.

Set Boundaries Regarding Who Pays for What

It's important that teens know what they will be expected to pay for and what their parents are going to cover. Like all boundaries, this is one that is best negotiated between parents and teens. In some cases, who pays for what really becomes an exercise in spending decisions. For example, if parents find that constant negotiations over the purchase of expensive clothing items is becoming a strain for everyone, they may propose a clothing allowance—a certain amount of money per month or season that will be given to their teens to buy all of their clothes. With a clothing allowance, parents should partner with teens by teaching them about shopping for bargains and assessing what clothes they need. But in the end, if the teen decides he would rather have one very expensive hoodie instead of two more moderately priced ones, that becomes *his* decision. Spending on entertainment or going out with friends are other areas that work well as teen responsibilities. It's also an excellent idea to encourage teens to earn their own money (or get creative making things) for gifts. (Nothing is a better example of the overfunctioning parent than the parent who gives her teens money so they can go off and buy their birthday gift for her!) And, if your teen is driving, there are a number of related costs that should also be discussed.

Sharing the Costs

I received the following email from a father:

"My wife and I didn't know how motivated our son was to go to university so we discussed a financial arrangement that would require him to make a commitment to his education. We told him we would partner with him on his savings plan: for every $1 he saved towards his education, we would match it. If he saved $4,000, we would give him $4,000. This partnership strengthened our relationship with our son because we no longer felt that we were carrying all the financial burden. It also helped our son get his act together—to focus on what he wanted. Although it took him a couple of years, he did eventually start to save seriously."

Jobs for Teens

I often get asked whether I recommend that teens get part-time or summer jobs. Parents are conflicted—they like the idea of their teens getting work experience and earning their own money, but they worry that working might reduce the energy and focus teens can put into their school work. How do you know if your teens are ready to work? What standards or guidelines should you set about the type of work, or the hours they spend at it?

I'm a strong supporter of young people having part-time jobs. I think working outside the home provides an amazing opportunity for teens to learn many skills (e.g., time management, people skills, money management, etc.). There is no magic age, however, at which kids are

Spending and the Yes and No Coin

Our teens live in a consumer society. Like the rest of us, they are bombarded with advertising, and are offered an unending supply of new products that promise to make life easier and more enjoyable. Before they even have the opportunity to land their first job, they may be spending every penny that comes their way. One good way to help your teens curb overspending is by introducing the no and yes coin technique described earlier in this chapter. For every purchase they want to make, suggest that they identify the thing or activity they will now not be able to afford (the no on the other side of the yes they want to say to the new purchase). Remind them that long-term goals are also on the other side of that no and yes coin. If they are saying no to a new pair of earrings, it doesn't necessarily mean they are going to have enough money to say yes to the ski trip, but the cost of the earrings could certainly go towards the trip instead, increasing the chances that they will have the money to go eventually.

ready to work. If your teens voice an interest in working, talk with them about your concerns and expectations. Make it clear that school has to be a priority and that if their marks, or their health, begin to suffer because of the work hours they are putting in, the job may have to go. You may want to establish boundaries around work: no late evenings on school nights, for example, or weekends only. If your teens are involved in a lot of extracurricular activities, they may want to consider working only in the summer and saving a significant portion of their earnings for spending money throughout the year. You may also want to negotiate the types of jobs your teens might do—do you want to rule out jobs in which the teens are required to work alone or in isolated locations in the evenings or at night, for example? You should also discuss transportation to and from work: will you be driving, will your teens drive or will they be required to bus, bike or walk?

What if your teens have not expressed any interest in working? If

FOCUS ON *Money Management, Allowance and Work*

they have a great number of after-school commitments—sports, music lessons, volunteer work and so on—and are learning time and financial management without paid work, a job may not be necessary or advisable. But if you are concerned that their motivation, work ethic, sense of responsibility and money management skills are not developing, you *should* ask yourself why your teens don't have the drive to earn their own money. Could it be that you are paying them $100 a week to clean their rooms? Or buying them everything on their wish list? Remember, as parents you can overfunction in many ways—including financially. Creating an environment in which teens can take financial responsibility for themselves in some way is not only the best way to teach money management—it's also a great self-esteem booster.

Card Tricks

There was a time when getting credit was no easy task. Employment records or income statements had to be produced, detailed risk assessments had to be undertaken. These days, however, credit is being offered to almost everyone, regardless of income or age. University and even high school students are often targeted by the card companies. Retailers, banks, financial institutions, payday loan and cheque-cashing companies are also happy to loan money—making it increasingly easy for us to get in over our heads.

We should acquire and use credit only once we have learned how to manage our money, budget, delay gratification and resist overspending. We also must first understand thoroughly how the credit system works (e.g., penalties and interest payments on credit cards, credit ratings and so on). For these reasons, many teens (and many adults for that matter) are not ready for credit cards.

But we live in a plastic age. Trips to the bank are time consuming and often inconvenient (and there are fewer and fewer neighbourhood branches around). If your teens have their own bank accounts, debit cards may be the answer. Before your teens arrange for a card, however, encourage them to find out all of the rules and fees involved in using their cards. If your teen does need a credit card for some reason, a prepaid credit card (on which the holder has to make a deposit and can charge no more than the balance on the card) is the best idea.

If you do allow your teens to use your credit card for some reason, make sure that you are repaid within a time frame that will allow you to make your payment to the credit card company on time. Agree in advance what the fine or interest penalty will be for your teens if their payment is late. Setting up boundaries is critical for them to learn how credit cards operate.

Educate your teen about credit card costs and the importance of your credit rating. Be aware of the financial services that target cash-starved teens and young adults, and educate your children about costs involved in using cheque-cashing companies and pay-day loans. (A recent report from Statistics Canada noted that loans from cheque-cashing and payday loan companies come at a very steep price—hidden fees and the interest charged for the transactions was the equivalent of between 335 percent and 650 percent per year—well outside the legal lending limit set out in Canada's criminal code!

Talk to your kids about the interest penalties and hidden costs in such retail offers as "Don't Pay for a Year" or "Rent to Own." Let them know that even if a financial institution or retailer wants to lend them money, it doesn't mean they can afford to borrow. Encourage them to investigate thoroughly all the details and fine print whenever they are being offered credit or delayed payment.

FOCUS ON *Money Management, Allowance and Work*

Money Reality Quiz

A. How much spending money do youth in North America have?

B. How much disposable income does a typical Canadian teen have per week?

C. True or false: People under 25 are one of the fastest-growing groups filing for bankruptcy.

D. According to the American Savings Education Council (ASEC), what percentage of college students and high school students have credit cards?

E. According to the American Savings Education Council (ASEC), what percentage of these students do not pay off their credit cards per month?

F. What percentage of grade twelve students passed a test about basic money management?

Answers:

A. $ 190 billion a year

B. $ 107 (from jobs, gifts, allowances)

C. True

D. 55 percent of college students, 7 percent of high school students

E. Nearly 33 percent

F. 50.2 percent

Focus on Teen Sleep and Nighttime Routines

The sleep habits of teens are almost always baffling for parents. It's just so hard to understand why the little boy who woke you every morning at six whether you liked it or not, will now snooze until the late afternoon if he could. Is it laziness or necessity? And if he's so tired, why won't he go to bed before midnight?

Most parents realize that small children need considerably more sleep than adults do. Until recently, however, most of us assumed that the sleep needs of teens were much closer to those of adults than of young children. Recent research into adolescent sleep patterns, however, suggests that teens need much more sleep to perform optimally and stay alert—9.2 hours on average notes a 1998 study from Brown University Medical School. Adults tend to need only 7.5 to 8 hours.

There may be a number of reasons for this need for sustained sleep. Studies suggest that the production of growth hormones is most intense at the end of a REM (Rapid Eye Movement) cycle of sleep. This stage, however, only comes at intervals after non–REM sleep. During the teen years, when most people are undergoing intense periods of growth, their bodies may need to have more of these REM periods, and therefore more sleep. Also, early adolescence is now known to be a time when there is burst of brain growth and development, which may impact a teen's need for sleep.

But despite evidence that there is a strong biological need for more than 9 hours of sleep a night during adolescence, surveys have found that most teens average only between 7 or 7.5 hours of sleep. Clearly, then, your irritable, monosyllabic teenager may simply be suffering from severe sleep deprivation!

Sleep deprivation affects not only our moods, however, and it should be a concern for all teens and parents. Recent brain research suggests that new knowledge and skills are committed to memory during our REM sleep cycles. So if we don't have enough sleep, we are going to have a tough time learning. Many different studies of academic performance and sleep seem to be bearing this out. What's more, sleep deprivation affects concentration and reaction time, and is cited as the cause of many teen accidents—including driving accidents. Sleep deprivation can also affect motivation and behavioural control, and exacerbate emotional issues and challenges.

But why exactly are teens not getting enough sleep? Almost all of the teens I talk with voice a preference for staying up late—and certainly parents note that late nights are common with their teens. Teens go to bed late in part because of social activities, including talking on the phone or chatting on the computer with their friends, homework, evening jobs, television or evening sports activities. Drinking caffeinated beverages may also keep them awake. But their body clocks are also keeping them up. Research has shown that a teen's "circadian rhythm" (the brain's timing system) shifts in early adolescence. While young children tend to work on an internal clock that makes them want to sleep at about eight or nine at night and wake early in the morning, teens' internal bedtime seems to be set much later—closer to midnight. Unfortunately, the world that most Western teens live in does not allow them to follow their natural sleep-and-wake cycles, and the necessary early mornings cut back drastically on their rest.

So how do you ensure that your teenaged children are getting enough sleep? Should you enforce a bedtime for teens?

While it's important for young children to have a strict bedtime, I don't recommend that parents insist their teens go to bed at a set hour. While teens need structure just like the rest of us, they also need to start taking responsibility for themselves—including for their health and well-being. Parents need to be partners in these things—not managers. As partners, parents can work with their teens to establish boundaries that will help them get the sleep they so desperately need. Start by asking them about how they feel they are managing their sleep. For example, parents should ask the following:

- How many hours of sleep do you need to feel really rested?
- What time do you need to get up in the morning to give you plenty of time to get ready for school?
- Therefore, what time do you need to go to bed to give your body the rest it needs?
- Think about what's worked in the past. What has helped you sleep well?

Healthy Sleep Habits for Teens

Keep in mind that everyone is different, and not all teens are going to need the same amount of sleep. But if your teens acknowledge that they are tired and are not sleeping well, the following boundaries and tips may help:

- Set a time that you need to be in your room for the night.
- Set a time that that all loud noise, generated by you or by other people in the house, must stop (TVs, music, phones, making food in the kitchen, etc.) at least a half hour before you want to go to asleep. The quiet will help you relax.
- Stick to a schedule, going to bed at the same time each night and getting up at the same time each morning. Most people will find that their bodies adjust to a new schedule after a few days. You can also try to move into the new schedule gradually: start by going to bed at the time that naturally feels right (even if it is late), but get up early enough for school in the morning. Then move the bedtime back by 15 minutes each night, until you are going to bed early enough to get the right amount of sleep (for teens, generally 9 to 9.5 hours).
- Create a relaxing bedtime routine that you can follow each night. The routine may include things like having a hot bath or reading, as well as brushing your teeth and so on. Repeating the same activities each night signals the body and mind that it is time to go to sleep.

- Dim the lights as you get ready for bed to help you relax. In the morning, turn your lights on right away to help you wake up.
- Avoid eating (especially sweets) just before bed.
- Avoid consuming caffeinated beverages or foods (like chocolate) in the afternoon or evening.
- Avoid exercising at night—exercise keeps the body and mind awake instead of getting them ready to fall asleep.
- Avoid naps, unless you're sick. Sleeping during the day can make it very difficult to get to sleep at an appropriate time of night.
- Avoid doing homework in your bed, as your mind may start to associate the bed with a place to think instead of a place to relax. Keep the bed for sleeping only.
- Turn off all gadgets in your room (e.g., computers, TV, music, cellphones).
- Get all your school stuff ready the night before (e.g., put your school bag together, choose what you're going to wear). Knowing that you are totally ready for the morning will help you to relax.
- Keep a pad of paper by your bed. If you think of things that you have to do, write them down and let them go from your mind.
- Set an alarm and get yourself up in the morning. Don't rely on your parents to keep you on schedule.

Encourage your teens to stick to these boundaries for a few days and see what happens. If after applying these simple daily habits they are still struggling with falling asleep, talk to your family doctor.

Getting Your Teens to Acknowledge a Problem

While I've seen all of the suggestions above work well for teens, they aren't going to try them out unless they recognize and acknowledge that they aren't getting enough sleep. If you spend every morning fighting to get your teens out of bed and off to school, but they still don't want to get to bed earlier, what do you do? Well, first and foremost, stop being a human alarm clock. That's overfunctioning. Make sure your teens have their own alarm clocks and make it clear that it is their responsibility to set them and to get up when they go off. Make sure, however, that you state this boundary in a loving and respectful way (see tips on how to communicate in Chapter 5). Resist the temptation to nag or remind your teens to get out of bed.

If you drive your kids to school, make it clear that this service is a privilege that will only be honoured if they are ready at the appropriate time. If they are late, the ride will no longer be available and they will have to get themselves to school. For most teens I've coached, it only takes two or three days of walking or paying their own bus fare for them to get themselves organized on time. And although they are often resistant at first, most teens feel great about themselves after learning this new habit because it means they are being responsible, feeling empowered and there is no fighting with or nagging by parents—a win-win situation!

If your teens normally get to school on their own, make sure that you don't bail them out by offering them rides or writing them notes when they sleep in. Allow them to suffer the natural consequences of being late for school or work. I know some families who have imposed a penalty each day a teen is late for school, and while this method seems to work for some of them, I prefer that the consequences are natural.

When you refuse to overfunction, your teens are much more likely to stop underfunctioning in the mornings. But remember, the transition can be a little tough. Once they have acknowledged that they need to change their morning routines, some teens ask that their parents give them one reminder of the time while they are getting used to getting up on their own. After a while, this reminder should become unnecessary. And when teens recognize that they may need more sleep to make their mornings easier, you can introduce them to some of the healthy sleep routines discussed earlier in the chapter.

Sleep Problems and Health Concerns

While most teens who have trouble falling asleep are being affected by body clocks that are out of synch with their schedules, by caffeine or by worries and anxieties that are making it difficult to relax, some sleep problems are signs of other health issues. Insomnia, late night or early morning waking or excessive sleepiness can be signs of depression. Trouble sleeping can also be a symptom of other medical issues. If your teen has tried all the tips listed in this chapter and still has trouble sleeping, see your family doctor.

Author's Note

I was chatting to one of my friends just after my twin boys were born, when I blurted out, "I instantly loved them, but now my greatest goal is to understand them—who they are, what makes them tick, what they need, what scares them, what excites them, what they love...." I think most parents love their children quickly and naturally, but in my experience, few parents really *understand* them. When we have a deeper understanding about what makes our children tick, it not only makes us more empathetic, it also changes how we communicate and leads to better parenting. My goal in writing this book was to help all parents have a greater understanding of their children.

I also wanted to assure parents that having exceptional relationships with their teens really is possible. There is hope! Yes, there are challenges and difficulties, but there are great opportunities even in difficult times. So regardless of your current situation—whether your relationship with your teen is "okay" or "terrible"—change really *can* happen. I've seen it happen hundreds of times.

I also wanted to answer the most common question I'm asked: "Karyn, where should I start?" First, try some of my communication tips and techniques the next time you're talking to your teenager. Make a list of goals or things that you would like to change about yourself or your teen, but don't try working on everything at once. The trick to achieving goals is to make sure they are ones you can control. Start with a single area (some examples: improving your parental attitude; improving your communication; learning how to set and follow boundaries). Next, I strongly recommend that you put together your own parenting group or book club. Use this book as a resource, along with any other books that you've found helpful, and assemble a group of four to seven friends you feel comfortable with; together you can talk, learn, challenge and encourage each other. Parenting shouldn't happen in isolation, and parenting groups provide support, hope, encouragement, great ideas—and perspective.

As you journey through the parenting process—and yes, it is a journey, since the job of being a parent is never done—I would love to hear your stories and feedback. Please visit my website at **www.drkaryn.com** and drop me a line.

Acknowledgements

I've often said that my education has been extremely rewarding and helpful, but nothing compares to the 7,000 hours I've spent listening to teens in my office. They are the ones who have told me what works and what doesn't. They've told me, bluntly and honestly, what they need from their parents to get them to talk. So first, I want to thank each and every teen I've worked with over the last 12 years. Thank you for letting me into your world, for trusting me and for sharing honestly and openly your thoughts and needs. I hope you believe this book accurately reflects your wisdom.

I also want to thank four of my dearest professors who introduced me to the world of counselling, and marriage and family therapy. Thanks to Dr. Brian Cunnington, who challenged us never to ask our clients to do something that we ourselves were not prepared to do. Thanks to Drs. Peter and Carol Schrek, who repeatedly told us, "Do your own work," because it is impossible to be an excellent counsellor/coach without first looking at ourselves. (It was during this time that my philosophy for inside-out parenting first began.) And thanks especially to Dr. Robin Smith. I so appreciate your wisdom, words of encouragement and guidance, and I particularly loved the way you challenged us to get curious and learn how to ask the right questions. I fully understand why Oprah loves you so much!

I am also grateful to have been inspired by the work of many extraordinary pioneers of marriage and family therapy, including Dr. Murray Bowen, Virginia Satir and Salvador Minuchin.

Thank you to Jackie Kaiser—the world's best literary agent! Thank you for your enthusiasm, unbelievable guidance and support for this book. It's been such a joy to work with you!

Thank you to Brad Wilson and the team at HarperCollins, who were immediately excited about this project. It's been a truly wonderful experience working with all of you. To Meg, the wonder woman who has spent endless hours editing my manuscript: The phrase "it takes a village to raise a child" is also true of books. It took a village to put this book together, and I so appreciate your gifts in editing and research, and your eye for detail.

To my mentor, Tony Chapman—you've helped me to focus, focus, focus! If it weren't for you, I would still be doing hundreds of different projects with little effectiveness. Thank you for challenging me to really think about my mission and to make decisions accordingly. Because of you I am such an advocate for the power of mentoring.

To my incredible and exceptional assistant, Andrea—you are such a superstar! Thank you for your wonderful spirit, huge heart and impeccable organization skills. You are such a tremendous gift to me.

To my parents, Mom and Dad—you are the models for inside-out parenting. Thank you for loving me but not rescuing me. Thank you for sharing your wisdom but for not taking over. Thank you for challenging me to see things differently but still allowing me to make my own choices. Your parenting skills were exceptional—and although you are not perfect, you were always open to admit your mistakes, ask forgiveness and model what you taught.

Finally, to my dear husband, Brent, who took such incredible care of me during my extremely difficult pregnancy so that I could make the deadline for this book: You are such a gift and treasure to me. And to the two newest little treasures in my life—my twin babies, Baron and Chase—your mommy loves and adores you. You are truly my inspiration for striving to be an inside-out parent!

Sources

American Academy of Child and Adolescent Psychiatry. (1999). Tobacco and kids. Facts for Families 68. Retrieved from http://www.aacap.org/cs/root/facts_for_families/tobacco_and_kids

American Academy of Child and Adolescent Psychiatry. (1999, December). Self-injury in adolescents. Facts for Families 73. Retrieved from http://www.aacap.org/cs/root/facts_for_families/selfinjury_in_adolescents

American Academy of Child and Adolescent Psychiatry. (2001). Bullying. Facts for Families 80. Retrieved from http://www.aacap.org/page.ww?section=Facts%20for%20Families&name=Bullying

American Academy of Child and Adolescent Psychiatry. (2003, January). Psychotherapies for children and teens. Facts for Families 86. Retrieved from http://www.aacap.org/cs/root/facts_for_families/psychotherapies_for_children_and_adolescents

American Academy of Child and Adolescent Psychiatry. (2004). Children and divorce. Facts for Families 1. Retrieved from http://www.aacap.org/cs/root/facts_for_families/children_and_divorce

American Academy of Child and Adolescent Psychiatry. (2004). Teenagers with eating disorders. Facts for Families 2. Retrieved from http://www.aacap.org/cs/root/facts_for_families/teenagers_with_eating_disorders

American Academy of Child and Adolescent Psychiatry. (2004). Teens: Alcohol and other drugs. Facts for Families 3. Retrieved from http://www.aacap.org/cs/root/facts_for_families/teens_alcohol_and_other_drugs

American Academy of Child and Adolescent Psychiatry. (2004, July). Bipolar disorder in children and teens. Facts for Families

38. Retrieved from http://www.aacap.org/cs/root/facts_for_
families/bipolar_disorder_in_children_and_teens

American Academy of Child and Adolescent Psychiatry.
(2004, July). Stepfamily problems. Facts for
Families 27. Retrieved from http://www.aacap.
org/cs/root/facts_for_families/stepfamily_problems

American Academy of Child and Adolescent Psychiatry. (2004,
November). Panic disorder in children and adolescents. Facts
for Families 50. Retrieved from http://www.aacap.org/cs/root/
facts_for_families/panic_disorder_in_children_and_adolescents

American Academy of Child and Adolescent Psychiatry.
(2004, November). Schizophrenia in children. Facts
for Families 49. Retrieved from http://www.aacap.
org/cs/root/facts_for_families/schizophrenia_in_children

American Academy of Child and Adolescent Psychiatry. (2006,
January). Gay, lesbian and bisexual adolescents. Facts for Families
63. Retrieved from http://www.aacap.org/cs/root/facts_for_
families/gay_lesbian_and_bisexual_adolescents

American Academy of Pediatrics. (2007). Alcohol abuse. Parenting
Corner Q & A. Retrieved from http://www.aap.org/publiced/
BR_Alcohol.htm

American Academy of Pediatrics. (2007). Becoming a stepfamily.
Parenting Corner Q & A. Retrieved from http://www.aap.org/
publiced/BK5_StepFamily.htm

American Academy of Pediatrics. (2007). Mental health. Parenting
Corner Q & A. Retrieved from http://www.aap.org/publiced/
BR_MentalHealth.htm

American Academy of Pediatrics. (2007). Suicide. Parenting Corner
Q & A. Retrieved from http://www.aap.org/publiced/BR_
Suicide.htm

American Academy of Pediatrics. Eating disorders. A Minute for
kids. Retrieved from http://www.multimedia.aap.org

American Academy of Pediatrics. Some things you should know
about preventing teen suicide. Retrieved from http://www.aap.
org/advocacy/childhealthmonth/prevteensuicide.htm

American Academy of Pediatrics. Substance abuse prevention. Parenting Corner Q & A. Retrieved from http://www.aap.org/publiced/BR_SubstanceAbusePrev.htm

American Academy of Pediatrics. Tobacco, alcohol, drugs and adolescents. Parenting Corner Q & A. Retrieved from http://www.aap.org/pubed/ZZZF1BEVR7C.htm?&sub_cat=23

American Medical Association. (2007). Obesity. Retrieved from http://www.ama-assn.org/ama/pub/category/11759.html

American Psychiatric Association. (2005). Eating disorders. Let's talk about brochures. Retrieved from http://www.healthyminds.org/letstalkfacts.cfm

American Psychiatric Association. (2005). Teen suicide. Let's talk facts about brochures. http://healthyminds.org/letstalkfacts.cfm

American Psychological Association Online. (1996). People with depression tend to seek negative feedback. 1996 press release. Retrieved fromhttp://www.apa.org.

American Psychological Association Online. Women and depression. Briefing sheet. Retrieved from http://www.apa.org.

Bowman, L. (2004, May 11). New research shows stark differences in teen brains. Scripps Howard News Service. Retrieved from http://www.ftnys.org/Newresearchshowsstark.htm

British Columbia Ministry of Attorney General. (2004). A teen guide to parental separation and divorce. Retrieved from http://www.familieschange.ca/teen_flash/index.htm

Caissy, G. A. (1994). Early adolescence: Understanding the ten- to fifteen-year-old. New York: Insight Books.

Canadian Association for Adolescent Health. (2007). Sexual orientation. Retrieved from www.youngandhealthy.ca/caah

Canadian Association for Adolescent Health. Depression. Retrieved from http://www.youngandhealthy.ca/caah/Informations/Mind+and+Soul/t430c440s548x414/Depression.aspx

Canadian Association for Adolescent Health. Suicide. Retrieved from http://www.youngandhealthy.ca/caah/Informations/Mind+and+Soul/t430c440s549x414/Suicide.aspx

Canadian Institute of Child Health. (1996). Suicide. Adapted from
The Health of Canada's Children: A CICH Profile 2. Child and
Family Canada. Retrieved from http://www.cfc-efc.ca/docs/
cich/00000012.htm

Canadian Mental Health Association. (2007). Children and family
break-up. Retrieved from http://www.www.cmha.ca/bins/
content_page.asp?cid=2-29-67&lang=1

Canadian Mental Health Association. (2007). Depression.
Retrieved from http://www.cmha.ca/bins/content_page.
asp?cid=284-1007-1110-1111-1141&lang=1

Canadian Mental Health Association. (2007). Separation and divorce.
Retrieved from http://www.www.cmha.ca/bins/content_page.
asp?cid=2-70-72&lang=1

Canadian Mental Health Association. (2004). High school: On the
front line of mental health. Public Health Agency of Canada.
Retrieved from http://www.canadianhealthnetwork.ca/servlet/
ContentServer?cid=1101055629164&pagename=CHN-RCS/
CHNResource/CHNResourcePageTemplate&c=CHNResource

Canadian Mental Health Association. Mental health and high school.
Retrieved from http://www.cmha.ca/highschool

Canadian Mental Health Association. Preventing suicide.
Retrieved from http://www.cmha.ca/bins/content_page.
asp?cid=3-101-102&lang=1

Canadian Mental Health Association. Suicide. Retrieved
from http://www.cmha.ca/bins/content_page.
asp?cid=3-101&lang=1

Canadian Mental Health Association. Youth and psychosis.
Retrieved from http://www.cmha.ca/bins/content_page.
asp?cid=3-105-106&lang=1

Canadian Mental Health Association. Youth and self-injury.
Retrieved from http://www.cmha.ca/bins/content_page.
asp?cid=3-1036&lang=1

Canadian Mental Health Association. Youth and suicide.
Retrieved from http://www.cmha.ca/bins/content_page.
asp?cid=3-101-104&lang=1

Canadian Paediatric Society. (2004). Dieting: Information for teens. Caring for kids. Retrieved from http://www.caringforkids.cps. ca/teenhealth/TeenDieting.htm

Canadian Paediatric Society. (1998). Eating disorders in adolescents: Principles of diagnosis and treatment. Paediatrics & Child Health 3(3): 189-92. Retrieved from http://www.cps. ca/english/statements/am/am96-04.htm

Canadian Paediatric Society. Dieting: Information for parents, teachers and coaches. Retrieved from http://www.caringforkids. cps.ca/teenhealth/DietingInfo.htm.

Carpenter, S. (2001, October). Sleep deprivation may be undermining teen health. Monitor of Psychology. Retrieved from http://www.apa.org/monitor/oct01/sleepteen.html.

Centers for Disease Control and Prevention, National Injury Prevention and Control. (2007). Youth violence: Facts at a glance. Retrieved from http://www.cdc.gov/injury

Centre for Addiction and Mental Health. (2007). My kid's on drugs: What can I do? Retrieved from http://www.camh.net/About_ Addiction_Mental_Health/Drug_and_Addiction_Information/ help_child_on_drugs.html

Centre for Addiction and Mental Health. (2002). Substance use and mental health concerns in youth. Youth scoop: Fast facts and topical tips for working with youth. Retrieved from http://www.camh.net/education/Resources_teachers_schools/ Youth%20Scoop/youth_scoop_subuse_menthealth.pdf

Centre for Addiction and Mental Health. Take action: Dealing with alcohol and other drug problems in your family. Retrieved from http://www.camh.net/About_Addiction_Mental_Health/ Drug_and_Addiction_Information/take_action_deal_with_ drugs.html

Centre for Addiction and Mental Health. Take action: How to get help and information links. Retrieved from http://www.camh. net/About_Addiction_Mental_Health/Drug_and_Addiction_ Information/take_action_help_info_links.html

Centre for Addiction and Mental Health. Take action: Preventing alcohol and other drug problems in your family. Retrieved from http://www.camh.net/About_Addiction_Mental_Health/ Drug_and_Addiction_Information/take_action_preventing_ drug_prob.html

Centre for Suicide Prevention. (2001). A closer look at self-harm. Suicide information and education collection. Retrieved fromhttp://www.suicideinfo.ca/csp/go.aspx?tabid=23

Chen, I. (2006). Teens are fastest growing group of bankruptcy filers. TBA News. Retrieved from www.tbacorp.com/news.html

Child and Family Canada. Helping your child cope with separation and divorce. Retrieved from http://www.cfc-efc. ca/docs/cafrp/00008_en.htm

Child and Family Canada. Smoking and teens: What you should know. Retrieved from http://www.cfc-efc. ca/docs/canps/00004_en.htm

Coats, E. J., et al. (1996, October). Approach versus avoidance goals: Differences in self-evaluation and well-being. Personality and Social Psychology Bulletin (10): 1057-67.

Coloroso, B. (2002). The Bully, the bullied and the bystander. Toronto: HarperCollins Canada.

Covey, Stephen. (1989). The 7 Habits of Highly Effective People. New York: Simon & Schuster.

Davidson, S., & I. Manion. (1995). Youth and mental illness. Canadian Psychiatric Association. Retrieved from http://www. mentalhealth.com/book/p43-yout.html

DeSimone, A., et al. (1994). Alcohol use, self-esteem, depression, and suicidality in high school students. Adolescence, 29: 939.

Department of Health and Human Services. Steps to preventing overweight and obesity. President's Council on Physical Fitness and Sports. Retrieved from http://www.fitness.gov/obesity_ america.htm

Department of Justice Canada. (2007). Dating violence: A fact sheet from the Department of Justice Canada. Retrieved from http:// www.justice.gc.ca/en/ps/fm/datingfs.html

Dugas, C. (2000). Teens need some training wheels. USA Today. Retrieved from http://www.usatoday.com/money/wealth/consumer/mcw074.htm

Duguay, D., & L. Strang. (2002). From bad to worse: Financial literacy drops further among 12th graders. Jump start financial smarts for students. Retrieved from http://www.jumpstart.org/upload/news.cfm?recordid=99

Ebernathy, T. J., et al. (1993). The relationship between smoking and self-esteem. Adolescence, Winter 30 (12): 899.

Epstein, R. (2007). The Case against adolescence: Rediscovering the adult in every teen. Sanger, CA: Quill Driver Books.

Epstein, R. (2007, April). The myth of the teen brain. Scientific American Mind. Retrieved from http://www.sciam.com/article.cfm?id=the-myth-of-the-teen-brain

Ericson, N. (2001). Addressing the problem of juvenile bullying. No. 27. Office of Juvenile Justice and Delinquency Prevention, U.S. Department of Justice. Retrieved from http://www.ncjrs.gov/pdffiles1/ojjdp/fs200127.pdf

Familydoctor.org. (2006). Depression hurts. Substance Abuse and Mental Health Services Administration, United States Department of Health and Human Services. Retrieved from www.family.samhsa.gov/monitor/depressionhurt.aspx

Familydoctor.org. (2006). Depression in children and teens. American Academy of Family Physicians. Retrieved from http://familydoctor.org/online/famdocen/home/children/parents/special/common/641.html

Familydoctor.org. (2006). Understanding your teenager's emotional health. American Academy of Family Physicians. Retrieved from http://familydoctor.org/online/famdocen/home/children/parents/parents-teens/590.html

Familydoctor.org. (2006). Know the warning signs—prevent suicide in young people. Substance Abuse and Mental Health Services Administration, United States Department of Health and Human Services. Retrieved from http://www.family.samhsa.gov/talk/suicidewarn.aspx

Farley, C. (2001). Teen clout. Toronto Star. D1.

French, S. A., et al. (1995, June). Changes in psychological variables and health behaviours by dieting status over a three-year period in a cohort of adolescent females. Journal of Adolescent Health, 16 (6): 438-47.

Gengler, C. (2005, August 24). Peer pressure on teens is often misunderstood. University of Minnesota Extension Service. Retrieved from http//www.extension.umn.edu/extensionnews/2005/peerteens.html.

Gibbs, N. (2006, June 4). The magic of the family meal. Time Magazine. Retrieved from http://www.time/magazine/article/0,9171,1200760,00.html.

Giesler, R. B. et al. (1996, August). Self-verification in clinical depression: the desire for negative evaluation. Journal of Abnormal Psychology, 105 (3): 358–68.

Government of Alberta. (2005). Bully-free Alberta. Retrieved from http://www.bullyfreealberta.ca

Gowen, K. (1998, August). Being teased by peers has a major impact on girls' body satisfaction. American Psychological Association Online (17): 1.

Health Agency of Canada. (2002). Eating disorders. A Report on mental illnesses in Canada. Retrieved from http://www.phac-aspc.gc.ca//publicat/miic-mmac/chap_6_e.html

Hope, J. T. , et al. (1993). Asessment of adolescent refusal skills in an alcohol misuse prevention study. Health Education Quarterly, 20 (3): 373-90.

Jenkins, K. (2004, October 15). Understanding teenagers' sleep habits. Canadian Health Network. Retrieved from http://www.canadian-health-network.ca/servlet/ContentServer?cid=1096654414508&pagename=CHN-RCS%2FCHNResource%2FCHNResourcePageTemplate&c=CHNResource&lang=En

Kelly, K. (2006). Violence in dating relationships: An overview paper. National Clearinghouse on Family Violence, Public Health Agency of Canada. Retrieved from http://www.phac-aspc.gc.ca/nc-cn

Kinnier, R. T., et al. (1994). Depression, meaninglessness, and substance abuse in normal and hospitalized adolescents. Journal of Alcohol and Drug Education, 39(2): 101-11.

Langlois, C. (1999, April). Teen angst. Parenting Magazine, p. 76.

Lay, K. Recognizing and responding to your child's learning style. Partnership for Learning. www.partnershipforlearning.org/article.asp?ArticleID=2113

Long, P. (2007). Eating disorders. Internet Mental Health. Retrieved from http://www.mentalhealth.com

Lyness, D., & L.A. Hawkins. (Eds.). (2006). Sexual attraction and orientation. Teens' Health, The Nemours Foundation. Retrieved from http://www.kidshealth.org/teen/sexual_health/guys/sexual-orientation.html

Marano, H. E. (2007, March/April). Trashing teens. Psychology Today. Retrieved from http://psychologytoday.com/rss/index.php?term=pto-20070302-000002.html

Mayo Clinic Staff. (2007). Teen sleep: Why is your teen so tired? Retrieved from http://www.mayoclinic.com/health/teens-healthCC00019

McCreary Centre Society. (2006). Self-harm: Pain from the inside out. Canadian Health Network, Public Health Agency of Canada. Retrieved from http://www.canadian-health-network.ca./servlet/ContentServer?cid=1140963343074&pagename=CHN-RCS%2FCHNResource%2FCHNResourcePageTemplate&c=CHNResource&lang=En&repGroupTopic=Mental+Health+KS

McCullough, P. M., et al (1994). The effect of self-esteem, family structure, locus of control, and career goals on adolescent leadership behaviour. Adolescence, Fall 29(115): 605-11.

Mental Health America. (2006). Depression in teens. Retrieved from http://www.nmha.org/index.cfm?objectid=C7DF950F-1372-4D20-C8B5BD8DFDD94CF1

Mintel International Group. (2006). Teen spending estimated to top $190 billion by 2006. Market Research World. Retrieved from http://www.marketresearchworld.net/index.php?option=content&task=view&id=615&Itemid=

National Eating Disorder Information Centre. 2005. Definitions. Know the facts. Retrieved from http://www.nedic.ca/ knowthefacts/definitions.shtml

National Institute of Mental Health. (2001). Teenage brain: A work in progress. U.S. Department of Health and Human Services. Retrieved from http://www.nimh.nih.gov/publicat/teenbrain. cfm

National Youth Violence Prevention Resource Center. Facts for teens: Bullying. Retrieved from http://stopbullyingnow.hrsa. gov/index.asp?area=main

Oster, G. D., & S. Montgomery. (1995). Helping your depressed teen. Toronto: John Wiley & Sons.

Overholser, J. C., et al. (1995). Self-esteem deficits and suicidal tendencies among adolescents. Journal of the American Academy of Teen and Adolescent Psychiatry, 34(7): 919-28.

Parents, Friends and Families of Lesbians and Gays (PFLAG), New York City chapter. (2002). For parents of gay children: Can we understand? A Brochure for parents of gay and lesbian youth. Retrieved from http://www.chebucto.ns.ca/health/teenhealth/ sexualhealth/orientation/orient-parentsbro.htm

Peikin, D. (1998, March). Boys and girls are cruel to each other in different ways, but effects are equally harmful. American Psychological Association Online.

Preschool Support Services. (1996). When parents separate or divorce: Helping your child cope. Child and Family Canada, Family Service Canada. Retrieved from http://www.cfc-efc. ca/docs/fscan/00000315.htm

Public Health Agency of Canada. (2005). Because life goes on ... Helping children and youth live with separation and divorce: A Guide for parents. Retrieved from http://www.phac-aspc. gc.ca/publicat/mh-sm/divorce

Public Health Agency of Canada. (2006). How can I stop drinking alcohol or taking other drugs? Retrieved from http://www. canadian-health-network.ca/servlet/ContentServer?cid=108109

8093207&pagename=CHN-RCS%2FCHNResource%2FFAQ
CHNResourceTemplate&c=CHNResource&lang=En

Pyper, W. (2007). Perspectives on labour and income. Statistics Canada 8 (4):220.

Rafferty, A. (2006). What if I'm not straight? Palo Alto Medical Foundation. Retrieved from http://www.pamf.org/teen/sex/whatif.html.

Richard, J. (2003, September 21). Running on empty: Who benefits from a full to-do list: child or parent? Toronto Sun. Retrieved from http://www.hyper-parenting.com/torontosun2.htm

SAMHSA's Family Guide. Effects of alcohol. Substance Abuse and Mental Health Services Administration, United States Department of Health and Human Services. Retrieved from http://www.family.samhsa.gov/talk/effects.aspx

SAMHSA's Family Guide. How can I protect my teen from underage drinking? Substance Abuse and Mental Health Services Administration, United States Department of Health and Human Services. Retrieved from http://www.family.samhsa.gov/set/underage.aspx

SAMHSA's Family Guide. Marijuana use rises during summer. Substance Abuse and Mental Health Services Administration, United States Department of Health and Human Services. Retrieved from http://www.family.samhsa.gov/monitor/marijuanarises.aspx?printid=1&

SAMHSA's Family Guide. Parents, parties, and preventing underage alcohol use. Substance Abuse and Mental Health Services Administration, United States Department of Health and Human Services. Retrieved from http://www.family.samhsa.gov/teach/parties.aspx

SAMHSA's Family Guide. Rising risk: Substance use and our daughters. Substance Abuse and Mental Health Services Administration, United States Department of Health and Human Services. Retrieved from http://www.family.samhsa.gov/talk/riserisk.aspx

SAMHSA's Family Guide. Teen popularity tied to alcohol, tobacco, and illegal drug use. Substance Abuse and Mental Health Services Administration, United States Department of Health and Human Services. Retrieved from http://www.family.samhsa.gov/teach/popularity.aspx

SAMHSA's Family Guide. Who's using alcohol? Substance Abuse and Mental Health Services Administration, United States Department of Health and Human Services. Retrieved from http://www.family.samhsa.gov/talk/alcohol.aspx

SAMHSA's National Mental Health Information Center. (2002). Teen mental health problems: What are the warning signs? Substance Abuse and Mental Health Services Administration, United States Department of Health and Human Services. Retrieved from http://mentalhealth.samhsa.gov/publications/allpubs/Ca-0023/default.asp

SAMHSA's National Mental Health Information Center. Child and adolescent mental health. Substance Abuse and Mental Health Services Administration, United States Department of Health and Human Services. Retrieved from http://mentalhealth.samhsa.gov/child/childhealth.asp

Shain, B. (2007, September). Clinical report: Suicide and suicide attempts in adolescents. Pediatric, 120(3):669-76. Retrieved from http://www.pediatrics.aappublications.org/cgi/content/full/120/3/669

Shields, M. (2005). Measured obesity: Overweight Canadian children and adolescents. Nutrition: Findings from the Canadian Community Health Survey. No. 1. Statistics Canada. Retrieved from http://www.statcan.ca/english/research/82-620-MIE/2005001/articles/child/cobesity.htm#1

Society of Obstetricians and Gynaecologists of Canada (SOGC). (2007). Talking contraception and sexuality with your child. Retrieved from http://www.sexualityandu.ca/parents/talk.aspx

Society of Obstetricians and Gynaecologists of Canada (SOGC). (2006). Sexual and gender orientation. Retrieved from http://www.sexualityandu.ca/teens/orientation.aspx

Spinks, S. (2007, August). Adolescent brains are works in progress. Frontline. Retrieved from http://www.pbs.org/wgbh/pages/frontline/shows/teenbrain/work/adolescent.html

Statistics Canada. (2000, September 28). Divorce. The Daily. Retrieved from http://www.statcan.ca/Daily/English/000928/d000928b.htm

Statistics Canada. (2001, May 30). National longitudinal survey of children and youth: Participation in activities. The Daily. Retrieved from http://www.statcan.ca/Daily/English/010530/d010530a.htm

Statistics Canada. (2005, December 13). Study: Divorce and the mental health of children. The Daily. Retrieved from http://www.statcan.ca/Daily/English/051213/d051213c.htm

Statistics Canada. (2007, May 23). Study: The busy lives of teens. The Daily. Retrieved from http://www.statcan.ca/Daily/English/070523/d070523b.htm.

Steinberg, L., & A. Levine. (1997). You and your adolescent. New York: Harper Perennial.

Steinberg, L., & A. Levine. (1990). You and your adolescent: A parent's guide for ages ten to twenty. New York: Harper & Row.

Swenson, R. (2004). Margin: Restoring emotional, physical, financial and time reserves to overloaded lives. Colorado Springs, CO: NavPress.

Turcotte, M. (2007, February 13). Time spent with family during a typical workday, 1986 to 2005. Statistics Canada. Retrieved from http://www.statcan.ca/english/freepub/11-008-XIE/2006007/11-008-XIE20060079574.htm#8

Underwood, N. (2007, August 24). The teenage brain: Why adolescents sleep in, take risks, and won't listen to reason. The Walrus. Retrieved from http://www.walrusmagazine.ca/print/2006.11-science-the-teenage-brain.

Wallis, C. (2004, May 10). What makes teens tick? Time Magazine. Retrieved from http://www.time.com/time/printout/0,8816,631970,00.html

Whitfield, D. (1995, October-November). Increasing interest and achievement motivation among adolescents: an overview. High School Journal 79(1): 33-40.

Index

abandonment, feelings of, 96–98
achievement
  academic, 11–14
  character development as context for,
    15–16
  vs. effort, 12
  as indication of teen's development,
    10, 20
  undue focus on, 10–11, 13–14, 16–19
alcohol use or abuse. *See* drinking
allowances, 261–64, 267, 272
alternative schools, 35–36
anger
  allowing teens to vent, 139, 190, 221,
    241
  boundaries instead of, 245
  at breakup of parents' marriage, 202,
    203
  link between self-esteem and
    response to, 102
  parking, 180–83, 241
  self-esteem and, 131
  as substitute for other emotions, 95,
    102
  at teens' poor choices, 235
  undue focus on, 245
anorexia, 73–74
anxiety
  and communication, 178–79, 183, 197
  disorders, 104, 106
  felt by children of underfunctioning
    parents, 47
  felt by underfunctioning parents, 48
  and low self-esteem, 124, 139–40
  and marriage breakdown, 200, 201,
    203, 207, 209

  in overachievers, 12, 17, 246–47, 249
  in "Overcircuited" parents, 82–83
  in "Overfunctioning" parents, 20–21,
    38, 222, 235, 243
  as a result of overscheduling, 246–49
  setting boundaries as a way to reduce,
    87, 245, 255, 260
  at teens' poor choices, 235
apologizing, 101, 196, 238
  inappropriate, 130, 134
assertiveness, 31–32, 130, 163–64
attention spans, 173
auditory learners, 34, 35
  and boundary plans, 231, 234
authenticity, 57, 174
authority
  exercised through intimidation, 50–51
  vs. influence, 21
  and inside-out parenting, 56

"Babbler" attitude, 51–52
balanced life, 243–50
bank accounts, 239, 264–65
"Basket Case" attitude, 47–49, 52, 82–83,
  222
bedrooms, searching, 63–64
bedtime boundaries, 221, 275–76
behaviour
  actions as symptoms, 22–23
  as clue to emotions, 98
  effect of character on, 22
  effect of self-esteem on, 11, 20, 24–25
  focus on instead of feelings, 11,
    96–103, 139, 227
  rooted in emotional problems, 140
  sudden changes in, 104, 108